COACHING PARENTS
OF VULNERABLE INFANTS

Coaching Parents
of Vulnerable Infants

THE ATTACHMENT
AND BIOBEHAVIORAL
CATCH-UP APPROACH

Mary Dozier
Kristin Bernard

THE GUILFORD PRESS
New York   London

Library of Congress Cataloging-in-Publication Data

Names: Dozier, Mary, 1954– author. | Bernard, Kristin, author.
Title: Coaching parents of vulnerable infants : the attachment and
    biobehavioral catch-up approach / Mary Dozier, Kristin Bernard.
Description: New York : Guilford Press, [2019] | Includes bibliographical
    references and index.
Identifiers: LCCN 2018047003 | ISBN 9781462539499 (hardcover)
Subjects: LCSH: Parents of problem children. | Attachment disorder in
    children. | Behavior disorders in children. | Parenting—Psychological
    aspects. | Problem children—Behavior modification.
Classification: LCC HQ773 .D69 2019 | DDC 649/.153—dc23
LC record available at *https://lccn.loc.gov/2018047003*

About the Authors

Mary Dozier, PhD, is Professor of Psychological and Brain Sciences and Amy E. DuPont Chair in Child Development at the University of Delaware. Since the 1990s, she has studied the development of young children in foster care and those living with neglectful birth parents. Dr. Dozier developed the Attachment and Biobehavioral Catch-Up (ABC) intervention and is currently conducting randomized clinical trials examining ABC's effectiveness with high-risk birth children, foster children, and internationally adopted children. She served on the Institute of Medicine's Committee on Child Abuse and Neglect, was an associate editor of *Child Development*, and serves on a number of advisory and editorial boards. Dr. Dozier is a recipient of the Translational Research Award from the International Congress on Infant Studies, the Urie Bronfenbrenner Award for Lifetime Contribution in Developmental Psychology in the Service of Science and Society from the American Psychological Association, and the Francis Alison Faculty Award from the University of Delaware, the University's highest faculty honor.

Kristin Bernard, PhD, is Assistant Professor of Psychology at Stony Brook University. As Director of the Developmental Stress and Prevention Lab, she is interested in how early-life stress influences children's neurobiological and behavioral development and how optimal caregiving and preventative interventions may buffer at-risk children from problematic outcomes. As a graduate student, Dr. Bernard worked with Mary Dozier on the development and evaluation of ABC and delivered the intervention as a parent coach. She continues to collaborate with Dr. Dozier and her team on evaluations of ABC's efficacy and is leading dissemination efforts in New York City in collaboration with Power of Two and the Administration for Children's Services. Dr. Bernard is a recipient of the Excellence in Attachment Research Dissertation Award from the Society for Emotion and Attachment Studies and was named a Rising Star by the Association for Psychological Science.

Preface

The work of this book began 25 years ago, or much longer ago when we consider the contributions of the people on whose shoulders we stood as we developed and tested our parenting program. The theory and research of John Bowlby (the architect of attachment theory) and Mary Ainsworth laid the foundation, and their work was developed further by Alan Sroufe, Mary Main, and many others.

Our work was motivated by our recognition of the challenges facing young children who experienced early adversity—children who suffered disruptions in their relationships and children who experienced neglect or abuse. These conditions were central to Bowlby's early formulation of attachment theory. Perhaps Bowlby's biggest departure from psychoanalytic thinking was his firm belief that children's actual experiences were key to their representations of themselves and others, with their experiences with primary attachment figures of particular importance.

Therefore, helping parents to behave in ways that provide infants with what they need was our goal. Based on our own findings and those of others, we identified several key issues that are important for parents of children who have experienced adversity. First, children who have experienced adversity are in special need of parents who behave in nurturing ways when their children are distressed—that is, parents who respond directly to them in reassuring ways. Nurturing parenting enhances children's ability to develop secure, organized attachments. Second, these children need parents who are very responsive in everyday interactions, essentially following the child's lead. This helps children develop their self-regulatory capabilities. And third, children need parents to avoid intrusive, harsh, and frightening behaviors because such behaviors undermine the child's ability to develop organized attachments and to develop adequate regulatory capabilities.

The parenting program we developed, Attachment and Biobehavioral Catch-Up (ABC), includes attention to these and only these elements. Parents are helped to behave in nurturing, responsive, nonfrightening ways through 10 sessions in their homes. A key requirement of the program is that clinicians or parent coaches provide "in-the-moment" feedback regarding parents' behavior that relates to intervention targets. In this way, parents get practice and feedback (about 60 times in a session) such that children's actual experiences with their parents change quickly.

This in-the-moment feedback also speaks to the following issue raised by Bowlby (1951): "If a community values its children, it must cherish their parents." When parents hear throughout the intervention sessions that they are behaving in very specific ways that support their children's development, they feel supported. Many parents with whom we work have not heard many positive things about their parenting. It would likely not mean much to them, or would not feel believable, if their parent coach made a general statement about their being good or loving parents. But when parents hear very specifically that the particular thing they did was important (whether it be patting the child on the back or handing the child the block that he or she wanted) and why it mattered—and when they receive such feedback over and over—they tend to glow and to feel cherished.

Indeed, the intervention is proving to be powerful. Through randomized clinical trials, we have found that children whose parents received the intervention are more likely to develop secure and organized attachments and to show more normative production of cortisol (a stress hormone), together with better regulation of behavior (as well as advantages in language, brain function, and autonomic nervous system regulation) than children who received a control intervention. These effects are now seen 8 years postintervention. Parents show improvements in sensitivity, as well as changes in neural activity and in the way they think about attachment—changes that persist over time.

This book provides an overview of the development of the intervention, effects of the intervention, and adaptations for different populations. To bring it to life, we have incorporated case examples of parents and their children, some of whom we follow throughout the book.

AUDIENCE

This book is designed for scholars with interest in attachment, and for clinicians, home visitors, and child welfare professionals who serve vulnerable young children and their parents. Emerging scholars and clinicians new to attachment will be introduced to the foundations of attachment theory and research, which served as the basis for ABC. For established researchers in the field of attachment, this book offers an example of translating attachment theory and research into clinical practice. In the classroom, this book could serve as a supplementary text for advanced undergraduate- or graduate-level courses focused on infant mental health, childhood maltreatment, and prevention and intervention. By integrating theory and research with clinical examples, we expect this book to be accessible to readers of diverse professional backgrounds and across levels of expertise.

ORGANIZATION OF THE BOOK

The book begins with an overview of the ABC intervention and of the book, featuring a case example that is followed throughout. In Chapter 2, we provide an introduction to attachment theory and discuss key empirical findings from the science of attachment that have informed our work. We then, in Chapter 3, discuss how we developed the intervention. Confronting critical issues such as how infants entering foster care form new attachments and to what extent disruptions in attachment relationships undermine children's stress physiology, our own research helped us identify the three components of ABC: provide nurturance even when the child does not elicit it and even if it does not come naturally; follow the child's lead with delight; and avoid behaving in frightening ways.

Over time, the intervention was adapted for birth parents living under high-risk conditions, foster parents, internationally adopting parents, and parents of toddlers (2- to 4-year-olds); adaptations for these populations are presented in Chapters 4–7, respectively. Although the intervention components and clinical approach of ABC remain the same, we describe unique considerations for these different populations.

Chapter 8 presents the research evidence from four different randomized clinical trials supporting the ABC intervention's efficacy on child and parent outcomes through middle childhood. From there we move to a description of the fidelity monitoring system we developed that facilitates the effective dissemination of ABC; Chapter 9 addresses how we conceptualize fidelity, details our microanalytic coding process, and describes some of the nuances of in-the-moment commenting. Chapter 10 describes the challenges to implementing the intervention in community settings, documenting the many mistakes we made in the process of dissemination, and presents recommendations for being successful when moving an intervention into the community. In Chapter 11, we describe other interventions that work to enhance the relationship of the parent and young child. We focus on several interventions that have the strongest evidence base. Chapter 12 describes the successful implementation of ABC through Power of Two in New York City. Although we have been cautious about adapting the intervention significantly, we were persuaded to adapt it for use in the context of visitation—that is, when children see their birth parents while in foster care. We describe Fostering Relationships, an adaptation of the ABC model for visitation, in Chapter 13. Finally, in Chapter 14, we discuss the exciting possibilities we envision for ABC in the future.

THE BOOK'S FEATURES

Throughout the book, we present detailed case stories about children and their parents with whom we have worked. These stories offer rich examples of how we conceptualize clinical issues, deliver in-the-moment comments to celebrate parent strengths, and gently target areas for growth through video-feedback. Although many case stories highlight our successes, we also describe the challenges of this work. The book's tables and figures visually summarize the intervention model (e.g., conceptual model, session topics, fidelity monitoring) and the key research methods and findings from our work.

Acknowledgments

We thank the families who trusted us enough to invite us into their homes for intervention, who came to the lab year after year for research assessments, and who became valued collaborators along the way. In this book, we describe various families, many of whom have experienced challenging conditions that are sometimes hard to fathom—and yet most are willing to put in the hard work needed to enhance the way they parent so that their children can have the best possible chance in life. We thank you so very much.

It takes courage for child welfare agencies to allow researchers to conduct studies in their systems because the attention they usually get is negative. But the Delaware Division of Family Services has boldly partnered with us from the beginning, and we thank the directors and staff so much for that. Also, we extend our appreciation to the Philadelphia Division of Human Services and the New York City Administration for Children's Services.

The National Institute of Mental Health provided support for most of the research described (R01 Grant Nos. MH074374, MH084135, and MH052135 to Mary Dozier), and Edna Bennett Pierce has provided annual support since 2006.

Thanks to all the undergraduate and graduate students, postdoctoral fellows, and staff who helped develop and implement the intervention, adapted it for various populations, and collected research data. The findings described throughout the book are a direct result of your engagement in the research process. We consider you all as partners in this work, which would not have been possible without you.

We attribute much of our success in moving the intervention into the community to Caroline Roben, who leads our large and committed dissemination team; EB Caron, who developed the in-the-moment fidelity coding system; Chase Stovall-McClough, who stayed involved years after graduate school to help us transition from implementing as part of randomized clinical trials to implementing in the community; and community partners, Lisa Berlin, Brenda Jones-Harden, Karen Carmody, Anne Heller, and Erasma Monticciolo.

Much of our work is translational and depends on the expertise of others. We thank Bob Simons, who worked with us to collect event-related potential data; Julie Hubbard, who collaborated with us on questions of peer relations; Tania Roth, who collaborated on DNA methylation; Jean-Philippe Laurenceau, who provided statistical consultation; Nim Tottenham, who collaborated on functional magnetic resonance imaging; Megan Gunnar and members of the National Institute of Mental Health–supported Early Experience, Stress, and Neurobehavioral Development Network/Center, who supported our work on stress neurobiology; Phil Fisher, who consulted with us as we developed the toddler intervention; Elizabeth Carlson, who coded our Strange Situations; the Circle of Security developers (Bert Powell, Glen Cooper, Kent Hoffman, and Bob Marvin) and Alicia Lieberman, who helped us think through issues in addressing parents' "voices from the past" when we were first developing the intervention; Charley Zeanah and Carole Schauffer, who helped us think through systemwide issues; and Lisa Berlin, Brenda Jones-Harden, Karen Carmody, Anne Heller, and Erasma Monticciolo, who helped us disseminate the intervention in the community.

We are grateful to the many supportive and talented professionals at The Guilford Press. Editor-in-Chief Seymour Weingarten helped persuade us that this was the time to write the book. C. Deborah Laughton, Senior Editor and Publisher, was an amazing support to us, providing advice, direction, and wisdom.

Thanks also to Katherine Sommer, Editorial Assistant; Oliver Sharpe, designer and typesetter; Katherine Lieber, Senior Copywriter; and Laura Patchkofsky, Senior Production Editor. Phil Shaver and Deane Dozier provided wonderful edits of the complete manuscript. Bernat Ivancsics of Columbia University took the cover photograph.

Finally, we thank family and friends who celebrated our progress. It's no accident that I (M. D.) began to develop this intervention shortly after my sons were born. I then understood the joy of having that sparkle in my eye for my boys and to know that I'd stand between them and whatever danger lurked as long as they'd allow it. Thanks to Ben and Zachary, who will always be the light of my life.

Contents

List of Abbreviations

AAI (Adult Attachment Interview): A semistructured interview for assessing attachment state of mind, developed by Mary Main and colleagues.

ABC (Attachment and Biobehavioral Catch-Up): A 10-session parenting intervention for infants exposed to early adversity.

ABC-T (Attachment and Biobehavioral Catch-up for Toddlers): An adaptation of the ABC intervention for toddlers.

ACEs (adverse childhood experiences): Experiences of maltreatment (e.g., child abuse, neglect) or family dysfunction (e.g., parental substance abuse, parental separation) that occur during childhood.

ACS (Administration for Children's Services): The government agency that oversees the child welfare system in New York City.

ACTH (adrenocorticotropic hormone): A hormone released by the pituitary gland as part of the body's stress response.

ASA (Attachment Script Assessment): A word-prompt procedure for assessing secure-base script knowledge, developed by Harriet Waters and colleagues.

ASD (autism spectrum disorder): A mental condition characterized by difficulties with social skills, language deficits, and repetitive behaviors or interests.

BMS (Brownsville Multi-Service Family Health Center): A community center that provides health care and social services in the Brownsville neighborhood of Brooklyn, New York.

CCC (Citizens' Committee for Children of New York): A nonprofit child advocacy organization in New York.

COS (Circle of Security): A group-based attachment intervention, developed by Glen Cooper, Kent Hoffman, and Bert Powell.

CPP (child–parent psychotherapy): An intervention for children birth to age 5 who have been exposed to trauma, developed by Alicia Lieberman and Patricia Van Horn.

CPS (Child Protective Services): The system responsible for responding to reports of child abuse and neglect and ensuring child safety.

CRH (corticotropin-releasing hormone): A hormone released by the hypothalamus as part of the body's stress response.

DB-DOS (Disruptive Behavior Diagnostic Observation Schedule): An observational procedure that challenges children's behavior and emotion regulation abilities, developed by Lauren Wakschlag and colleagues.

DCCS (Dimensional Change Card Sort): Procedure for assessing children's set-shifting ability, developed by Philip Zelazo and colleagues.

DEF (Developmental Education for Families): A comparison intervention targeting cognitive, language, and motor development, used in randomized clinical trials of ABC.

EEG (electroencephalogram): A recording of electrical activity of the brain.

ERPs (event-related potentials): Changes in electrical activity in the brain in response to a stimulus.

fMRI (functional magnetic resonance imaging): A method for measuring brain activity based on changes in blood flow.

GABI (Group Attachment-Based Intervention): A group-based attachment intervention, developed by Anne Murphy, Miriam Steele, and Howard Steele.

HARC (Home Visiting Applied Research Collaborative): A research collaborative that aims to strengthen the impact of home visiting, directed by Anne Duggan.

HIPAA (Health Insurance Portability and Accountability Act)
Established in 1996, the primary goals of the law are to make it easier
for people to keep health insurance, protect the confidentiality and
security of health care information, and help the health care industry
control administrative costs.

HomVEE (Home Visiting Evidence of Effectiveness): An initiative that
reviews the quality of research evidence for home-visiting programs.

HPA (hypothalamic–pituitary–adrenal) axis: The biological stress
response system that produces the hormone cortisol.

LPP (late positive potential): A positive-going ERP component that
indexes brain responses to emotionally salient stimuli.

mABC (Modified Attachment and Biobehavioral Catch-Up): A
modified version of ABC for opioid-dependent mothers.

**MIECHV (Maternal, Infant, and Early Childhood Home Visiting
Program)**: A funding program that supports the implementation of
evidence-based home-visiting programs.

NFP (Nurse–Family Partnership): A home-visiting program for low-
income first-time mothers delivered by nurses, developed by David
Olds.

OT (occupational therapy): Services aimed at supporting the
development of skills needed for activities of daily living.

PT (physical therapy): Services aimed at enhancing motor skills.

RSA (respiratory sinus arrhythmia): A variation in heart rate during
the respiratory cycle; an index of parasympathetic nervous system
activation.

VIPP (Video-Feedback to Promote Sensitive Parenting): A short-term
intervention targeting parenting behaviors through video-feedback,
developed by Femmie Juffer, Marian Bakermans-Kranenburg, Marinus
van IJzendoorn, and colleagues.

WIN (Women In Need): A family shelter in the Brownsville
neighborhood of Brooklyn, New York.

CHAPTER 1

Introduction to Attachment and Biobehavioral Catch-Up

Eleven-month-old James banged his head against the bedside table in the motel room. He reached his hand to his head and cried out "Momma!" and crawled quickly to his mother, Sonya. She reached out for him and said, "Oh sweet baby, that hurt, didn't it?" James sank into his mother for a minute while she rubbed his head. Gabriella, sitting on the other bed, said, "Oh my gosh, that was just beautiful nurturing him. That so lets him know you're there for him." Then James smiled up at his mother and pointed to the toy on the floor. Jumping off his mom's lap, he picked up the toy and held it out to his mother.

When Gabriella first met Sonya and James, they looked very different than they do now. At 8 months, James was withdrawn and passive, interacting very little with his mother or with the world. When he accidentally shut his finger in a drawer, he had a pained expression on his face but just sat on the floor and cried. Sonya commented that he did things like that sometimes but that she did not know how to deal with him. When asked to play "as she usually would" (a standard preintervention procedure to allow observation of parental sensitivity), James was limp and uninvolved. His mother took his hands and put them on toys, but he had little interest.

1

But now, nearly a year old, James is energetic and engaged. He smiles broadly at his mother, asks her to pick him up when he's hurt, and looks for her to be engaged when he plays. Even though James and Sonya continue to live in a dreary motel room, James's world has changed. So much of his world is defined by his interactions with his mother, and his mother has become a responsive, nurturing partner on whom he can depend.

Sonya has been enrolled in a parenting program, Attachment and Biobehavioral Catch-Up (ABC). The intervention consists of 10 home-visiting sessions that focus on enhancing parents' ability to follow their children's lead, nurturing children when they are distressed, and avoiding frightening behaviors. Parent coaches make frequent "in-the-moment comments" regarding parents' behaviors that are relevant to intervention targets. These comments call attention to and reinforce these behaviors. In the incident with James and his mother, the parent coach commented on Sonya's nurturing her distressed child. Parents become accustomed to such comments but still notice them and are affected by them.

Throughout the 10 weeks of the ABC intervention, Sonya lived in the motel with her son. As would be expected, the motel was in an unsafe section of town, such that she and James could not spend much time outdoors. The motel room did not have a refrigerator or cooking appliances, so they ate fast food, crackers, and cookies. Sonya did not have many people to depend on. Her own mother had died several years earlier, but even before that Sonya hadn't had family support. She had been in foster care nearly all of the time since she was 10 years old. Her last foster mother, with whom she lived between the ages of 14 and 18, had stayed involved with her over the years, providing her the limited support that she did have. This foster mother sometimes helped out with James during the day when Sonya was able to find work.

Sonya came to the ABC parenting program with a host of issues, problems, and concerns. Her parent coach, Gabriella, was respectful of all Sonya had to deal with but was also focused on the ABC targets. The challenges of living in a motel, coping with a failed romantic relationship, and wishing for more support from

her family fluctuated throughout the 10 weeks of the intervention, but these concerns were never the focus of intervention.
Rather, the intervention addressed Sonya's nurturing James when
he was upset, following his lead, and avoiding harsh and frightening behavior through manualized content, video presentations
of other mothers and of Sonya, and in-the-moment comments. In
some ways, Sonya and James's circumstances at the end of the
10 sessions were as challenging as they had been at the beginning. Nonetheless, James's world had fundamentally changed. His
mother had become nurturing, sensitive, and nonfrightening.

ATTACHMENT AND BIOBEHAVIORAL CATCH-UP

ABC was first developed for foster parents of young children.
We later extended the program to parents such as Sonya, who
were living under challenging conditions but whose children had
not been removed from their care. The program has since been
extended for use with parents who adopt internationally. The children all experienced early adversity, such as neglect, placement
into foster care, or orphanage care, as well as other challenges.
Along with other researchers, we have found that children who
have experienced early adversity are in particular need of parents
who are nurturing (i.e., who soothe their distressed child), follow
their children's lead in play, and consistently avoid behaving in
ways that are harsh, frightening, or intrusive. These are the issues
targeted in the ABC intervention.

Why Is Parenting So Critical to Infant Development?

The ABC intervention, similar to many programs that target
development in infancy, focuses on enhancing parental sensitivity. So why is it that parenting is seen as so critical for infant
development? Humans are an altricial species—that is, infants
are born fully dependent on their parents. In terms of our evolutionary history, human infants would not have survived without

parents. Consider human infants at birth: They have no locomotor abilities; it is 6 months or more before they can crawl, and they cannot hold onto their parents at birth. Indeed, human infants can do less to hold onto and follow parents than monkey and ape infants, and therefore are even more dependent on parents for locomotion and sustenance than are these other primates. In human evolutionary history, infants would not have survived without the care of others, and thus the infant human brain and behavioral systems are programmed to "expect" input from other people—most often, but not necessarily, parents (Greenough, Black, & Wallace, 1987). Social input is key to the development of many brain regions. Synapses, proliferated over the course of prenatal growth, serve as the building blocks for the brain's architecture. When fired repeatedly, connections are strengthened, and larger, more complex networks are created over time. When particular synapses are not fired over time, they are pruned. Experience is thus integrally involved in the brain's architecture—or in the connections made between neurons and eventually between brain regions.

> We may think of early experience as the foundation for the building. The foundation cannot be more important than solid supporting beams or a sturdy roof; without these, the house will not last. But at the same time, a house cannot be stronger than its foundation, and the foundation frames or structures what the house can become. . . . (Sroufe, Egeland, Carlson, & Collins, 2005, pp. 10–11)

Developing abilities to regulate attention, emotions, and behavior are dependent on parental responses. Young children who experience neglect or abuse adapt in ways that "make sense"—that is, in ways that help them cope at the time. Nonetheless, these means of coping have downstream consequences that often compromise optimal development at physiological, emotional, and behavioral levels. The quality of parenting is therefore key, especially for children who have experienced adversity.

In the case of James, chances are that, not only was his behavioral repertoire diminished as a result of his mother's failure to interact with him as a baby, but his early experiences also affected the synapses created and neural networks formed. Had his mother continued to interact with him so minimally, paying inadequate attention to his distress, he would likely have experienced consequences ranging from stunted intellectual development to an insecure attachment to later problems with peers. But fortunately, his mother's behavior changed dramatically as the result of intervention, and so did his behavior—and quite likely his brain development.

Whereas the brains and behavior of young humans are strikingly plastic and thus vulnerable to adversity, this plasticity also renders them open to change as the result of improved conditions. This is where intervention comes in. The ABC intervention targets parental nurturance, following the child's lead and avoiding frightening behavior because we see these behaviors as key to healthy development, especially during this sensitive period.

Nurturance

Belinda

When her 10-month-old son, Juwan, cried, Belinda could hear her mother saying, "You'll spoil that baby if you pick him up." But somehow Belinda knew that Juwan needed to be picked up, and she usually went right over to him and said something like, "Hey, what's wrong, buddy? Come here." Providing nurturing care to Juwan was critical for him—he could trust that his mother would be there when he needed her. Even though Belinda's own mother had said Juwan would cry more if he were picked up than if he were not picked up, that wasn't Belinda's experience. He had cried lots when he was several months old, but he became less fussy over time. He cried when he got hurt or when he got scared, but she found that he was easily soothed when she picked him up and held him.

Clara

Clara's own mother had warned her not to pick up her baby when the baby cried, and Clara heeded the advice. She hated the sound of her baby crying. She had tried a number of solutions, such as putting her baby in another room with the door closed, telling the baby to hush, and acting like she was crying herself when the baby cried. She was convinced that trying to soothe her baby would make things harder for the baby to learn to soothe herself. Her baby, Eloise, sometimes became so upset crying that she couldn't catch her breath. Clara often said to her at such times, "I told you not to cry like that. Look what you're doing to yourself." As Eloise got older, Clara noticed that Eloise acted like she didn't notice when Clara came home from work and often turned away when she was hurt.

These two mothers provide very different experiences to their children. When Juwan feels scared or worried, he can trust that his mother will respond—that she'll be there for him and will help him get through difficulty. Eloise's experience is so different—she learns that her mother will not be there and instead will push her away or make light of her distress. She finds that she cannot trust that her mother will reassure her when she is distressed. As a baby, she needs that reassurance. So Eloise learns to adapt in ways that may not be optimal. In her case, she gets to a point where she learns to turn away when she needs her mother.

The ABC intervention helps mothers such as Clara learn the importance of behaving in nurturing ways with their babies, and it reassures parents such as Belinda that nurturance is important, despite messages they might get from others. We know that providing nurturing care is critical, especially for children who have experienced adversity. From attachment theory and research, we know that nurturance is the key to children learning that they can depend on their parents being available when needed. When children have parents who respond to their needs as Belinda does with Juwan—offering reassurance when he is distressed—the children develop a sense that they can depend on parents, which serves as a model for other relationships. The ABC intervention helps Clara see that her child does things that make it hard for her to nurture, and it also helps her see that she has her own issues that get in the way of providing nurturance. So, even though nurturance, the first component of the ABC intervention, does not "come naturally" for Clara, she can override her natural tendencies and provide the support her child needs.

Following the Lead

Jonathan

When Jennifer picked up her stuffed rabbit, her father, Jonathan, said, "What you got there, girl?" Jennifer beamed, held her rabbit up, and said, "Bunny bunny." Jonathan laughed and said, "You got your bunny!" Jonathan, the father of 18-month-old Jennifer, had not had an easy early life. He was in and out of foster care from the age of 3 and was in juvenile detention for 2 years as a teen. Still, since starting ABC, he quickly embraced the notion of following Jennifer's lead. He had realized that he didn't know how to interact with her comfortably, so he had done things like tickling her, throwing her into the air, and talking with a booming voice—actions that got her attention but seemed unsettling to her. When his parent coach talked about following her lead, Jonathan almost seemed to breathe a sigh of relief. He said at one point, "Wow, I don't have to try as hard." Indeed, for both the parent and the child, following the child's lead makes the interaction simpler, more rewarding, and less jarring than it otherwise would be.

Cassie

Cassie, the parent of Brian, a child adopted from eastern Europe, was especially concerned about her son's cognitive delays, so she tried to turn every interaction into a learning experience for him. When he reached for a toy she held in her hand, she asked him to use his words to say what he wanted. When he held out a truck for her to look at, she asked what color the truck was. As a result, she did not follow Brian's lead well. He quickly lost interest in play with her and shifted from one activity to another. The advice she got from physical therapy/occupational therapy reinforced her belief that it was essential that she push Brian to "use his words."

When Cassie and her husband, Greg, started working with their ABC parent coach, what they heard surprised them. The parent coach gently urged them to follow Brian's lead, telling them that children will develop language skills best when parents follow their lead. Cassie, in particular, resisted, convinced that Brian's cognitive development would suffer if she did not persist in her approach. She gradually came around and found it wonderfully rewarding to have Brian so much more responsive to her when she followed his lead than when she had not.

Following the lead is the second component of the ABC intervention. When parents follow their children's lead, they serve as effective "co-regulators" for their children (Hofer, 1994), helping children regulate physiology, emotions, and behavior. Over time, with many experiences of smooth interactions in which parents serve in this capacity, children gradually become better able to self-regulate. Following-the-lead interactions are often rich with child-directed speech that builds on the child's focus of attention—like Jonathan commenting on Jennifer's interest in her stuffed animal. In contrast to what Cassie initially believed, these child-directed interactions, rather than "teachy" or parent-led interactions, best support children's early language development (Golinkoff, Can, Soderstrom, & Hirsh-Pasek, 2015).

Harsh and Frightening Behavior

Rochelle

When the parent coach first began meeting with Rochelle, Rochelle's behavior with her 22-month-old daughter, Addison, was concerning. Rochelle glared at Addison when Addison asked her a question while she was talking; she told Addison she would tell her father if she continued crying; she smacked Addison's hand when she reached for her mother's soda; she yelled when Addison pulled a toy from a neighbor child. On each of these occasions, Addison looked frightened in one way or another—she stared blankly when threatened with her father's punishment and jumped when her mother yelled.

Rochelle's own mother had also been a scary figure; she threatened her often and frequently followed up with beatings. Rochelle felt that she had worked hard to avoid being abusive in similar ways with her child, but she was unaware that less overt frightening behaviors could also have adverse effects on her daughter.

We know from the research literature on attachment and stress neurobiology that frightening parental behavior undermines children's ability to develop organized attachments and to regulate their physiology (Bernard & Dozier, 2010; Schuengel, Bakermans-Kranenburg, & van IJzendoorn, 1999). Thus, helping parents recognize and avoid behaving in frightening ways is critical. This is the third component of the ABC intervention.

THE ABC INTERVENTION

The ABC intervention targets nurturing care, following the child's lead, and frightening behavior (see Figure 1.1). It targets these behaviors through both manualized content—that is, content included in a treatment manual—and parent coaches making comments in the moment when they observe relevant behaviors.

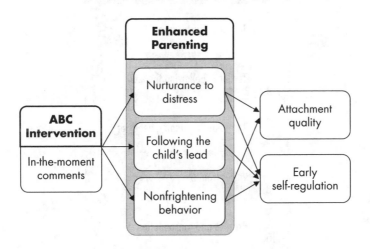

FIGURE 1.1. Overview of the ABC model.

Manualized Content

The ABC manualized content provides the structure for sessions with parent coach, parent, and child. The session content introduces parents to the intervention components of providing nurturance, following the lead, and avoiding frightening behavior (see Table 1.1). Parent coaches present research evidence that highlights the importance of each component. Parents view videos of other parents who show high or low levels of the relevant behaviors (e.g., high or low levels of following the child's lead) to clarify their understanding of exactly what the behaviors are. Parent coaches review on a behavior-by-behavior basis just how the parents in the video are following (or not following) the child's lead. In many sessions, parents are then asked to engage in activities that challenge their ability to follow their child's lead (or other relevant behaviors). Having viewed and discussed the videos, and having the parent coach scaffold them, parents are almost always able to exhibit some following-the-lead (or other relevant) behaviors.

TABLE 1.1. ABC Session Topics	
1	Target 1: Nurturance
2	
3	Target 2: Following the lead
4	
5	Target 3: Frightening behavior
6	
7	Voices from the past
8	
9	Practice and consolidation
10	

Sessions 1 and 2: Nurturing Care

The first two sessions introduce parents to the concepts of nurturing children and following the children's lead, and then go into greater depth in considering nurturing behavior. In the first session, parent coaches introduce common ideas about parenting, which they talk through. For example, parent coaches ask parents to react to the idea that "babies get spoiled if they are picked up when they cry." When Gabriella presented this idea to Sonya, Sonya responded in the affirmative—that she thought James would get spoiled and cry more if she picked him up. Gabriella said, "Yes, that's what you would think, wouldn't you?" As indicated in the manual, Gabriella went on to describe Mary Ainsworth's finding that children actually cried less when they had been picked up quickly than when they had not. The purpose of the discussion of common ideas about parenting is not to dissuade parents of their beliefs, but rather to have them articulate these beliefs and be introduced to one of the primary issues of the intervention in a nonthreatening fashion. Despite thinking that children would cry more if they were picked up, Sonya was surprisingly open to the idea that it was useful for parents to pick up their children when they cried.

Sessions 3 and 4: Following the Lead

In Sessions 3 and 4, parents are introduced to the importance of following their children's lead. In Session 3, after seeing videos of other parents, parents are asked to play with blocks and/or books with their children, with parent coaches making frequent comments to scaffold the parents' behavior. The interactions are video-recorded. Between sessions, parent coaches select one or more video clips to present the following week in which the parent followed the child's lead successfully. These are often very brief clips of about 2–5 seconds.

Sonya watched the videos of the mother who was following her child's lead and was able to articulate ways in which she did this. Nonetheless, when given the chance to play with blocks with

James, she was initially passive, sitting while James hit one block against another. Gabriella provided very gentle scaffolding, commenting that Sonya could just do what James was doing. Sonya banged the blocks together, and James looked back at her surprised; he then broke out in a smile and banged his blocks again. It was this sequence that Gabriella showed at the beginning of Session 4.

In Session 4, parents are asked to make pudding with their child (or engage in a similar activity if the child is too young or if the parent is too uncomfortable to engage in pudding preparation). As in Session 3, parents are first shown a video of a parent following her child's lead, as well as a video of a parent not following her child's lead. The task is intentionally challenging because parents are so accustomed to taking the lead under similar circumstances.

Sessions 5 and 6: Avoiding Harsh and Frightening Behavior

From following the lead, we move in Session 5 first into behaviors that are intrusive and then, in Session 6, into behaviors that are harsh and frightening. This process represents a natural continuum from responsive behaviors that are smooth and regulating (Sessions 3–4) to behaviors that are somewhat perturbing (Session 5) to behaviors likely to undermine a child's ability to regulate (Session 6). Both Sessions 5 and 6 are introduced gently because they are often threatening to parents. In Session 5, parents are helped to think about times when adults behaved in ways that were intrusive to them when they were children. Tickling represents a good example because, although many adults tickle children, parents often recall disliking being tickled as children but being unable to communicate that effectively. Parents are helped to think of other behaviors that seemed intrusive to them. Playing with puppets is an activity that often elicits intrusive behavior. Parents are shown videos of a parent playing with puppets sensitively and of a parent playing in intrusive ways. They are then given puppets to play with and are reminded that the puppets will likely elicit intrusive behavior.

Despite being somewhat passive at times, Sonya was also intrusive at other times. Before ABC, Sonya would have tickled James with puppets or acted as if the puppets were growling in his face. Having increased success with following his lead, however, she was able to hold the puppets out to him and await his response. When James shied away from them, she put them down and said, "They scare you, don't they, honey?"

Session 6 asks parents to think about times from their childhood when they felt frightened by an attachment figure. By Session 6, parent coaches will typically have seen frightening parental behavior if it is a problem for the parent. When frightening behavior is a problem, the parent coach usually presents one video in which the parent has managed to avoid behaving in frightening ways, even though the child's behavior or the context may have elicited it, and another video in which the parent behaved in frightening ways. We emphasize to parents that even if they make changes in other behaviors, their efforts will be undermined if they occasionally behave in harsh or frightening ways. Given that the subject matter is so threatening, introducing this gently and sensitively is key.

Sessions 7 and 8: Voices from the Past

In Sessions 7 and 8, parents are helped to think about how their own attachment experiences affect their parenting. The primary objective is to change parental behavior rather than provide insight into previous relationships for its own sake. Therefore, these sessions are very much driven by the parent coach rather than by the parent. That is, the parent coach identifies the issue or issues that the parent is struggling with behaviorally (i.e., nurturing, following the lead, and/or avoiding frightening behavior), focusing on "voices from the past" relevant to these issues.

The assumption we make is that many parental behaviors are "automatic"—that is, parents engage in these behaviors without thinking or without considering alternatives. One reason for this automaticity is that the parent may have received care consistent with this approach (e.g., her own parents may not have picked her up when she cried), or she may have heard her parents comment on appropriate parenting (e.g., "Don't pick up that baby—you'll spoil him"). What we seek to do is help parents become aware of this influence such that they can interrupt the process. For example, Sonya may have the following run through her head as she overrides a "voice from the past":

> "James hit his head, and I can just hear my mother saying, 'He's OK! Don't pick him up.' But I realize that that's my mother's voice, and does not reflect what James needs. I know he just needs me to pick him up."

Through this process, Sonya (and other mothers and fathers) can interrupt the previously automatic cycle in which the event is "child is hurt" and the response is "Get up, you're OK." What had previously been an automatic response becomes no longer automatic, and the parent can override the voices from the past (see Figure 1.2). For many parents, nurturing or following the lead may never quite come naturally; rather, they may always need to override their voices from the past.

Typically, parent coaches use videos showing parents' strengths and weaknesses (in nurturing, following the lead, or frightening behavior) to provide a context for thinking through voices from the past. As with Session 6, it is critical to provide parents with support and to introduce potentially threatening topics gently. For example, for a parent who struggles with nurturance, the parent coach may bring in a video clip from a session when the parent picked up the child when he cried. When introducing the video clip, the parent coach describes specifically what aspect of the parent's response was nurturing. Then, the parent coach shows a time from an earlier session when the parent was not nurturing—for example, a time when the parent mockingly fussed back at the child when he cried—and asks the parent, "That was a bit different than the other video. Did you notice what

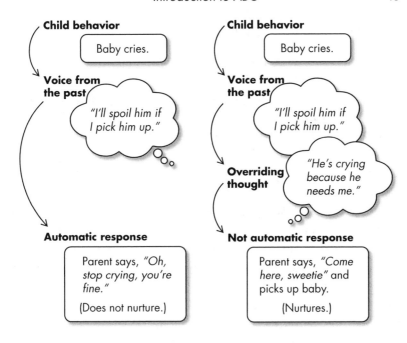

FIGURE 1.2. Voices from the past: Making automatic responses not automatic.

happened then?" Assuming the parent acknowledged that she fussed at or made fun of her child, the parent coach comments, "That's such a strength that you noticed that. You saw that you missed an opportunity to be nurturing. That was a voice from the past that got in your way of being nurturing in that moment." This type of video review allows the parent coach to help parents see how their "voices from the past" affect their behavior. Although parents vary in their ability to connect their own parenting challenges to the way their parents responded to them, most become aware that they struggle to be nurturing or to follow their child's lead, or they may behave in frightening ways at times. This awareness opens the door for making the automatic become no longer automatic. With continued video review and in-the-moment comments that focus attention on the targets in sessions, Session 8 allows the parent to generate and practice ways to override voices from the past.

Sessions 9 and 10: Consolidation

Sessions 9 and 10 help parents consolidate strengths. Typically, no new content is introduced at this point. Nonetheless, given that we have only 10 hours with parents, we use these final two sessions to work to make changes when parents are not yet nurturing, when they are not following their children's lead, or when they are behaving in frightening ways. For example, if frightening behavior is first seen in Session 9, we work on it even though it is the last or next to the last session.

At the end of Session 10, we present parents a montage set to music containing video clips from earlier sessions in which they behaved in nurturing ways and followed their child's lead. This is intended to celebrate parents' accomplishments as well as to remind parents of the importance of nurturing and following the lead in the weeks and months after the intervention ends. It is sometimes tempting for parent coaches to make this the centerpiece of Session 10, but again, we emphasize the importance of using all 10 sessions fully. Sonya's montage was lovely—it included beautiful clips of James going to her crying and settling in her arms and of her following his lead while he lit up with a smile. Sonya teared up as she watched the video and talked about feeling that she could be a good parent to James now, something she wasn't confident in before.

In-the-Moment Comments

Perhaps the most unusual part of the ABC intervention is that parent coaches are expected to make comments about parents' behavior, and to do so at a very high rate. Every opportunity a parent has to behave in a nurturing way (e.g., her child bumps his head) or to follow her child's lead (e.g., her child hands her a toy) is a trigger for a parent-coach comment. Parent coaches need to be aware of opportunities to make comments regarding nurturance and following the lead in ongoing parent–child interactions, even as they are presenting manual content. These comments are important in drawing attention to the parents' specific behaviors (so that parents are clear about what is referred to), link behaviors to the intervention targets (so that parents can see how a specific behavior relates to intervention targets), and point out the effects of the parents' behaviors on children (so that parents can see the importance of the behaviors for children's short- and long-term outcomes).

Early in the intervention, these comments are almost exclusively positive, highlighting the parent's responding to the child's overtures, however fleeting. For example, if the child fell and bumped his head, the parent coach might say, "That's such a good example of nurturing him. He fell and you said, 'Oh honey.'" Over time, the parent coach should be increasingly able to make comments when parents failed to nurture or follow the child's lead. These comments could support or scaffold the parent's behavior (i.e., suggesting a way to nurture or follow the lead) or could even point out that the parent was not nurturing or following. For example, if the mother took the lead by asking what letter was on a block, the parent coach might say, "What would be a way you could follow his lead now?" or "Who is leading right now?"

The effect of these comments is to draw attention to intervention targets. Rather than merely having discussions about the importance of nurturance and following the lead, parents experience having their own behaviors pointed out to them time and again. Parents essentially practice the target behaviors over and over again, receiving feedback from their parent coach as they do. This approach is strikingly different from most other approaches. Parent coaches sometimes resist making comments initially, fearing parents will be put off by them. However, we almost uniformly find that parents find the in-the-moment feedback rewarding even early on in the intervention and can be seen to light up in response to comments.

ALL ABOUT CHANGE IN PARENTING

Some parenting programs focus on changing parents' feelings and thoughts about their children. Other programs focus on parents' own attachment experiences, reasoning that parents will not be able to provide nurturance to their children if they are still conflicted about not receiving nurturance themselves. Still others help parents work through traumatic experiences they have encountered because, as a field, we know that not working through such experiences can adversely affect parents' ability to respond in optimal ways to their children (Schuengel et al., 1999). We recognize the importance of each of these issues, but we focus almost exclusively on changing parents' behaviors. Rather than focusing on parents' thoughts, feelings, awareness of their own attachment experiences, or their own trauma, ABC works to change the way parents respond to their children.

We focus on parents' behavior because, in the words of Zero to Three (2016), "Babies can't wait." For the baby's sake, it is critical that parents learn to behave in sensitive and nurturing ways right away. Working through a parent's traumatic issues can be very important, but we argue that parental change can occur before or even without that. In a meta-analysis of over 80 studies of attachment-based interventions, programs that focused solely on changing parents' behaviors were more effective than interventions that focused on changing parents' attachment representations (i.e., cognitive models about attachment relationships) or on providing support (Bakermans-Kranenburg, van IJzendoorn, & Juffer, 2003). In fact, interventions with an exclusively behavioral focus were even more effective than those that tried to change behavior *and* provide social support or change attachment representations. These findings, which held for studies focused on high-risk families, suggest that a targeted behavioral approach, like ABC, may be ideal.

IMPLEMENTING IN THE HOME

It would be so much easier if this intervention could be conducted effectively in an office or a clinic. Intervening in the home is more expensive in terms of staff time than intervening in a clinic.

Rather than being able to see six to eight clients a day in a clinic, parent coaches can usually see only two to four families a day through home visitation.

Why is it so important to implement this intervention in the home? At home, parents can practice nurturing their child and following the child's lead while experiencing the same challenges that they experience in their everyday lives. Generalizing skills from sessions is much easier than it would be if the intervention were implemented in an office. In an office setting, parents might come to understand the concepts and even practice them during a session, but it might be harder to engage in these new behaviors at home. Consider some of the key differences. For example, Cheryl has two children but lives in a house with her mother and sister and her sister's three children. Sessions in the home are noisy, busy, and somewhat chaotic, and often five children and three or four adults are present. If Cheryl were to go through the intervention in a clinic with one or two of the children present, the conditions would not resemble those in which she lives. Although she might change her behavior in the clinic, it would be hard to generalize the new behaviors to her home. Many factors distinguish the two settings. In addition, other caregivers (e.g., sister, mother, boyfriend) are also exposed to the intervention. Having these other caregivers exposed to the intervention makes for a much better buy-in.

ADAPTING FOR DIFFERENT POPULATIONS

The ABC intervention was originally designed for foster parents, with whom we began our work. Children in foster care often return to the care of their birth parents. In our first randomized clinical trial, we planned to intervene with parents wherever children moved, and so we intervened with birth parents when children were reunited with them after living in foster care. To our surprise, the intervention did not require major revamping for use with birth parents. The primary change needed, as detailed in Chapter 4, was paying attention to frightening and intrusive behavior.

Children adopted internationally are quite different from children involved with the child welfare system in the United States. Although internationally adopted children have often experienced severe early adversity, they enter homes where parents have impressive resources. One of the primary challenges to our intervention targets (especially following the lead) is that many internationally adopting parents are deeply concerned about children catching up developmentally. We emphasize to them that responsive parenting helps children develop regulatory capabilities that are key to school success, but it is sometimes difficult to help them overcome their "teachy" approach, which is at odds with following the child's lead. Although the concerns of parents adopting internationally might be quite different from foster or high-risk birth parents, our intervention did not need major revision for this population. Other than incorporating attention to issues specific to them (e.g., quasi-autistic behavior and indiscriminate sociability), attention to nurturing care and following the lead remained at the intervention's core.

EFFECTIVENESS

Chapter 8 provides evidence of the effectiveness of the ABC intervention. In brief, through randomized clinical trials, we found that more of the children whose parents received ABC developed secure attachments, and fewer developed disorganized attachments than children whose parents received a control intervention. The ABC children also showed more normative regulation of biological systems and better regulation of emotions and behaviors than control children. Parents and children continued to exhibit the benefits of ABC at least 8 years postintervention. We now have findings from four randomized clinical trials: with neglecting birth parents, parents adopting internationally, and foster parents of both infants and toddlers. In all four cases the interventions were effective in enhancing child outcomes.

DISSEMINATING THE INTERVENTION

Given that the intervention is effective, we have begun to disseminate it to other places. There are many challenges in implementing interventions successfully in new locations. As we describe in Chapter 9, one key challenge is ensuring that the intervention is implemented with fidelity. We have developed a coding system that both parent coaches and supervisors use to help ensure that the intervention is being implemented as intended. This system focuses on the quality and frequency of in-the-moment comments. Other challenges include developing criteria to identify individuals who will be effective parent coaches and ensuring that we collaborate with agencies that will provide the necessary support for parent coaches to master the intervention.

OVERVIEW OF THE BOOK

In this book, we provide an overview of the ABC intervention, incorporating extensive case material from parents with whom we have worked as we developed and tested the effectiveness of the program. For example, we describe how the intervention worked with Sonya as well as with parents for whom progress was not as straightforward. Given that attachment theory heavily influences the intervention, we begin with an overview of attachment, providing a summary of infants' quality of attachment and how we measure it and of adults' attachment state of mind and how that is measured.

We then describe the development of the intervention—how it came to include its present components and to be implemented in specific ways. The need for intervention among children who have experienced different kinds of adversity, and for adaptations of the intervention for these children, is then developed. We start with what the intervention looks like with parents of infants who had experienced maltreatment and with foster parents. Although high-risk birth parents and foster parents are very different, their tasks are similar: they need to help children overcome a history of insensitive care, whether at their own hands or the hands of others. We describe the intervention as implemented with young children adopted following orphanage care, including a description of how we deal with issues specific to this population (i.e., indiscriminate sociability and quasi-autistic behaviors). We next present the intervention model as adapted for toddlers, which involves the most significant differences because toddlers present different challenges.

Following our presentation of the models, we describe the evidence base for the ABC intervention. We move from there to the fidelity coding system that we developed to ensure that the ABC model is implemented as intended. We encountered a number of other challenges when disseminating the intervention to new populations and places. We describe these challenges and explain how we worked to create conditions that increased the likelihood that the intervention would have the same effectiveness in the community as when it was implemented through randomized clinical trials. Power of Two, an agency in New York City that is working to scale up ABC for use throughout the city, is described in depth as an example of successful dissemination of the intervention.

We have generally been cautious in making adaptations to ABC that go far beyond our original intentions of enhancing parental sensitivity. However, given that we have seen children in foster care and learned that their birth parents and foster parents struggle with the challenges posed by visitation, we developed an intervention to make visitation work better for all parties. We describe this program, called Fostering Relationships, in Chapter 13.

In Chapter 14, we describe possibilities for the future. Throughout the book, we weave in stories of actual parents with whom we have worked.

CHAPTER 2

Attachment

While 12-month-old Aaron was visiting a neighbor's apartment with his mother, the neighbor's dog barked loudly. Aaron startled and cried out immediately. He turned and crawled quickly to his mother, and then pulled himself up to a standing position and looked into her face. She picked him up and asked, "Did you get scared when that doggy barked?" He clung to her for a minute and quickly calmed down. He then looked at the dog and said, "Doggie?" looking back and forth at the dog and his mother. It was not long before he had slipped down off his mother's lap and crawled cautiously toward the dog, saying "Doggie?"

As with nearly all 12-month-olds, Aaron is attached to his mother. And like about 60–70% of children, he behaved in a way that is characteristic of a secure attachment. That is, he could go to his mother directly when he needed her for reassurance, using her effectively as a safe haven. After getting the reassurance needed, he could then use her as a secure base from which to explore. Likely because Aaron had many experiences in which his mother reassured him in the past, he could make a direct bid for comfort when he was frightened, confident that she would provide the reassurance he needed. Once reassured, he could turn back to his goal of exploring the world.

ATTACHMENT THEORY

John Bowlby (1969/1982) was the architect of attachment theory. Although he was trained as a psychoanalyst, his approach represented a stark departure from previous psychoanalytic thinking in many significant ways. One of the most important differences was his belief that children's *actual* experiences with their parents were key to their representations of attachment figures and of self and others—representations were not primarily "fantasies."

Bowlby proposed that nearly all infants form attachments to their parents or caregivers and do so under nearly all conditions. From an evolutionary perspective, the attachment system functions to ensure that the infant seeks out the parent and maintains proximity to him or her under conditions of threat. Thus, the system has enhanced survival by keeping infants close to parents when conditions feel threatening—such as when children are sick or when unfamiliar people are present. As Bretherton (1985) pointed out, the attachment system fully kicks in before infants are capable of mobility. Therefore, when the infant is capable of crawling away from the parent, he or she has a strong drive to maintain proximity if conditions feel threatening.

Infants develop attachments to figures who are "older and wiser" than themselves, and they seek to maintain proximity with these attachment figures under threatening conditions. The infant's repertoire of crying, smiling, clinging, and following represents an organized system, evolved to maintain or restore proximity to the caregiver when threat is experienced (Bowlby, 1990; Sroufe & Waters, 1977). Whereas the presence of an attachment relationship is essentially universal except under unusual conditions, there is variability in the quality of attachment relationships. Mary Ainsworth worked closely with Bowlby, providing empirical support for some of Bowlby's key theoretical ideas. An astute observer of parent–child interactions, Ainsworth noted individual differences in children's ability to rely on their parents when they were distressed and in their parents' presence. Some, like Aaron, seek out their parents directly for reassurance and are soothed; these infants have secure attachments to their parents (Ainsworth, Blehar, Waters, & Wall, 1978). Other babies turn away when distressed or give the appearance that they are too engaged with toys or other things to go to their parent; these children have avoidant attachments. Still others may go to their parent, but they remain unsettled and upset; such children have resistant or ambivalent attachments.

INFANTS' ATTACHMENT QUALITY

These three types of attachment—secure, avoidant, and resistant (see Table 2.1)—are considered "organized" attachments because they represent strategies that maximize the availability of a particular caregiver (Main, 1990). In the case of an infant with a secure attachment, the strategy is thought to derive from a history of experiences in which the parent was generally available and responsive, causing the child to seek the parent out directly. Such a child can move directly to his or her parent, confident that bids for reassurance will not be rebuffed.

In the case of an infant with an avoidant attachment, the parent is assumed to have been rejecting of attachment needs. For example, the parent may have been clearly and directly rejecting, saying to the child who bumped his head, for example, "You're not hurt. Get up." Or the parent may have turned the child away in more subtle ways, such as by trying to distract the child. The

TABLE 2.1. Attachment Quality	
Classification	Description
Secure	Child seeks out whatever comfort is needed from parent; can be soothed and calmed by parent and can return to exploration of environment.
Avoidant	Child turns away from parent when distressed; does not seek proximity.
Resistant	Child is fussy and irritable when distressed; appears to desire proximity but resists.
Disorganized	Child lacks a strategy or the strategy breaks down when child is distressed and with parent; shows anomalous or contradictory behaviors.

child's strategy of appearing not to need the parent diminishes the likelihood that the parent will reject the child's attachment needs, effectively maintaining proximity to the parent to the extent permitted (Bowlby, 1969/1982; Cassidy, 1994).

In the case of the resistant infant, the parent has typically been inconsistent in his or her availability; the infant's strategy of high-level support seeking (and fussing) maximizes the likelihood of responsiveness by an inconsistent caregiver. That is, the parent, who might be preoccupied with other children or with her own internal states, may provide nurturance to the child but only intermittently. If the child fusses often, although the rate per request may not increase, the absolute number of times or amount of time the parent is nurturing may well increase (Bowlby, 1969/1982; Cassidy, 1994).

For the first decade after Ainsworth and colleagues (1978) published the tripartite classification system, researchers used the three categories to classify children's attachment. Main and Solomon (1986, 1990), however, observed that some children exhibited behaviors that were not captured by the three categories. Indeed, some of the behaviors observed that fell outside this system appeared anomalous, but without further specification they could not be considered in coding. As the result of their very careful observations, Main and Solomon introduced disorganized attachment as a fourth distinct category. About 15% of children in typical samples fell into this disorganized attachment category (Main & Solomon, 1986). Disorganized attachment represents a breakdown in attachment strategy, with children appearing to lack a solution for dealing with their distress (Main & Solomon, 1990).

An infant's attachment quality is typically assessed in what Mary Ainsworth called the Strange Situation—a laboratory procedure in which the child and parent are separated and reunited twice in a series of episodes that are increasingly stressful for the child (see Table 2.2). Ainsworth and colleagues (1978) developed the Strange Situation to provide a standardized and efficient way to assess attachment quality. A believer in observational data,

TABLE 2.2. Strange Situation Procedure Episodes	
Episode	**Description**
1	Parent and baby brought into the room.
2	Parent and baby alone.
3	Stranger enters, sits quietly, talks to parent, plays with baby.
4	Parent leaves (first separation), stranger and baby alone.
5	Parent returns (first reunion), stranger leaves, parent and baby alone.
6	Parent leaves (second separation), baby alone.
7	Stranger returns, stranger and baby alone.
8	Parent returns (second reunion), stranger leaves, parent and baby alone.

Ainsworth had spent about 72 hours observing each of 24 infants in her Baltimore sample, which was the basis of her typology.

The Strange Situation was designed to assess attachment under controlled conditions that clearly and powerfully elicited attachment behaviors. In this procedure, the child and parent are brought into a room that has attractive toys laid out on the floor. After the child has a few minutes to play with the toys, a stranger enters the room; at first, the stranger sits quietly, then begins talking with the parent, and next tries to engage the child. The parent then leaves the room and stays out for 3 minutes unless the child becomes very upset, in which case the separation time is reduced. The parent returns for 3 minutes, with the stranger leaving. After 3 minutes, the parent leaves again, with the child left alone in the room. The stranger then returns, with the parent returning after another 3 minutes, or earlier if the child is very upset. The child's reunion behaviors are key to classifying his or her attachment quality. These reunion behaviors are thought to reflect the child's expectations regarding the parent's responsiveness to his or her distress. Some children appear to expect their parent to be responsive to their distress and seek out whatever comfort they need; such children are classified as securely attached. Other children do not appear to have confident expectations of their parent's responsiveness. In the case of avoidant children, they turn away from their parent upon reunion. In the case of resistant children, they are difficult to soothe despite appearing to desire proximity to their parent. Disorganized attachment behaviors can be observed throughout the various episodes of the Strange Situation, although the strongest indicators are observed in the reunion episodes. Examples of disorganized behaviors include freezing or remaining still for a period of time, showing contradictory attachment tendencies (distress and avoidance) sequentially or simultaneously, or showing apprehension or fear of the parent.

Earlier in this chapter, 12-month-old Aaron was described as looking to his mother for protection when a dog barked and getting the reassurance he needed to allow him to explore. His behavior in the Strange Situation was similar to his behavior observed in the home. During the first separation from his mother, he protested her leaving and cried a little, but at the stranger's suggestion he was willing to continue playing, however listlessly. When his mother returned, he crawled to her quickly and insisted that she pick him up. Very shortly thereafter, he was ready to get down to play with the toys, showing his mother each toy as he played. When she left the next time, he cried vigorously until she returned. Upon reunion, he held onto her for a full minute, with his head on her shoulder and his arms around her neck. He was then able to turn his attention to the toys, first pointing at them from his mother's lap and then sliding off her lap to play with them on the floor. Aaron represents the picture of a prototypical securely attached child.

In normative (i.e., low-risk) samples, about 62% of children are classified as having secure attachments, 15% as avoidant, 8% as resistant, and 15% as disorganized (van IJzendoorn, Schuengel, & Bakermans-Kranenburg, 1999). In our own studies of children whose parents have Child Protective Services (CPS) involvement, only 33% of the children develop secure attachments. As can be seen in Table 2.3, more of these children whose parents are involved with CPS have avoidant and disorganized attachments than one finds in samples of low-risk children. Among foster children and internationally adopted children, the numbers are intermediate between the low-risk and CPS-involved groups, with 54% and 52% secure and 36% and 39% disorganized, respectively, in our samples (see Table 2.3).

It may be obvious why we would expect to see relatively higher rates of attachment security and lower rates of attachment disorganization among low-risk children than among children in high-risk samples. Indeed, CPS has identified high-risk parents in our studies as being at risk for maltreating their children. It would surely be surprising if attachment differences were *not* seen between the CPS-involved and the low-risk children. It may be more surprising that *any* disorganization would be seen in low-risk samples and/or that any security is seen among high-risk samples.

Frightening behavior from parents is one of the purported causes of infant disorganized attachment (Jacobvitz, Leon, & Hazan, 2006; Schuengel et al., 1999). Main and Solomon (1986) proposed that when parents are frightening, infants have an unsolvable dilemma; they need to seek reassurance from the

TABLE 2.3. Percentages of Attachment Patterns across Samples

Sample	Secure	Avoidant	Resistant	Disorganized
Low-risk	62%	15%	8%	15%
High-risk/CPS-involved	33%	10%	0%	57%
Foster	54%	5%	5%	36%
Internationally adopted	52%	6%	3%	39%

Note. Sources of data: *Low-risk:* based on meta-analytic findings of middle-class, nonclinical groups in North America (*N* = 2,104), from van IJzendoorn et al. (1999); *High-risk/CPS-involved:* based on distribution of classifications in CPS-involved control (non-ABC) group, from Bernard et al. (2012); *Foster:* based on distribution of classifications in foster control (non-ABC) group, unpublished data from our lab; *Internationally adopted:* based on distribution of classifications in internationally adopted control (non-ABC) group, unpublished data from our lab.

parent, but they are frightened of him or her. It is difficult for them to move toward their parent because of the fear, but it is difficult to move away because they need protection or reassurance. Overtly frightening parental behaviors, such as threatening looks, yelling, and harsh physical behaviors, are indeed seen primarily among maltreating parents or high-risk parents. Nonetheless, there are other paths to disorganized attachment. When parents have their own experiences of unresolved loss or abuse, they may behave in ways that frighten children, even though the behaviors do not seem overtly frightening. For example, parents with unresolved abuse are at increased risk for dissociating or "spacing out" (Schuengel et al., 1999). Behaviors associated with dissociation can be disconcerting and even frightening to children. These behaviors are seen most frequently among high-risk parents but are nonetheless also seen among low-risk parents.

It may seem unusual that secure attachment is seen among any of the children with CPS involvement. Although all CPS-involved parents face many challenges and have come to the attention of CPS because of concerning caregiving, some of these parents may not be the source of the abuse or neglect and may have the resources to provide children with nurturing care. For example, parents may come to the attention of CPS due to difficulty in meeting their child's needs for food or stable housing. Such parents may be able to provide nurturing, responsive care under challenging environmental conditions. Alternatively, some children may develop secure attachments even though their parents behave in frightening ways at times or fail to protect them from threat.

There have been far fewer studies of children in foster care than of children living under low-risk conditions, but our findings of intermediate levels of security are consistent with the existing studies (e.g., McLaughlin, Zeanah, Fox, & Nelson, 2012; Oosterman, De Schipper, Fisher, & Dozier, 2010), and they are also consistent with studies of other effects of foster care (e.g., Bernard, Butzin-Dozier, Rittenhouse, & Dozier, 2010). We reason that foster children do not show rates of secure attachment as high as seen in low-risk samples, both because they have experienced challenging conditions prior to foster placement and because of the inherent instability of foster care. Although we did not expect this when we began our research, we and others have found that foster parents often provide a regulating environment for children. Thus, children have better outcomes across the board in foster care than when living with high-risk birth parents. Among these outcomes, children show higher rates of secure attachment and lower rates of disorganized attachment than children living with their high-risk birth parents.

ATTACHMENT'S ASSOCIATION WITH LATER OUTCOMES

Attachment quality reflects children's expectations of parental availability when they are distressed. These expectations of a key relationship partner are thought to be the basis of children's emerging internal working models of self and others. Confidence in the availability of parents allows the child to process attachment-related experiences openly and nondefensively.

In line with this theory, attachment quality predicts a host of relational and nonrelational outcomes. The theory was tested in the Minnesota Study of Risk and Adaptation from Infancy to Adulthood, a study of longitudinal outcomes associated with attachment initiated by Alan Sroufe and Byron Egeland (Sroufe et al., 2005). In designing the Minnesota project, Sroufe and Egeland considered key developmental tasks that are salient at each point in development. The developmental tasks at one age might appear quite different from the tasks at another age, but an underlying continuity in the system's organization might still be detectable. In terms of outcomes, the study did not focus on attachment to the parent per se at various ages, but rather on markers of competent functioning at each age. For example, a key task for 2-year-old Aaron is to become increasingly autonomous while still relying effectively on his mother for help when necessary. Thus, in a laboratory procedure called the Tool Task, children are presented with a toy inside a transparent cylinder; the toy can be dislodged only by joining several tools together to push it out. The 2-year-old cannot succeed at this task alone but must rely on his parent for help. Differences in the child's effective reliance on the parent, and enthusiasm and competence in performing the task, can be assessed in this context.

Aaron, who showed a prototypically secure attachment to his mother at 12 months, took on the Tool Task with enthusiasm at age 2. He studied the toy inside the cylinder and tried each of the tools one by one. He talked to his mother as he worked. She was able to scaffold the task, eventually saying, "I wonder what would happen if you screwed the pieces together." When he experienced trouble screwing them together, he handed the pieces to his mother, who started the connection but left it for Aaron to finish. Aaron suddenly realized that the combined pieces would fit into the cylinder to push the toy out, which he eagerly executed. He exclaimed, "Look Mommy!" and she exclaimed in response, "You did it!" Consistent with this example, Matas, Arend, and Sroufe (1978) found that children who were securely attached at age 1 showed more enthusiasm for the task and relied more effectively on their parents for assistance than did other children.

Children with secure attachments show better outcomes across a range of domains than children with avoidant, resistant, or disorganized attachments. Social competence with peers has been assessed in 80 independent samples of children whose attachment was assessed in infancy (Groh et al., 2014). Secure children are more socially competent in their peer interactions than children from any of the other attachment categories. Insecurity of attachment, and avoidance in particular, is associated with heightened levels of internalizing problems, including symptoms such as depression and anxiety (Groh, Roisman, van IJzendoorn, Bakermans-Kranenburg, & Fearon, 2012). Disorganization is especially predictive of externalizing behaviors, which include problems such as oppositional behavior, impulsivity, attention problems, and aggression. Avoidance and resistance also predict externalizing behavior but not as strongly as does disorganized attachment (Fearon, Bakermans-Kranenburg, van IJzendoorn, Lapsley, & Roisman, 2010). Disorganized attachment also predicts dissociative symptoms in middle childhood and adolescence (Carlson, 1998).

Sroufe (2016) is careful to point out that as members of a field we should be specific in what we expect attachment and parental sensitivity to predict. Whereas attachment quality should predict interpersonal outcomes, Sroufe and colleagues initially did not expect it to have implications for language development and other cognitive outcomes. However, attachment quality and sensitive parenting do indeed predict cognitive outcomes, with effects at least as large as for social outcomes (Raby, Roisman, Fraley, & Simpson, 2015).

Our understanding of the role of sensitive interactions in language development has evolved in recent years. Parents who talk more to their children during the child's early years have children with larger vocabularies at school age and beyond (Hart & Risley, 1995; Klebanov, Brooks-Gunn, McCarton, & McCormick, 1998). Not only is it better that children hear more words, but speech that involves the child or is responsive to the child (i.e., child-directed speech) is the critical factor (Golinkoff et al., 2015; Hirsh-Pasek et al., 2015). A mother responding contingently to her child's babbling, commenting on her baby's focus of attention, and repeating her child's vocalizations are all examples of such child-directed interactions. These responsive interactions provide a social context that supports children's development of early language.

In addition to predicting cognitive and language outcomes, secure attachment also predicts physical well-being. In longitudinal studies, insecure attachment in infancy was associated with the increased likelihood of being overweight or obese at preschool age (Anderson & Whitaker, 2011) and in adolescence (Anderson, Gooze, Lemeshow, & Whitaker, 2012). Similar to the findings linking sensitive parenting to cognitive and language outcomes, these findings linking attachment quality to physical health were not predicted by early attachment theorists. However, emerging evidence regarding the mechanistic links between physiological stress regulation, inflammation, and physical health provides a rationale for why we may expect attachment relationships to influence obesity and other aspects of physical well-being.

PARENTS' STATE OF MIND WITH REGARD TO ATTACHMENT

Attachment is theorized to be the basis of internal working models that are carried through to subsequent relationships and to the processing of attachment-relevant memories, thoughts, and feelings. The Adult Attachment Interview (AAI; George, Kaplan, & Main, 1985) was designed with the goal of assessing internal working models and the processing of information related to attachment. "Attachment state of mind" (see Table 2.4) is reflected in discourse coherence when discussing attachment experiences, as well as in the manner with which one processes information about attachment-related thoughts, memories, and feelings.

Mary Main and her students/colleagues Carol George and Nancy Kaplan developed the AAI, and the scoring system was first developed by Main and Ruth Goldwyn. In this interview, adults are asked to describe their childhood relationships with their parents, to instantiate more general characterizations with specific memories, and to reflect upon relationship influences, among other things. On the basis of discourse analysis, adults are classified as autonomous, dismissing, preoccupied, or unresolved (with unresolved also receiving a secondary classification of autonomous, dismissing, or preoccupied).

Adults classified as having autonomous states of mind are coherent in their discourse and show a valuing of attachment. For example, if they describe an attachment figure as having been

TABLE 2.4. Adult Attachment State of Mind	
Classification	Description
Autonomous	Open, flexible processing of information, valuing of attachment
Dismissing	Lack of recall for attachment-related memories and/or idealizing of attachment figures
Preoccupied	Angry involvement with attachment figures and/or vague or rambling discourse
Unresolved	Lapse in reasoning regarding loss or trauma

emotionally available, they can support the claim with episodic memories, such that the picture that emerges is consistent with their more abstract, overall characterization. Such parents often have children who are securely attached to them—that is, children who come to them when distressed and make clear bids for reassurance. This connection between autonomous parental state of mind and secure infant attachment is presumed to result from autonomous parents being comfortable with their children's bids for reassurance, such that they are reassuring to their distressed infants; they neither feel a need to shut down negative affect, nor do they get so caught up in their own issues that they are unresponsive.

Adults classified as having dismissing states of mind idealize attachment figures and attachment experiences and/or have little recall for attachment experiences. Idealization is seen when interviewees choose very positive adjectives to describe their childhood relationships with parents (e.g., loving, wonderful, always there), but fail to provide specific examples as evidence. For example, when asked about a time when their mother was "loving," an adjective they selected themselves, they may describe a general memory, such as "you know, soup and ginger ale when you were sick," but specific episodic memories elude them, or alternatively, fail to support the glowing summary adjectives altogether. This strategy of limiting access to their own distressing attachment-related memories and feelings likely contributes to parents' needing to shut down their children's display of distress. Such parents are likely to be rejecting of their children's bids for reassurance—for example, indicating that children should hop up quickly if they fall or should never have stood on top of the chair in the first place. Or they may avoid children's distress by urging them to "look at the birdy outside the window" rather than cry. Each of these behaviors sends the message to children that they should not bring their distress to parents. Parents with dismissing states of mind often have children with avoidant attachments—children who turn away from them when hurt, frightened, or upset. Attachment theorists have suggested that this strategy is well suited to maximize proximity to the parent. The child does not make a bid for reassurance because the parent is not comfortable providing reassurance, and therefore the child is not actively rejected for making a bid (Bowlby, 1969/1982; Cassidy, 1994).

Parents with preoccupied states of mind become lost in their discourse about attachment memories, rather than clearly answering questions asked, and/or they may show an angry preoccupation with attachment figures. For example, when asked to recall a time when she was upset as a child, a mother first described the event, then moved to the present to say that her mother still lets her down, and finally went on to talk about other slights she had experienced. Such parents are often inconsistent in their responsiveness to their children's distress. They do not have the same aversion to distress that characterizes parents with dismissing states of mind, but their own issues impinge upon their attention, and they do not respond in ways that lead to children having confident expectations of their availability. Children of parents with preoccupied states of mind often develop resistant attachments to their parents, fussing and failing to soothe easily. Using the logic that children's strategies are designed to maximize proximity to their parents, attachment theorists have suggested that these children ramp up their requests for reassurance because the rate of favorable response is low (Bowlby, 1969/1982; Cassidy, 1994).

Parents who are "unresolved with respect to attachment" display a breakdown in reasoning or a breakdown in their discourse when discussing incidences of trauma or loss. For example, a mother recalled her father coming up the stairs to beat her and her sister, and she then became seemingly lost in the memory, describing the pounding and vibration of his footsteps as if it were happening at that moment. A father talked in the present tense about his grandmother who had raised him even though his grandmother died 25 years earlier. Parents who are unresolved with respect to attachment are at risk for behaving in ways that are frightening to their children. One of the concomitants of unresolved abuse or trauma is a tendency to dissociate. During the AAI, this is seen when parents become lost in their discourse. In their interactions with their children, such parents may "space out" occasionally for brief or even extended periods of time. As has been well documented in the Still Face Paradigm (Weinberg & Tronick, 1996), children become dysregulated when parents become unresponsive to them by briefly holding a neutral expression, but they seem to recover quickly when their parents resume normal interaction. If, however, such behavior is experienced more often, it is likely to be highly dysregulating.

Parents with unresolved loss or trauma are also prone to behave in ways that are overtly frightening (Jacobvitz et al., 2006; Schuengel et al., 1999). For example, parents may use an unreal, odd voice in ways that frighten the child, or they may yell or threaten the child. When children experience a parent who dissociates frequently in their presence or is frankly frightening, they are likely to experience "fright without solution" (Hesse & Main, 2006). Such children often exhibit a breakdown in their attachment strategy when distressed (Main & Solomon, 1986, 1990).

The attachment state of mind classification system was largely empirically derived; that is, adults were grouped as parents of secure infants, avoidant infants, resistant infants, and disorganized infants, with discourse similarities and differences used as the defining features. Given this procedure, it may not be surprising that parent state of mind predicts infant attachment (Verhage et al., 2016) (see Table 2.5). Indeed, parent state of mind is currently the *strongest* predictor of infant attachment. We have been discussing parental behaviors that are associated with state of mind as the mechanism explaining the association between state of mind and attachment, but this link between parental behaviors, state of mind, and attachment is still somewhat theoretical. At

TABLE 2.5. Parent State of Mind, Parental Behavior, and Infant Attachment

State of Mind	Parental Behavior	Infant Attachment
Autonomous	Nurturing	Secure
Dismissing	Rejecting	Avoidant
Preoccupied	Inconsistent	Resistant
Unresolved	Frightening/frightened	Disorganized

best, parental behaviors have been found only to partially mediate the association (Verhage et al., 2016). Although we are first and foremost empiricists (i.e., believers in what data tell us), we do suspect that relevant parenting behaviors may not be captured fully through our measurements. It is hard to envision how parental state of mind could be transmitted to children's attachment quality in ways other than through parental behavior, especially in the case of parent–child dyads who are not biologically related.

Hazan and Shaver (1987) developed a taxonomy of adult attachment that also parallels the Ainsworth categories. Rather than rely on discourse analyses, the original Hazan and Shaver system used single-item self-report categorization. Adults endorsed one of three descriptions as most characteristic of themselves in close (e.g., romantic or couple) relationships. People who indicated that they find it easy to get close to others and do not worry about having others get too close to them were classified as having a secure attachment style. Those who indicated discomfort with others getting too close were classified as avoidant, and those who indicated concern about not being loved enough were classified as resistant. This system, which was later expanded into two highly reliable multi-item scales measuring attachment anxiety and attachment-related avoidance, has been used extensively in studies by social psychologists (see review by Mikulincer & Shaver, 2016). Findings are often compatible with findings using the AAI (Jones, Cassidy, & Shaver, 2015), even though the two measures seem to tap different things (Roisman et al., 2007).

RELEVANCE TO ABC

Both child attachment quality and parents' state of mind with respect to attachment are central constructs undergirding the ABC intervention. One key targeted outcome of the intervention is attachment quality. The quality of a child's attachment is developed through many social interactions with his or her parent over time. Thus, when parents change as the result of the intervention, becoming more nurturing, for example, the child's expectations of availability are not necessarily immediately updated. The child has many previous experiences that are likely integrated with the new information. Nonetheless, there is "plasticity" in behavior and biology—and in children's expectations. Children's expectations of availability are expected to gradually—or eventually—change. Measured attachment quality provides information regarding those expectations. Therefore, we expected more of the children whose parents received the ABC intervention to develop secure attachments than those whose parents received a control intervention. That is exactly what we found, as we discuss more fully in Chapter 8. More children whose parents received ABC developed secure attachments and fewer developed disorganized attachments than children whose parents received a control intervention.

Parental state of mind matters in the context of intervention for several reasons. First, as discussed earlier in this chapter, parents with different states of mind with respect to attachment tend to interact with their children differently, especially in attachment-relevant contexts (such as when the child is distressed and needs the parent). Even when a mother with an autonomous state of mind is not responding in a nurturing way with her child, we find it is much easier to convince her of the importance of nurturance than it is to convince a dismissing mother. It often feels like a relief to a mother with an autonomous state of mind to hear that it is fine to pick up her crying baby, but this is often not the case with a mother with a dismissing state of mind.

Moreover, a collaborative relationship between parent and parent coach is much easier to achieve when the mother has an autonomous state of mind than when she has a dismissing state of mind. In research that we conducted many years ago, we found that adults with schizophrenia and bipolar disorder who were more dismissing with regard to attachment were more rejecting of treatment providers than were others (Dozier, 1990). Therefore, we approached ABC anticipating that parents with autonomous states of mind would be more collaborative as treatment partners, whereas parents with dismissing states of mind would be less so. Nonetheless, this does not mean that ABC or other interventions will not be effective with nonautonomous parents, just that building the relationship is likely to be somewhat more challenging, and the intervention targets will not be perceived as intuitive as with autonomous parents. Indeed, we have found that nonautonomous parents are able to become nurturing, responsive parents with support and coaching.

Given that early adversity poses direct threats to children's ability to form secure attachment relationships, attachment theory has provided a critical framework for designing the ABC intervention and evaluating its efficacy. In the next chapters, we describe how ABC was informed by attachment theory and how we targeted attachment issues.

CHAPTER 3

Development of
the ABC Intervention

One night I (M. D.) was watching the news and saw a social worker taking a screaming 2-year-old away from her foster mother. The child was being moved to another foster home because she was a different race from that of her foster mother. At this point, I can't remember if the foster mother was white and the child black, or vice versa. What I remember clearly, though, is that the child was reacting as if the world was ending. Indeed, for an infant, losing one's attachment figure would feel as if the world were ending. From an evolutionary perspective, this makes sense: In times past, if infants did not have someone to protect them from the dangers of predators or falling off a cliff, they would not have survived. The attachment system developed to ensure that by the time babies had the capacity to move away from their attachment figures, they would have a strong drive to stay close when conditions were threatening.

This 2-year-old who was being taken away from her foster mother screamed because she needed to hold onto her at all costs. At the time, my first child was a little more than a year old. It occurred to me that this child on the news was reacting to being taken away from her foster mother just as my son would have reacted if he were taken away from me. My child would surely have screamed and reacted as if the world were ending—indeed, the world as he had known it, with me as the primary attachment figure, would have ended. This child on the news was experiencing this same type of loss. She understood nothing of foster care or of differing racial backgrounds; she knew only that she was being taken away from her attachment figure.

Until this point, I had been conducting research in a very different area. I had been studying how adults' attachment state of mind affected receptiveness to treatment among people with serious psychiatric disorders. Over time, I had become somewhat frustrated with this area of research. Although the research had indirect implications for treatment, it did not have *direct* implications. For example, sometimes when I gave a talk to a group of clinicians, they asked how my findings should affect their work with their clients. My findings were perhaps somewhat useful, but only somewhat. Furthermore, I had been studying how adults, many of whom had experienced severe early adversity, talked about and represented their attachment experiences. Again, this was indirect, and I was eager to explore these early adverse experiences directly.

I was poised for a change in research directions. After seeing the news segment in which the child was taken from her foster mother, I immediately started talking to students in classes about the important issues raised by this example. How would this child (and other children) be affected by this disruption in care? Would the child be able to form a new attachment to a new caregiver? How would the child's relationship with her foster mother be carried forward in future relationships, and in the child's representations of herself and others? Perhaps one of the most important questions was: How could we help the child and subsequent caregivers be able to forge the strongest, most secure relationship that was possible under the circumstances?

We started with these larger questions in mind, but we quickly became aware that there were some basic things that were critical to address first. For example, as a field, we did not know what the process of forming a new attachment looked like, or indeed how to study this process, or how long it would take for a child to form a new attachment. These seemed very basic questions, integral to attachment theory. Indeed, John Bowlby had been very interested in how separations from attachment figures affect children. But relatively few attachment researchers had studied foster or adopted children, and little attention had been paid to the issues of how children form new attachments, the process by which they formed new attachments, and the effects of losing attachment figures. We therefore began our program of research with little previous work to inform us specifically about these questions.

CHILDREN PUSH CAREGIVERS AWAY

As we began to study the process by which children formed attachments to their new foster parents, it occurred to us that we did not have the tools we needed to answer the questions. If we wanted to look at the quality of the attachment once it was formed, the Strange Situation was appropriate, but we did not know how long it would take after a child was placed into a new foster home before he or she would consolidate an attachment, or how we would know when he or she had a fully formed attachment. (Although this was the situation in 1994 when we began this work, Elizabeth Carlson [reported in Zeanah, Smyke, Koga, Carlson, & the Bucharest Early Intervention Project Core Group, 2005] has since developed an assessment of attachment formation that has proven useful in determining the extent to which children have developed clear attachments to their parents following institutional care.)

A graduate student at the time, Chase Stovall (now Chase Stovall-McClough) developed a diary methodology (Stovall & Dozier, 2000) that allowed us to examine attachment behaviors on a daily basis. Using the diary, foster parents reported how their children behaved when they were hurt, separated, or upset. Parents used a checklist to indicate the child's initial behaviors, the parents' behaviors in response, and the child's behavior in response to the parents. Parents also wrote brief narrative accounts of the incidents, which allowed us to verify the behaviors they had indicated on the checklist. This diary was not a perfect instrument because, of course, it relied on parental report, and attachment theory and research make us keenly aware of the differential filters that different parents use in reporting (e.g., Stokes, Pogge, Wecksell, & Zaccario, 2011). Still, we reasoned that by reporting on specific incidents in a recent time frame (rather than reporting on general behavioral tendencies) and in specific behavioral interactions with children with whom they did not have a relationship history full of expectations, this reporting bias would be minimized (e.g., Scheeringa, Peebles, Cook, & Zeanah, 2001).

Foster parents were asked to keep daily diaries of their children's attachment behaviors from as close to the first day of placement as possible throughout the first 3 months (see Figure 3.1).

This allowed us to examine what affected children's attachment behaviors and how those behaviors changed over time. We found that autonomous foster parents reported that young infants (younger than about 10 months of age) started showing secure behaviors toward them in the first to second weeks, and this reflected a stable, perhaps even consolidated, pattern of behaviors (Stovall & Dozier, 2000; Stovall-McClough & Dozier, 2004). This finding was startling to us at the time: How could a child organize his or her attachment behaviors so quickly when placed with a new caregiver? But it occurred to us that a week in the life of a young infant is a very long time. In terms of evolutionary significance, it would have been critical to the child's survival to have the ability to depend on a new caregiver quickly if the child lost his or her parent. There are consequences for children when they experience disruptions in care, which we consider later, but in terms of attachment, an infant younger than about a year seems able to organize attachment behaviors around a new caregiver and, from the perspective of the new caregiver, to do so relatively quickly.

With older infants (between 1 and 2 years old), the picture was different. Even autonomous foster parents did not report that their children showed secure behaviors. These older infants continued to show avoidant and resistant behaviors over the first several months of the placement. Figure 3.2 provides an example of

1. Think of one time today when your child got physically hurt (includes anything like falling down, scraping a knee, bumping into something, etc.) and answer the following:

   Describe this situation in two to three sentences (including how you responded to your child):

   Alice was standing holding onto a kitchen chair and fell

   down. She bumped her head on the floor and started to cry.

   I went over and picked her up and rubbed her head.

   A. What did your child do to let you know he/she was hurt? Number your child's reactions, in order. Only put a number if the behavior occurred.

   ___ looked at me for assurance
   ___ went off by him/herself
   ___ acted as if nothing was wrong
   ___ acted angry/frustrated (e.g., stomped feet, kicked legs)
   ___ called for me
   ___ looked at me briefly then looked away and went on
   ___ came to me
   _2_ signaled to be picked up or held, reached for me
   ___ cried
   ___ did not indicate he/she wanted or needed me
   _1_ cried and remained where he/she was, did not signal for me
   ___ moved closer to me (but actual contact did not occur)
   ___ other(s) _____

   B. After you responded to your child, what did your child do next? Number your child's reactions, in order. Only put a number if the behavior occurred.

   _2_ was soon calmed or soothed
   ___ pushed me away angrily or in frustration
   ___ continued to play, did not notice me
   ___ stomped and/or kicked feet
   ___ hit or kicked at me
   ___ remained upset, was difficult to soothe
   ___ turned from me angrily or in frustration
   ___ did not indicate he/she needed my help
   ___ ignored me
   ___ became quiet and then fussy again
   ___ turned away when picked up or made contact
   _1_ sunk into me or held on to me until calmed down
   ___ did not easily let me hold him/her but remained upset (e.g., arched back)
   ___ held on to me or went after me if I tried to put him/her down or go away
   ___ turned, walked, or crawled away from me as if nothing was wrong
   ___ other(s) _____

FIGURE 3.1. Parent attachment diary.

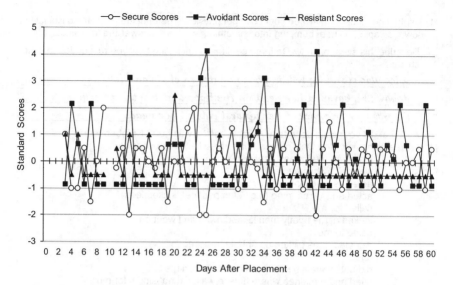

FIGURE 3.2. Parent attachment diary: Example of child placed at 14 months. From Stovall and Dozier (2000). Copyright 2000 by Cambridge University Press. Adapted with permission from Cambridge University Press.

a child placed in the home of an autonomous foster mother at the age of 14 months. The filled squares denote avoidant behavior; the relative frequency of the behavior is on the Y (vertical) axis and the day since placement on the X (horizontal) axis. A preponderance of avoidant behaviors can be seen through the first 2 months of placement. Whereas the younger infants showed secure behaviors quickly, such was not the case for infants older than about a year.

What troubled us most was that foster mothers responded "in kind" to their infants' cues. When infants cried and looked to them, autonomous foster parents went to their babies, picked them up, or soothed them in some way. However, when infants turned away from them, foster parents acted as if their babies did not need them—and did not act in comforting ways. This was the case even for foster parents with autonomous states of mind who would otherwise be expected to respond in nurturing ways to their infants. Similarly, when their babies behaved in resistant ways (i.e., were fussy and inconsolable), foster mothers acted frustrated or annoyed. This self-perpetuating cycle was truly troubling.

Although this surprised us at the time, it makes a great deal of sense. Some social behaviors powerfully elicit complementary behaviors from others. Help-seeking behaviors (and help-rejecting behaviors) are perhaps among the most powerful. Think of your own experience. Can you imagine saying to a friend, "I'm so sorry that your father died," and having your friend say, "I'm OK—we were never that close." Most of us would react by pulling away—by not offering any more support—and that was the effect foster children had on their foster parents. These children acted as if they didn't need their foster parents, and their foster parents responded in kind.

One might first think that the situation is very different for high-risk birth parents, but we have found the situations analogous. As birth parents work to become more nurturing, their children's expectations often lag behind (based on what we saw among foster children, we think this is the case especially if children are older than about a year).

Take the example of Sonya who was living in the motel room with James. Sonya worked hard to notice when James bumped his head or scraped a toe or had other similar experiences. As she went through the ABC intervention, she became invested in having James trust in her availability. When James was hurt, however, he looked quickly away from his mother. For example, he sometimes seemed totally engaged with his toys after bumping his head, even more than prior to hurting himself. If Sonya were to be nurturing, she needed to provide nurturance to James even though he did not signal a need for nurturance.

In summary, when babies have had experiences of adversity, whether from previous or current relationships, they often behave in ways that fail to elicit nurturing care. This is especially troubling because the children's expectations of unreliable relationships will be confirmed by their parents. Even though their parents may be capable of being loving and nurturing, the infants' behaviors will fail to elicit nurturance—and parents will respond in kind.

Intervention Component 1a: Provide Nurturance Even When the Child Does Not Elicit It

Helping parents provide nurturance even when the child's behavior suggests that he or she does not need it, or cannot be soothed by it, is the first intervention component and is introduced to parents in the first ABC session. Having an expert in parenting come into one's home can be threatening. But this initial focus on the child pushing the caregiver away makes it less so. Parents are encouraged to see their task as especially difficult; they need to be more than sensitive parents. Indeed, they need to be therapeutic parents. If they respond to their child only as elicited by the child's behaviors, the child's behaviors will elicit non-nurturing behaviors, and the child's expectations will be confirmed. Therefore, our first intervention target is helping parents provide nurturance even when children fail to elicit it.

Helping parents think about how their children push them away is the easiest aspect of the intervention. We have found that both foster and high-risk birth parents are comfortable with the idea that their children have experienced adversity, which then makes it hard for them as parents to provide nurturing care. For example, when Gabriella mentioned that sometimes children who have experienced difficult times push their parents away, Sonya said immediately, "Well, I can tell you that's true with James—he's had hard times!" The door was open for Gabriella to talk about how this could make it harder for James to signal clearly to his mother when he needs her.

PARENTS' OWN ISSUES GET IN THE WAY OF NURTURANCE

We know that nurturing care is especially important for young children who have experienced adversity. But two things can get in the way. First, as discussed, these young children often behave in ways that fail to elicit nurturing care. Second, responding in nurturing ways comes easier to some parents than it does to others. For some, especially those with dismissing states of mind, there is a strong urge to move children past their distress quickly. For example, when a child falls down, the mother may say something to the effect of "Get up, you're okay," or "Look outside—there's a big bus going by," or even "I told you not to stand on that chair. That's what you get." In each of these instances, the mother is trying to move the child past the distress quickly and is sending the message that the child does not need the parent's soothing or calming. The mother whose own parents rejected her attachment needs has learned to push away such needs herself; she is uncomfortable with her child's distress and is convinced that the child will be better off if he or she does not experience distress any longer than necessary. The idea that her child may just need to feel the distress and be calmed and soothed by her is foreign to her.

We know, however, that it is important for children who have experienced adversity to have nurturing parents. We know that children who have experienced adversity are at especially high risk for developing disorganized attachments if their parents are not nurturing (Dozier, Stovall, Albus, & Bates, 2001). Whereas children from low-risk families typically develop avoidant attachments when their parents have dismissing states of mind, children who have experienced adversity are more likely to develop disorganized attachments rather than avoidant attachments. Given that disorganized attachment is associated with problematic long-term outcomes (e.g., Carlson, 1998; Fearon et al., 2010), we reasoned that it is important to help parents provide nurturing care even if it does not come naturally to them.

Intervention Component 1b: Provide Nurturance Even When It Does Not Come Naturally

In ABC, we seek to help parents recognize important influences from their own attachment experiences, become aware of how these influences affect their parenting behaviors, and then learn to "override" their automatic responses, providing nurturance even when it is not elicited. Importantly, our purpose is not to process past experiences in a way that will change attachment at a representational level; rather, we expect that attention to these topics will change parents' behavior.

Parent coaches approach "voices from the past" with a clear objective in mind (or perhaps several objectives). The concept is introduced late in the intervention (Sessions 7 and 8 of the 10-session intervention). At that point, parent coaches have worked to create behavioral change in nurturance, following the lead, and reducing frightening behavior. They typically know where parents have the most difficulty and where parents are likely to experience the most problems after the intervention is over. Our approach to voices from the past is therefore to target the issue or issues seen as most problematic behaviorally, which is not necessarily the area that the parent is most likely to resonate with in terms of past influences.

Sonya had made real progress in following the lead and in nurturing James by Sessions 7 and 8. Nonetheless, she sometimes became distracted by the demands on her and annoyed with James's needs for reassurance. In Sessions 7 and 8, her parent coach Gabriella helped Sonya think of her own experiences when she needed reassurance as a child. Sonya's memory of her early childhood was very patchy, but she had a vivid memory of falling at a playground at the age of 5. Her face and arm were cut and bleeding, but her sister was able to help her get home. When she walked into her apartment, her mother began yelling at her sister that they should not have been at the playground. Her mother came and looked at Sonya's cuts and said, "What were you doing at that playground? You should have known not to climb up there. I've told you about that." Even as her mother cleaned her up, her words dismissed Sonya's distress: "What are you still crying for? You're fine—you're not even bleeding anymore." From this interaction and many others, Sonya got the message that she should not come to her mother for reassurance.

Gabriella pointed out that Sonya's "automatic" response to James might well be to fuss at him when he got hurt or was distressed. It made it all the more impressive that she was able to provide nurturance when she did. Gabriella showed Sonya a short video clip of Sonya reassuring James when he was frightened. She pointed out that it must have been hard to be nurturing because her mom was often not nurturing to her. She then showed a short clip from an early session in which Sonya told a crying James that he wasn't really hurt. Gabriella asked what she noticed in the video. Sonya said emphatically, "He *was* hurt! He wouldn't have been crying if he wasn't. And I just told him he was fine." Gabriella said, "Yeah, and that was like your mom's voice, right?" Gabriella highlighted what a strength it was that Sonya recognized the voice from the past in the video, noting that we all have such voices that can influence parenting.

Sonya was helped to see that her automatic response had been, and might always be, to minimize James's distress. But if she recognized this automatic response, she did not have to respond in accord with the historically automatic response; she could essentially make the automatic no longer automatic. She could thus "override" her initial (automatic) response and choose to respond in a way that was in keeping with James's needs. This is how we deal with voices from the past.

STRESS NEUROBIOLOGY

With no expectation that the intervention would ever be informed by neuroscience, I (M. D.) attended a talk at our university by Seymour, or Gig, Levine. Levine had moved to Delaware following a long career as a neuroendocrinologist at Stanford studying squirrel monkeys, rodents, and other mammals. In his talk that day in 1995, he described how the hypothalamic–pituitary–adrenal (HPA) axis of the infant squirrel monkey was affected by separations from its mother. The HPA axis (see Figure 3.3) is an evolutionarily prepared system reserved for responding to uncontrollable stress (Dickerson & Kemeny, 2004). When the organism is stressed, the hypothalamus releases corticotropin-releasing hormone (CRH), which travels to the pituitary gland, which then releases adrenocorticotropic hormone (ACTH). ACTH travels to the adrenal cortex, which releases glucocorticoids (cortisol in primates and corticosterone in rodents). Cortisol can be studied as an end product of this axis, providing information about the level of the response and the recovery poststressor.

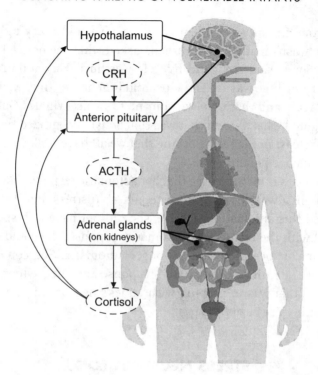

FIGURE 3.3. Hypothalamic–pituitary–adrenal (HPA) axis. When an individual encounters a stressor, the HPA system responds through a series of biochemical reactions, resulting in the output of cortisol. The hypothalamus releases corticotropin-releasing hormone (CRH), which stimulates the release of adrenocorticotropic hormone (ACTH) from the anterior lobe of the pituitary gland. ACTH then stimulates the adrenal glands to produce glucocorticoid hormones (cortisol in humans). Cortisol then feeds back to the hypothalamus and the pituitary gland to suppress CRH and ACTH production.

Levine described behavioral and neuroendocrine responses to infant squirrel monkeys being separated from their mothers. When the infants were separated within earshot of their mothers, where they could hear and smell her, their cries were frequent and intense 24 hours later. When placed in a distant cage, such that they could not hear or smell their mothers, their cries diminished (S. Levine, personal communication, April 1999). If one paid attention only to the behaviors of the infant squirrel monkeys, one might have thought that the infants who could not see their mothers were no longer as distressed as the other infants. But their neuroendocrine response (measured by the production of cortisol) showed something very different. The monkeys that could not see their mothers showed a robust cortisol response, with levels of cortisol remaining very high at the end of the 24-hour period. This divergence between the behavioral response and the neuroendocrine response was striking.

The parallels between the research on nonhuman animals and children in foster care were remarkable. It seemed plausible that children in foster care might show perturbations in their cortisol production following placement into foster care, even though foster parents often remarked that behaviorally they seemed "fine." In collaboration with Seymour Levine, we began asking questions about the HPA functioning of children who had experienced adversity.

Whereas the animal research had focused on stress reactivity, we found that differences in diurnal patterning were the most compelling. Stress reactivity and diurnal patterning are two independent functions of the HPA axis. As humans, when we wake up in the morning we are typically producing a relatively high level of cortisol (peaking about 30 minutes after wake-up), with levels going down in the morning and reaching near zero levels at bedtime. This diurnal pattern (see Figure 3.4) is evolutionarily adaptive, helping us function as diurnal creatures, awake and active when other members of our species are also awake. The high morning level does not reflect increased stress in the morning; rather, we are metabolizing more glucose to help us take on the day.

We found that children who had experienced adversity showed different patterns of cortisol than children growing up under less challenging conditions (Bernard et al., 2010; Dozier et al., 2006). In particular, children who lived under the most high-risk conditions (children living with high-risk parents) showed a very flat pattern of cortisol production with low morning values, as can be seen in Figure 3.5. Children living with foster parents showed a somewhat steeper slope, and children living with low-risk birth parents showed the steepest slope. What this told us is

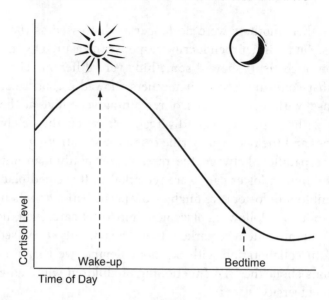

FIGURE 3.4. Typical diurnal rhythm of cortisol production.

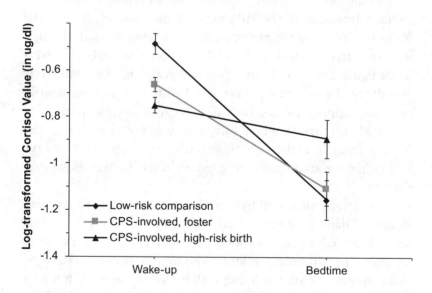

FIGURE 3.5. Diurnal cortisol rhythms among low-risk, foster, and CPS-involved children.

that adversity had affected a very basic biological function. Such changes to the diurnal patterning could interfere with sleep, with daytime alertness and attention, and with other critical functions.

This finding provided us with evidence that children who experienced adversity had trouble regulating their physiology. Phil Fisher and his colleagues reported very similar findings at about the same time (Bruce, Fisher, Pears, & Levine, 2009; Fisher, Stoolmiller, Gunnar, & Burraston, 2007), leading us both to have confidence that the results were robust. Many studies have found that children who have experienced adversity also have trouble regulating emotions and behavior (e.g., Pears, Kim, Buchanan, & Fisher, 2015; Tottenham et al., 2010). So we were presented with the next issue we needed to target in our intervention—enhancing children's regulatory capabilities.

Whereas the first issue we targeted (i.e., helping parents provide nurturance even when their children pushed them away) was readily linked with an intervention target, it was less clear how to change children's regulatory capabilities. We scoured the literature in search of ideas. We found that mothers who were very responsive, that is, mothers who followed their children's lead, had children with better self-regulation than mothers who were not responsive (Raver, 1996). We reasoned that if we helped parents follow their children's lead, children would develop enhanced regulatory capabilities. This, then, was our second intervention component.

Intervention Component 2: Following the Child's Lead

Children who have experienced adversity need help in developing regulatory strategies. The intervention stresses the importance of parents following their children's lead to help them develop adequate self-regulatory capabilities.

We help parents learn to follow their children's lead through their actions or their comments. At the behavioral level, a parent might simply take something offered from the child. For example, if the child hands her a toy, she might take it from him. She could engage in the same behavior the child is engaging in. For example, if the child takes a spoon and bangs it against a pan, she could do the same. Or she might follow the child's action with an action that is consistent with the child's action (i.e., not the same but not changing the game). For example, if the child puts a horse in a barn, the mother might put another animal in the barn. At the level of the parent's comments, the parent could comment on what the child does. For example, she might say, "Thanks for giving me that," or "Wow, you're banging the spoon, aren't you?," or "The horsey is in the barn now."

In each of these cases, the parent's actions are following the child's actions. They are not changing the direction of the activity but rather are continuing what the child started. These interactions typically feel smoother for the child than when the parent changes the interactional flow, and for this reason we expect these interactions to be regulating (Beebe et al., 2010; Kopp, 1982; Tronick & Cohn, 1989). Jack Shonkoff of Harvard's Center on the Developing Child refers to these as "serve-and-return" interactions.

We aspire to help parents follow their children's lead routinely, such that it becomes a consistent pattern of interacting with their children. To clarify what we mean by following the lead, we provide examples of what does not constitute following the lead. Following the child's lead does not mean offering the child a choice between whether to wear blue socks or red socks for the day; rather, it means noticing the child's focus of attention while putting on the socks and commenting on it (e.g., "Oh, does that sock feel bumpy?"). Following the lead does not mean letting the child play on his or her own with whatever toys are chosen; rather, following the lead involves active behaviors through which the parent becomes involved in the child's world.

Intervention Component 2a: Expressing Delight in the Child

Initially, we had planned to focus only on following the lead for component 2. What we observed was that sometimes parents learned to follow the lead, but they did so in a very rote fashion. In such cases, they appeared to be having no fun. This wasn't what we intended, but we realized that we had not specified that parents should take joy in their child when following the child's lead.

We went back to our own findings to learn more about the importance of this issue. We had found that delight was a signal of commitment among foster parents. That is, foster parents who indicate that they are committed to long-term relationships with their foster children show more delight in their children at the behavioral level than foster parents who are not as committed (Bernard & Dozier, 2011). In a personal communication (August 2001), Mary Main suggested that parental delight communicates to children how important they are to their parents, a sentiment that she indicated Mary Ainsworth shared.

A parent delighting in her child can take many forms— smiling when her baby looks at her, clapping and saying "Yay!" when her child knocks down a block tower, laughing as her child does a silly dance. We think that all of these expressions of delight communicate to the child that he or she matters.

PARENTAL FRIGHTENING BEHAVIOR

The two components of nurturance and following the lead constituted the intervention initially. And yet when we intervened with some families living under very challenging circumstances, we saw parents behave in frightening ways at times: yelling, smacking their child, glaring, threatening. We knew that failure to address frightening behavior would undermine any other progress parents might make.

Both attachment and stress neurobiology literatures provided us with evidence that parental frightening behavior leads to problematic outcomes for children. From the attachment literature (Jacobvitz et al., 2006; Schuengel et al., 1999), we knew that frightening parental behavior was predictive of disorganized attachment. Main and others had argued that, when parents behaved in frightening ways, children experienced "an unsolvable dilemma" (Main & Hesse, 1990). Children needed to seek proximity to their parent for safety but were frightened by the very person on whom they needed to rely. The seemingly anomalous behaviors these children show, such as turning in circles, freezing, or simultaneously showing avoidant and resistant behaviors, were evidence of this dilemma.

The stress neurobiology literature also provides evidence of the undermining influence of parental frightening behavior. Frightening parental behavior appears to render parents ineffective in their role in buffering children from the effects of toxic stress. We and others have seen this in children's cortisol response to threatening conditions (such as the Strange Situation). Babies are "built" to avoid elevations in cortisol, likely because high levels of circulating glucocorticoids are dangerous for the developing brain. But when parents are frightening, it seems that they fail to buffer children as would be expected, and children sometimes show elevated levels of cortisol when threatened (Bernard & Dozier, 2010; Hertsgaard, Gunnar, Farrell, Erickson, & Nachmias, 1995; Spangler & Grossman, 1993).

These findings from the attachment and stress neurobiology literatures, as well as our own observations of the frequency with which some parents behaved in frightening ways with their young children, impressed upon us the importance of intervening to affect frightening behavior. These observations and the knowledge of the research findings led to our third intervention component.

Intervention Component 3: Avoid Behaving in Frightening Ways

Parental frightening behavior undermines children's ability to organize attachment behaviors and regulate their physiology. This intervention component helps parents become aware of ways in which their behavior may be frightening to their children and then to develop alternatives to frightening behavior.

ABC addresses three issues and three issues only: helping parents nurture their distressed child, follow their child's lead with delight, and avoid frightening their child (see Table 3.1).

TABLE 3.1. ABC Components	
Component	**Description**
1: Nurturance	a: Be nurturing, even when child fails to elicit nurturance.
	b: Be nurturing, even when it doesn't come naturally.
2: Following the lead	a: Follow the child's lead.
	b: Express delight.
3: Nonfrightening behavior	Avoid behaving in intrusive, harsh, and frightening ways.

These three components are targeted in every session, every activity, and every comment.

Many other issues might be tempting to address, such as helping parents when housing problems arise, when developmental milestones are not reached, or when problems emerge with domestic partners. But the intervention is squarely focused on just three intervention targets and these three targets only. The crises that parents experience are very real and riveting, but paying attention to them will take the focus off these targets. We argue that a disciplined approach to these three issues will fundamentally change how parents care for their children. Although the pull to help with housing or developmental milestones will be compelling, moving away from the focus on the three intervention targets will undermine the intervention's effectiveness. Furthermore, although the crises are very real and urgent, there will continue to be crises in parents' lives. We are intervening with the objective of helping parents interact in ways that buffer their children from these crises.

We made substantial changes in the intervention later, as we began to disseminate it to other places, particularly with regard to commenting "in the moment." We describe those changes later in this book.

CHAPTER 4

ABC for High-Risk Birth Parents

CRYSTAL

On the day she met her parent coach, Crystal was living in an efficiency apartment with three of her four children. Her fourth child stayed with an aunt, and her boyfriend was in and out of the picture. The apartment had little play space other than the bed, the sofa, and the several feet surrounding them. Crystal was occasionally engaged with the baby, but the two other children were fully ignored or told to be quiet and stay off the bed with the baby.

Crystal's parent coach noticed immediately how tired Crystal seemed. It was little wonder—Crystal worked all day while her aunt looked after the kids, and she then came back to a crowded apartment with three kids. As it turned out, she was not only tired but depressed as well, and she had difficulty feeling any energy or sense of hopefulness on the best of days.

When Crystal was a child, her mother struggled with substance abuse (both alcohol and cocaine) and spent some time in jail. Her father was in the picture only rarely. Although Crystal can recall enjoying the occasional times she was able to see her father, her mother spoke disparagingly about him and discouraged contact. When her mother's substance abuse was particularly out of control, Crystal stayed with her aunt or grandmother. By the time she was 16, though, Crystal was fending for herself much of the time. It had been challenging, to say the least, but she prided herself on never landing in jail during her teens.

PARENTS WHO NEGLECT THEIR CHILDREN: THE CONTEXT FOR INTERVENTION

Like Crystal, parents who neglect their children are more likely than other parents to have a host of other problems, including substance abuse, psychiatric disorders, domestic violence, and problems with basic life needs, such as inadequate housing, employment, and access to food. These issues are often integrally related to parents' difficulties in parenting, both directly and indirectly.

Substance Abuse

Neglecting parents are disproportionately likely to have problems with substance abuse, including excessive use of alcohol and use of illegal drugs, especially marijuana, amphetamines, crack cocaine, and opioids (Dube et al., 2001; Dubowitz et al., 2011; Oliveros & Kaufman, 2011). Even after accounting for related factors, such as lack of social support, depression, and socioeconomic status, a strong association remains between parental substance use disorders and child neglect (Dunn et al., 2002). There is extensive evidence that substance abuse interferes with parenting capabilities (e.g., Bernstein, Jeremy, & Marcus, 1986; Mayes & Truman, 2002). Research on addiction and parenting suggests that substance abuse significantly impairs neural circuits of reward and stress regulation, which are critical for sensitive and effective parenting (Rutherford & Mayes, 2017). In addition, hormones, especially oxytocin and cortisol, which are involved in motivating parenting behavior, become dysregulated as the result of the use of opiates (e.g., McGregor & Bowen, 2012).

Mental Health Problems

Parents with substantiated allegations of maltreatment are more likely than other parents of similar backgrounds to be diagnosed with serious psychiatric disorders, including depression, bipolar affective disorder, schizophrenia, and borderline personality disorder. Although the evidence regarding the effects of psychiatric disorders on parenting is mixed (see Seifer & Dickstein, 1993, for a review), depressed mothers have been found to be less responsive to their infants' cues than other mothers (Bernard, Nissim, Vaccaro, Harris, & Lindhiem, 2018; Field, 1984), and children of depressed mothers show impairment across development (Goodman, 2007). Depression or other psychiatric disorders may interfere with sensitive parenting through multiple mechanisms, including blunted neural responses to infant cues (Laurent & Ablow, 2013), reduced emotion regulation ability (Haga et al., 2012), negative cognitions about infant crying (Leerkes et al., 2015), and physical fatigue (Thomas & Spieker, 2016).

Domestic Violence

Domestic violence refers to violence directed toward adults in the home. There is substantial overlap between children exposed to domestic violence and children who experience neglect and abuse (Hazen, Connelly, Kelleher, Landsverk, & Barth, 2004). Not surprisingly, parents who are victims or perpetrators of domestic violence are considerably more likely than other parents to be reported for child maltreatment (Hazen et al., 2004). The experience of domestic violence interferes with parents' ability to provide adequate care for their children and has significant effects on children who witness violence (e.g., Gustafsson, Coffman, & Cox, 2015; Vu, Jouriles, McDonald, & Rosenfield, 2016).

Poverty and Lack of Resources

Most cases referred to CPS for neglect involve families living in poverty (Connell, Bergerson, Katz, Saunders, & Tebes, 2007; Wald, 2015; Yang, 2015). Extreme poverty affects parents' ability to care for their children (Vernon-Feagons & Cox, 2013). Furthermore, poverty affects the response of the child welfare system, with children of poor parents more likely than other children to be placed into foster care when allegations of maltreatment are substantiated and more likely to stay in foster care longer than other children (Lindsey, 1991; Rivaux et al., 2008).

ABC INTERVENTION WITH CRYSTAL: A FOCUS ON PARENTING IN THE CONTEXT OF ADVERSITY

ABC focuses on enhancing parenting but not on such things as helping a parent find permanent housing, get adequate child care, or deal with depression. Crystal had many challenges and relatively few external resources, similar to most of the parents with whom we have worked. Certainly, many interventions focus at least partially on dealing with the life crises at hand. ABC, however, doggedly focuses on the three intervention targets and only those targets. Why is that? Why not help Crystal find housing? And why not help her find help for her depression?

Helping Crystal to find help with housing, child-care, or mental health needs could surely be helpful. But our concern is that, if we are not focused and disciplined, our intervention time will be hijacked. We have limited time to work with Crystal, and, on one hand, if we are not very careful, we will come to the end of 10 sessions having dealt with a host of very real crises, but Crystal will not be parenting in fundamentally different ways than she was initially. If, on the other hand, we use nearly every minute of our time focusing her attention on things that she is doing to follow her children's lead, to nurture her children, and to delight in her children, we are convinced that we can change her behavior substantially by the end of the 10 sessions. Although we appreciate the importance of permanent housing, improved mental health, and child care, these will be ongoing issues, and "babies can't wait" for these other issues to be resolved (Zero to Three, 2016). Rather, they need adequate, loving parenting now.

When the parent coach first arrived at the motel, Crystal was quiet and seemed to feel awkward. The two preschoolers were interested in the parent coach but they were reserved and heeded their mother's directive to stay on the other bed. The baby (8-month-old Carter) was on the bed with Crystal. Before the parent coach set up her camera for video recording, she commented, "You know, Carter just looked up at you and smiled, and you smiled right back. You're following his lead—that's the kind of thing that makes him feel like he's important. We'll be talking about that more during these 10 sessions." Crystal looked directly at the parent coach for the first time, shrugged, and smiled slightly. Carter then reached for a goldfish cracker, and his mother handed it to him. The parent coach commented, "Wow, there you did it again. He reached for the cracker and you handed it to him. These things are so natural to you that you may not even notice that you're following his lead." Crystal sat up straighter on the bed and smiled fully at the coach.

When parent coaches are first learning the intervention, they often anticipate that they will seem condescending to parents or offend parents by making in-the-moment comments. But almost without exception, we find the opposite to be the case. Parents feel respected when they are complimented for something that they are actually doing. Whereas it might seem condescending or disingenuous if parent coaches commented on global behaviors or qualities (e.g., "You're such a good parent"), commenting specifically on behaviors the parent has engaged in feels genuine. We find that parents seem disarmed quickly, even at the beginning of the first session.

Crystal visibly brightened and relaxed when hearing her parent coach's comments. During this first session, as well as the next several sessions, her parent coach made only positive comments regarding Crystal's parenting. She took note of other issues that she would want to address later but did not yet make any suggestions. She did indicate that the older children were welcome to join in activities in hopes that she could help Crystal engage with them more, but she did not push when it was clear that Crystal preferred that they not join in.

The first two sessions include more "content" than most other sessions. These sessions involve asking parents about their own beliefs about parenting (e.g., whether they think babies are spoiled by being picked up), as well as watching videos of children behaving in ways that elicit nurturance easily and in ways that fail to elicit nurturance. The risk of these content-heavy sessions is that parent coaches may fail to attend to what is going on between parents and children. The parent coach in this case, though, maintained a very high rate of comments, noting each time Crystal delighted in Carter or followed his lead. This was important in reminding Crystal that it was her behavior with Carter (and eventually with her other children) that was of primary importance.

For example, in Session 2, the parent coach began playing a video on her laptop showing a child crying loudly. Carter looked up with a concerned expression at the computer, and the older two children stopped playing and stared at the screen. Crystal looked at Carter and touched his head. The parent coach said, "You could tell he was worried there, and you touched his head. That really lets him know you're there for him." As the 3-year-old reached out for the laptop, Crystal said very gruffly, "Stop—don't touch that," providing an example of frightening behavior that the parent coach filed away for later.

Sessions 3 and 4 focus on Crystal's following her child's lead. In Session 3, the activities involve reading books and playing with blocks, and in Session 4, making pudding or some other food (or messy) activity. The parent coach brought enough books, blocks, and pudding for all three children to be engaged in the activities and encouraged Crystal to allow all three children access to her bed. This was, after all, an infant intervention, so it may seem odd that we were working to change parents' behaviors with all of their children. There are several reasons for this. First and most centrally in all such interventions, we want the parents' behavior to change in ways that will generalize to their real worlds. The more closely we can approximate their real worlds while working with them, the more likely behaviors will be sustained. At the extreme, working alone with a parent in an office would make generalizing the most challenging (and least likely to occur). However, even though conditions for generalizing to their environments are much more favorable when parents are in their own homes, we think that conditions aren't as similar to their everyday life if other children (and partners, mothers-in-laws, etc.) aren't part of the interactions. We worry that parents might be able to learn to be sensitive and responsive while interacting with only one child, but they may rarely experience that. We want parents to gain experience under their normal life conditions in behaving in nurturing, sensitive, and nonfrightening ways.

There are additional reasons we think it's important to attend to the other children as well. First, Carter's mother, Crystal, is able to attend to him at least some of the time while he's a baby, and she may well have attended to the older two children at his age. We don't want Carter to get pushed out as he becomes a toddler, losing the attention and delight he received as an infant. Second, helping parents to focus on the infant could potentially have iatrogenic effects on older children if it leads to attention being given to the infant to the exclusion of the older children.

As the intervention went on, the parent coach increasingly targeted the most challenging issues for Crystal—engaging the other children, reducing Crystal's occasional frightening behaviors (glares, fussing, and smacking), and helping Crystal become engaged even when she was tired or preoccupied.

ATTACHMENT STATE OF MIND: INFLUENCES ON PARENTING AND OPENNESS TO ABC

As a reminder, attachment state of mind refers to the adult's way of thinking about his or her attachment experiences and to the ways of processing attachment-related information. As detailed in Chapter 2, Mary Main and colleagues developed their adult attachment coding system by grouping parents based on infants' attachment classifications and then looking for commonalities in parents' discourse regarding their attachment experiences. Therefore, it is not entirely surprising that a parent's attachment state of mind coded from the AAI predicts her child's attachment classification, but how well it has done so has been impressive (e.g., Verhage et al., 2016). From the standpoint of a parenting intervention, the AAI is clearly very important because it is so closely associated with parenting behavior and with child attachment. As can be seen in Table 4.1, fewer of the CPS-involved parents have autonomous states of mind, and more of these parents have dismissing and unresolved states of mind than the low-risk, foster, and internationally adoptive parents. Indeed, only 30% of the

TABLE 4.1. Percentages of AAI Classifications across Samples

Sample	Autonomous	Dismissing	Preoccupied	Unresolved/CC
Low-risk	56%	16%	9%	18%
High-risk/CPS-involved	30%	34%	5%	31%
Foster	55%	19%	1%	25%
Internationally adoptive	75%	9%	5%	11%

Note. From Raby et al. (2017). Copyright 2017 by Cambridge University Press. Reprinted with permission from Cambridge University Press.

CPS-involved parents have autonomous classifications, in contrast with 56% of a comparison group of parents. In addition to the other issues faced by such high-risk parents, having a nonautonomous state of mind makes the task of parenting in nurturing, sensitive ways less "natural" and more challenging for these parents than for parents living under relatively low-risk conditions.

Autonomous State of Mind and ABC

Parents who have autonomous states of mind are "free to evaluate attachment," in Mary Main's words. They allow themselves to consider the negative influences as well as the positive, thus presenting a picture of attachment figures that is consistent with the interviewer's (or reader's) impressions of the attachment figures. General characterizations of parents and other figures are consistent with specific memories. An example of an AAI with a high-risk mother who has an autonomous state of mind illustrates this openness.

Jess: Autonomous State of Mind

Jess is a 32-year-old mother of three. Her grandparents raised her for the most part. Her mother was in and out of her life from time to time. She described her mother and her grandfather as drinking too much most of the time while she was growing up, but she was nonetheless able to get some of what she needed from them. It was her grandfather, though, whom she sees as the one who got her through. Here are some of her observations as expressed in the interview (with the interviewer's comments *in parentheses*):

> "Well, he was loving and caring. Even though he drank way too much, he still tried to look out for his granddaughters as much as he could. (*OK.*) Like, he would be, 'You all right, Grandbaby? You worried about something?' He'd sit and talk with me for hours. He would always be that one. Even though he was drunk too, but somehow he still just made sure I was all right. (*OK.*) My grandmama did too, but my grandpa was more of the one I would tell, you know, everything. He really looked out for me."

Throughout the interview, Jess showed a valuing of attachment and an open appraisal of her attachment experiences. Despite having had very challenging life conditions, Jess had managed to develop an autonomous state of mind. She did not show the involving anger or rambling discourse seen among parents with a preoccupied state of mind, nor did she show the idealization or lack of memory often seen among parents with a dismissing state of mind. Egeland, Jacobvitz, and Sroufe (1988) found that a supportive person can exert a powerful influence on someone's life even if primary attachment figures are not available.

As a parent, Jess faces significant challenges: She has struggled with alcohol addiction since her early 20s, has not had a stable partner or other source of support, and has occasionally been homeless. She reports that she has had trouble being the mother she wants to be at times. Nonetheless, she looks very different from a parent with a dismissing state of mind. First, she is thoughtful about the ways in which parenting is difficult and the ways in which she wants to parent differently. As a result, she is open to suggestions from her parent coach. For example, when her parent coach commented that her child might need her to pick her up when she fell, Jess said, "Oh my gosh, yes. I was just so wrapped up with what we were talking about that I didn't think!" Second, she values attachment, a hallmark of an autonomous state of mind. Therefore, a focus on her child and her relationship with her child feel right to her; the messages of ABC are consistent with her natural tendencies.

This case example is consistent with our earlier findings suggesting that people with an autonomous state of mind may be more open to treatment than people with dismissing states of mind (Dozier, 1990; Dozier, Lomax, Tyrell, & Lee, 2001).

Dismissing State of Mind and ABC

About 30% of the CPS-involved parents we've worked with have dismissing states of mind, as contrasted with 16% from the low-risk comparison sample. Parents with dismissing states of mind are characterized by discomfort with and devaluing of attachment, thus presenting challenges in an intervention designed to enhance nurturing care. We found in our earlier work that therapy clients with dismissing states of mind often push clinicians away (Dozier, 1990; Tyrell, Dozier, Teague, & Fallot, 1999). Therefore, it could be expected that parents with dismissing states of mind would not readily allow themselves to feel supported by parent coaches.

Claudette: Dismissing State of Mind

Claudette was a 23-year-old mother of four. She had her first child at the age of 14, her second at 16, and the other two in the last 3 years. She described her mother in much more positive terms globally than did Jess, saying that her mother was always there for her and was always loving. But when asked for memories to instantiate the more general description, she totally faltered and was not able to come up with any memory of her mother earlier than the age of 12. When asked about memories of being hurt, upset, or rejected, she responded, "I don't remember nothing when I was young." Her earliest memories of her mother were between the ages of 12 and 14 when Claudette ran away to live on the streets. When asked how her experiences as a child affected her adult personality, she said, "It never affected me." When this statement was probed, she said, "Everything was good, you know what I mean? Everything was really good."

Serving as a prototypical example of a parent with a dismissing state of mind, Claudette both idealizes her mother and remembers almost none of the details of her early attachment experiences. It is clear from the interview that Claudette, like Jess, had many very challenging experiences as a child and lacked supportive attachment figures. Unlike Jess, though, Claudette dismisses the importance of early experiences and maintains idealized representations of attachment figures that are not supported by her memories.

The effects of this dismissing state of mind can be seen in her parenting. When asked in Session 1 to respond to the commonly held opinion that picking up a baby spoils him, Claudette said emphatically, "Yes, it will! That baby will never stop crying if you pick him up. That's why I never pick Mickey up until after he's done crying." In session, this situation played itself out a number of times in the first 2 weeks of ABC, as Claudette insisted that Mickey didn't really need her when he cried. She sometimes checked to see if his pacifier had fallen out or if his diaper was dirty, but she resisted the idea that he might need to be held or hugged.

Claudette's parent coach found it necessary to be much more cautious than did Jess's. Whether asking her to think about the importance of picking up her baby or about difficult experiences she had as a child, Claudette seemed defensive and even a bit hostile. Claudette's parent coach needed to keep in mind that Claudette had adopted this strategy for dealing with her own challenging attachment experiences and that she had employed the strategy fairly consistently throughout her life. Suggesting that she make changes was asking a lot. Sensitive to this attitude, her parent coach approached the issues gently. It can be especially useful to help parents with dismissing states of mind see that recognizing voices from the past is a *strength*. Typically, acknowledging a problem is seen as a weakness, and this is especially the case for people with dismissing states of mind. However, we present voices from the past as universal, with everyone having voices from the past; that is, everyone is affected by their attachment experiences. The ability to recognize those voices represents a strength. Thus, we are attempting to reframe what might be seen as a weakness (i.e., identifying a problem) into a strength. Indeed, Claudette resonated to this. Although not able to recall difficult memories from her early childhood, she could recall her mother saying how spoiled her cousins were when their parents picked them up. Upon reflection, she asked herself whether that might have suggested that her mother hadn't picked her up when she was upset. This realization of course did not emerge readily, but rather after she came to believe that she needed to pick up her own daughter, and after recognizing that it wasn't easy or natural for her to do so.

Unresolved State of Mind and ABC

About 32% of the CPS-involved sample were given Unresolved classifications, contrasted with 23% of the comparison sample. Unresolved state of mind is associated with frightening behavior shown toward infants (Jacobvitz et al., 2006; Main & Hesse, 1990; Schuengel et al., 1999).

Maria: Unresolved State of Mind

Maria was a single mother of three boys. When she started ABC, her older son Marcus was 7 years old, Dominic was 2½, and Damion was 18 months old. All three boys were removed from her care when Damion was about 6 months old due to concerns of neglect after he broke his leg falling out of bed. Maria was devastated by this separation: "When they took my kids I thought I was gonna kill myself, but I couldn't—because they needed me, you know? Like it was so painful, you don't know. It was so painful— like I always lost everybody." Soon after they returned home, she was referred for ABC. What was obvious when talking with Maria and observing her interactions with her children was how invested she was in protecting them. When asked during the AAI about what she had learned from her own childhood, she said, "Well, I learned to protect my kids. And I've learned to provide stability for them. And I've learned that, um, even on days when I don't feel like it, I always tell them I'm there for them." Protection and stability, though, were not comforts that Maria had experienced growing up.

During the AAI, Maria shared overwhelming memories of abuse inflicted by her father. When she failed to clean the kitchen well, which was her assigned chore at age 9, her father's punishment was extreme. "He took out this dog leash, and it scared the daylights out of me. I thought I was gonna die. I thought he was gonna beat me with it because he used to beat my sister. And he took the leash and I thought I was gonna die. And he said, 'Get upstairs in your room.' And I must have been up there for 2 days."

Maria was classified as having an unresolved state of mind. There were times during the interview when she denied that abuse had occurred: "You know, I wasn't abused when I was younger. I mean I got smacked a few times. And I can count on one hand. And um, but I was . . . I wasn't abused." This denial of the occurrence and intensity of abusive experiences is one indication of disorientation with respect to trauma. In addition, Maria showed other lapses in monitoring her reasoning and discourse with respect to loss. She described extreme behavioral reactions to her father's death, experienced at age 16, such as wanting to die and attempting to get hit by a train. When discussing the circumstances of her mother's death, she incorporated unusual attention to detail, becoming completely absorbed in her memories of the day that she died.

When parents are unresolved with regard to loss or trauma, they are susceptible to behaving with their children in frightening ways (Schuengel et al., 1999). Indeed, Maria, like many of the birth parents we have worked with, behaved in frightening ways toward her children. Given high rates of unresolved attachment among CPS-involved birth parents and evidence that frightening behavior heightens risk for disorganized attachment, it was important to help parents become aware of their frightening behavior and learn to inhibit it.

FRIGHTENING BEHAVIOR: A KEY TARGET FOR HIGH-RISK BIRTH PARENTS

We implemented ABC among children in the child welfare system, first working with foster parents and then with CPS-involved birth parents. When we began intervening with birth parents, several things were striking. First, the basic focus on nurturance and following the lead worked very well. Even our mode of delivery worked well. Things that we envisioned we would need to modify often did not need modification. For example, one of the first things we emphasized to parents in the first session was that their task might be more difficult than it would otherwise be because their child had experienced early adversity. This concept was not threatening to foster parents because they were not the source of this adversity, and it helped some parents buy into the intervention. That is, it suggested that the child's history made it difficult to parent him or her and that as the foster parents, they needed to have skills beyond those needed by sensitive parents. We anticipated that birth parents might bristle at the notion that their child had experienced adversity because they would feel somewhat responsible. However, this was not the case. It seems that the idea that their children had experienced adversity resonates with virtually all birth parents with whom we've intervened. As with foster parents, the message that CPS-involved birth parents need to be especially sensitive or even therapeutic was appreciated.

In our work with high-risk birth parents, one thing was very striking that we had not witnessed as much with foster parents: frightening behavior. Not every parent engaged in frightening behavior, but it was pervasive enough that we realized that the positive effects of following the lead and nurturance would be undermined if we did not address it. We saw a mother smack the hand of an 8-month-old reaching for a lamp, a mother glaring at her 18-month-old when he made noises, and a mother yelling loudly and angrily when her children were wrestling.

Given that we primarily comment on parental behaviors in positive, supportive ways, intervening to change frightening behavior had to be approached very differently. We commented on times when parents followed their children's lead and nurtured their children, but commenting in the moment regarding frightening behavior was likely to be threatening to parents—at least early in the intervention. Frightening behaviors needed to be tackled more gently than this.

Maria: Addressing Frightening Behavior

Despite her own harsh parenting, Maria was quite nurturing with her boys. When Dominic tripped over her leg in Session 1, Maria picked him up, rubbed his foot, and said, "You okay?" Her parent coach immediately commented, "That's all he needed, huh? He fell down and you picked him up and checked in with him. That's exactly what we're talking about with providing nurturance." Following the lead also came easy to Maria. During Session 3, while playing with blocks, Damion put a block on Maria's head and Maria followed by putting a block on Damion's head, and they both laughed as the blocks slipped off. "Great following his lead! When you follow along with him, he gets the sense that he matters." Then, when clean-up time came, there was a momentary shift in Maria's behavior. As Dominic threw a block, Maria's voice deepened, and she loudly and gruffly said, "Bad! Bad! Bad!" while pushing Dominic down and tickling him roughly. The parent coach was startled, and Dominic was too. He squirmed and pulled away. Within a few seconds, Maria shifted back to her normal tone and gently said, "Don't throw the blocks, Dom. Be nice." This was a moment of frightening behavior in a sequence of otherwise sensitive interactions. The parent coach filed this observation for later. In Session 4, there was a similar moment. Dominic approached Maria, who was sitting on the couch next to the parent coach. Maria had been describing how Dominic was a very affectionate child. As Dominic approached, Maria lifted him above her head, shook him roughly, and said in a deep voice, "He's just trouble! That's what he is, that's what he is. That's all he ever wants is trouble!" The parent coach was again startled by how roughly she handled Dominic and by her threatening tone, despite her benign words. In Session 5, as Dominic and Damion clamored on her lap,

Maria, seemingly out of the blue, leaned quickly toward the boys' faces, and with a deep voice said, "I'm baaack!" as she grabbed the boys roughly and laughed. Dominic pulled away, seemingly startled by the abrupt shift in his mother's demeanor.

The concept of frightening behavior is introduced directly in Session 6. By this point, parents have come to trust their parent coaches and to feel supported by them. In this session, the coach introduces the idea that children have difficulty coming to parents if their parents are frightening to them. Examples of frightening behaviors are discussed, such as threatening to leave children or send them away, yelling at children, and engaging in physically harsh behaviors. Parents are asked to think about their own experiences growing up and whether there were times they were scared of their parents.

Maria openly recalled times when she felt afraid of her parents, some of which she had described during the AAI; there were times when her dad threatened to beat her or her mom slapped her in the face. Maria knew she had difficulty turning to her parents when she needed help as a child, and she recognized that this was because she was afraid of them.

Even when parents can recall their own experiences of being frightened and even with established trust in their parent coach, we consider it critical that parent coaches are careful when turning attention to the parent's own behaviors that may frighten her children. We often start by presenting a video in which the parent did not frighten her child, even though elicitors of angry behavior might have been present in the situation, such as the child misbehaving. Then, we show a video clip of a time when the parent behaves in a frightening way. The parent is asked to consider what is different between the two clips. The parent coach scaffolds the discussion to help the parent recognize the behavior that was frightening. For parents who struggle with frightening behavior, this is often just the start of a conversation that continues into Sessions 7 and 8, with a more explicit focus on recognizing and overriding potentially frightening behaviors.

Maria's parent coach showed her a clip of a time when Dominic approached her with a pretend golf club and swung the toy in a way that almost hit his brother. In the clip, Maria said, "Oops" and caught the toy before it hit Damion; then she smiled at Dominic and said, "Going golfing?" Her parent coach highlighted how Maria followed Dominic's lead, despite it being a time when she might have reacted harshly to concerns about safety. The parent coach then said that she wanted to show Maria a clip that looked a little bit different. She played the clip of Maria cleaning up the blocks with her boys from Session 3. In this clip, in response to Dominic throwing a block, Maria yelled "Bad!" multiple times while roughly pushing and tickling Dominic. After the 5-second clip, the parent coach asked Maria what she noticed. Maria laughed and said, "Oh yeah, he likes to be tickled." To the parent coach's surprise, Maria did not seem to notice her harsh tone of voice, her rough physical approach, or how Dominic squirmed and pulled away. "Let's watch it again," said the parent coach, "I wondered whether your response here might have been a bit overwhelming to Dominic." Maria still struggled to notice the behaviors that were frightening; despite the potential discomfort while watching a negative behavior, the parent coach showed the video multiple times, pointing out some specific aspects of the shift in her voice and behavior, and Dominic's response. "I know some of these may seem like small moments," the parent coach said, "but if children are frightened of their parents, even if just once in a while, it can undo all of your efforts to be nurturing and follow their lead."

In Sessions 7 and 8, the parent coach further helped Maria consider her voices from the past, focusing specifically on frightening behavior. Her parent coach suggested, "It makes sense that you behave in frightening ways sometimes; that is your voice from the past. Your father was threatening to you in many ways. When your voice changes, when you are rough with your children— either because you are angry or even at other times—that is your father's influence." Maria increasingly recognized these behaviors. She shared an example from the week between sessions when she yelled at her older son, Marcus, and caught a glimpse of herself in the mirror. "When I saw the expression on my face, I looked just like my father," she said, "and when I looked back at Marcus,

I could see just how afraid he was." In the remaining sessions, the parent coach helped Maria think of strategies to override this voice from the past. They discussed how Maria could catch herself in moments when she was angry and frustrated before she responded in harsh ways and how she could be mindful that her children needed her to follow their lead and keep a gentle tone of voice, rather than engaging in interactions that were overstimulating or overwhelming.

RESEARCH FINDINGS IN BRIEF

The ABC intervention was designed to increase parental sensitivity, with effects on children's ability to develop secure, organized attachments, and their ability to regulate physiology, emotions, and behavior. We describe intervention outcomes more fully in Chapter 8, but we overview them briefly here.

Parents in the ABC intervention interact with their children in more sensitive ways than parents randomized to the control intervention (Bernard, Simons, & Dozier, 2015). More of the children whose parents received the ABC intervention develop secure attachments, and fewer develop disorganized attachments, than children whose parents received the control intervention (Bernard et al., 2012). Children in the ABC intervention show more typical patterns of cortisol production, with higher wake-up values and steeper slopes, than children in the control intervention (Bernard, Dozier, Bick, & Gordon, 2015; Bernard, Hostinar, & Dozier, 2015). Also, children show better behavioral regulation, with greater success at inhibiting touching a set of attractive toys during a compliance task, than children in the control intervention (Lind, Bernard, Yarger, & Dozier, in press).

CHAPTER 5

ABC for Foster Parents

JACKIE

After her own children left for college, Jackie decided to explore becoming a foster parent. She attended the required parenting classes for foster parents, completed a home study such that her home was approved as a foster placement, and waited several weeks. Then, late on a Saturday night, she received a call asking if she was willing to foster an 8-month-old girl whose parents had been jailed because they were arrested for involvement in a heroin distribution ring. She said yes.

Over the next several weeks, she found herself developing some of the same feelings toward the child, Raja, that she had when her own children were babies, 20 years earlier. After the first several days, Raja looked to Jackie for reassurance when she was upset, and Raja was readily soothed. Raja cried on the rare occasions when Jackie could not take her with her. Jackie's own children were somewhat skeptical at first but gradually developed affection for Raja as well. Although she had not anticipated it, Jackie began to wonder whether she might be able to adopt Raja.

Raja's birth mother, Amanda, was released from prison 2 months later and began visitations with Raja. Jackie had mixed feelings—she had come to think of Raja as her own child, and yet

Raja's mother was surely committed to the child. Despite her misgivings, Jackie went with Raja to visits. She found herself quickly becoming fond of Amanda, even though Amanda missed two of the first visits. Five weeks later, Amanda was arrested for cocaine distribution. Jackie then let the child's case worker know that she would like to begin the adoption process if Amanda's parental rights were terminated. To Jackie's surprise, the child welfare system began putting calls out to maternal and paternal relatives who might want to adopt Raja. A paternal aunt, with whom the child had never spent any time, came forward and said that she would take Raja. Raja was, by that point, 14 months old and had been with Jackie for 6 months. Jackie fought to have Raja stay with her, but the child was placed with the aunt. Jackie let the child welfare agency know she was available if Raja ever needed to be placed again but that she did not want to foster other children.

JANE AND TREVOR

Like Jackie, Jane and Trevor were fostering their first child, an 18-month-old child named Jimmy. The first night felt like it would never end. Jimmy was upset throughout the night, crying so hard that he had trouble catching his breath. He cried almost continuously and could not be comforted. The next morning he continued to be distressed, but over the next several days he settled down considerably. What was disconcerting to both Jane and Trevor, though, was that Jimmy didn't look to them for reassurance. He most often appeared unperturbed when separated from them, and he showed little joy upon reunion. When he did become upset, he was almost inconsolable. This pattern went on for weeks. Both foster parents found it increasingly difficult to behave in nurturing ways. They got to the point where they didn't go to him when he fell, convinced he wouldn't need them. A self-perpetuating cycle had begun: Jimmy was behaving as if he didn't need nurturance, and his foster parents were responding in kind.

ELISE AND BOB

Elise and Bob had fostered over 100 children when 8-month-old Parker was placed with them. Parker joined two other young children (1- and 3-year-olds) that Elise and Bob were already fostering. Foster care workers had valued Elise and Bob's willingness to take in children any time, day or night, but they had also worried that Elise and Bob did not show the level of commitment to the children that some other foster parents did.

Elise indicated that she wanted to foster infants rather than older children because they were easier to care for—a sentiment not shared by many foster or birth parents. When the parent coach first came to Elise and Bob's home, Parker was in a baby carrier facing toward the wall so that he couldn't see his foster parents or the other children in the house. He occasionally made whimpering noises but generally asked for very little.

These examples illustrate the range of issues that both foster parents and foster children bring to their relationships. At one end of the continuum, foster parents think of the children as their own. Anecdotally, we often find that these parents are more invested in working to enhance their relationship with their children and are easier to engage in treatment than other parents. At the other end of the continuum, foster parents seem to be doing a job—providing care for children but not appearing to invest as much in their long-term development or their relationship with the child as other parents. They accept their role as temporary caregivers but do not think of themselves as parents. Such parents are often more difficult to work with than others because they may feel they already have the expertise they need, and they may not be motivated to change things that could increase the demands placed on them.

FOSTER CARE

In the United States, children who are removed from the care of their birth parents are usually placed in foster care. Approximately

23% of the children in foster care are younger than 3 years old (U.S. Department of Health and Human Services [DHHS], 2017). When children are placed in foster care, the most frequent reasons include neglect and parental drug abuse. About half of all children (45%) stay in care less than a year. When leaving foster care, children are often reunified with parents (51%) or are adopted (23%).

The Foster Care System

Although foster care is an imperfect system, it is far preferable to the alternative of institutional or orphanage care (Dozier et al., 2014; Dozier, Zeanah, Wallin, & Schauffer, 2012; Zeanah, Humphreys, Fox, & Nelson, 2017). Foster care systems vary in the way foster parents are recruited, the preparation and support provided to foster parents, and the extent to which foster parents are involved as partners in the process. Poor systems of foster care surely exist and are associated with many problematic outcomes, and poor foster parents exist even within relatively strong systems. But when foster care works well, foster parents help children regulate their physiology and behavior effectively. Children who are placed in foster care while being removed from their neglectful birth parents' care show better physiological and behavioral regulation than children who continue to remain in the care of neglecting parents (Bernard et al., 2010; Lind, Goldstein, Bernard, & Dozier, 2018).

Quality Parenting Initiative is an approach developed by the Youth Law Center in San Francisco to strengthen foster care through its "rebranding." The stereotype of foster parents is often negative, with some people believing that foster parents take care of children "for the money" or that foster parents are unusually likely to abuse children. Although there are widely publicized incidents of maltreatment among children in foster care, the nonrelative foster parent has been found to be the perpetrator of maltreatment in only about 0.1% of all cases (i.e., a foster parent is the perpetrator in about 1 in 1,000 maltreatment cases) (DHHS, 2013). Sometimes the foster parents' negative experiences with the system, such as having limited involvement in or knowledge of decision making, also affect the "brand" negatively. Quality Parenting Initiative seeks to change how foster parenting is perceived, thus altering how potential foster parents are recruited and who will be interested in taking on the role. Moreover, Quality Parenting Initiative seeks to define the expectations of foster parents in empowering ways that are consistent with the rebranding. Key changes include keeping foster parents informed about decision making (e.g., whether a child is returning home) and having roles for them in transitions (e.g., providing support to birth parents).

Foster parents' roles vary from one foster care system to another. In some systems (such as those involved with Quality Parenting Initiative), foster parents are treated as partners who are engaged in decisions, informed about upcoming transitions and visitation arrangements, and so on. In other systems, foster parents are not partners and are not fully informed. As an extreme example, case workers may pick up children at daycare to transport them to their birth parents' home without informing foster parents ahead of time, requesting at the last minute to have suitcases ready for pick-up. In this latter case, it is difficult to retain foster parents who wish to be partners in the process and who wish to have continued relationships with the fostered children over time.

A system that enhances commitment among foster parents to the children in their care is in the best interests of children. Nonetheless, there is a paradox for foster parents and for the system because foster parents also need to be able to support reunification efforts when they occur, optimally providing support to birth parents and children. Commitment to the children could make this task challenging, but we argue that highly committed foster parents can provide support for reunification if they receive the needed support themselves.

One of the tensions in the child welfare system is often between maintaining stability of "placements" and placing children with relative (kin) caregivers. From a developmental standpoint, stability of care with a trusted caregiver who wants to continue caring for a young child is preferable to placing the child with a relative whom the child doesn't know. Indeed, young children experience challenges coping with separations from caregivers (e.g., Lewis, Dozier, Ackerman, & Sepulveda-Kozakowsi, 2007). Although biological relatedness may be relevant for later identity issues, it is not salient to an infant or a toddler. However, child welfare and judicial systems often prefer kin caregivers, even when the relative has not been part of the child's life. We argue (e.g., Zeanah, Shauffer, & Dozier, 2011) that if kin care is considered optimal, it should be the first placement for a young child rather than the impetus for a disruption in care. One principle that we and others suggest when making decisions about children's placements is that placements be based on an assessment of children's needs, not on adults' "rights." Similarly, although long-term relationships with siblings are desirable, it is preferable to place the children together initially rather than disrupt attachment relationships later in order to reunite siblings.

When foster parents are engaged as partners in the process and are recruited with this objective in mind, relationships between foster parents and infants can go beyond the current placement. That is, sometimes foster parents can help to support birth parents following reunification, can become an emergency placement if needed and an occasional weekend visitor if wanted, and can continue to be important figures in the child's life.

Foster Parent Commitment

"This Is My Baby" (or "This Is Not My Baby")

Foster parents differ in how much they feel that the child they are taking care of is "theirs." I (M. D.) once saw a foster mother at a child welfare agency carrying her foster infant as though he were a sack of potatoes—head out one side of her arm and feet out the other side. I contrasted this foster mother with another I knew who seemed to feel as committed to her child as I felt to my own young children. It occurred to me how different life was for these two children—one whose mother appeared to treat him like a "sack of potatoes" and one who thought of her child as "my baby." Based on these observations, we developed an interview that we call the "This Is My Baby" Interview, in which we assess differential commitment of foster parents to the children in their care. In this interview, we ask parents to talk about the extent to which they feel committed to the child or would miss the child if he or she were taken from them (see Figure 5.1).

Consider, for example, these responses from two different foster parents to the second question in the "This Is My Baby" Interview, "Do you ever wish you could raise her?"

> "All the time. From the day she came to my door. . . . I mean for, she's been with us, when she came to us, she was a month old. So she, she is, she's our little pride and joy. . . . I don't think I would be able to let her leave me at this point—though I know that might be something I can't control."—Foster Parent 1

> "Sometimes, but that's not what we do. We take them, help them, and send them back where they're supposed to be, or wherever it's good for them to be."—Foster Parent 2

The first foster parent conveys that she has invested in this child emotionally and psychologically as her own; her response shows no evidence of withholding feeling or limiting the extent of her bond to the baby. Regardless of whether or not the child's placement plan involves adoption, you get the sense that this

---

1. I would like to begin by asking you to describe [child's name]. What is [his/her] personality like?

2. Do you ever wish you could raise [child's name]?

3. How much would you miss [child's name] if [he/she] had to leave your care?

4. How do you think your relationship with [child's name] is affecting [him/her] right now?

5. How do you think your relationship with [child's name] will affect [him/her] in the long term?

6. What do you want for [child's name] right now?

7. What do you want for [child's name] in the future?

8. Is there anything about [child's name] or your relationship that we've not touched on that you'd like to tell me?

FIGURE 5.1. "This Is My Baby" interview questions.

parent would keep this child and protect this child as if the child were her own. The second foster parent's response lacks these indicators of commitment. Although she sees herself as playing a role in the child's life, she does not express a desire for her role to be ongoing. She does not appear to be investing emotionally in this particular child and likely considers her involvement as temporary.

We think commitment matters because infants and young children need someone who has a strong commitment to them—someone who would protect them from danger at the caregiver's own peril. People become foster parents for many reasons. We initially expected that the original motivation might be important in distinguishing foster parents who became more committed to their children versus those who did not. After all, it seems logical that foster parents who are doing it "for the money" might be less likely to become highly committed than those whose motives were more altruistic. In fact, however, initial motivation for fostering did not predict later commitment or child outcomes (Bates & Dozier, 1999). At the anecdotal level, what we observed is that, despite initial motivation, foster parents might fall in love with their children—or might not.

What we found is that foster parents who had fostered fewer children indicated that they felt more highly committed to their current child than foster parents who had fostered more children. Some foster parents had fostered more than 100 children, and although there were surely exceptions, it tended to become harder to commit to the next child as the number of previously fostered children grew (Dozier & Lindhiem, 2006). Foster parents who were more highly committed seemed to take more joy in their children (i.e., showed more delight) than parents who were less committed. Indeed, we studied this issue and found that foster parents who indicated in our interview that they were highly committed to their foster children showed more delight behaviorally than foster parents who were not as committed (Bernard & Dozier, 2011). Children whose foster parents were less committed to them showed more behavior problems over time than children with more highly committed foster parents (Lindhiem & Dozier, 2007).

Earlier Is Easier

Our work and the work of others have suggested that the task of the foster, adoptive, or birth parent is easier when the child is younger at the time of placement than when the child is older. We have focused specifically on the attachment behaviors shown by children when they are first placed into a new foster home. Within a short time, younger infants behave in ways that make it easier for parents to be nurturing than older infants. And foster parents reported feeling greater commitment to infants who were placed with them at younger ages than at older ages (Dozier & Lindhiem, 2006).

INTERVENING WITH FOSTER PARENTS

With these individual differences in mind, we intervene to help foster parents provide nurturing, sensitive care to infants. Some foster parents work in a system in which they are treated as partners, whereas others do not. Some become committed to the children in their care, and others do not. Differences in parental attachment state of mind are certainly important as well.

About 55% of foster parents have autonomous states of mind, which is a substantially larger percentage than among CPS-referred parents and not much lower than among community parents. Most of the foster parents with nonautonomous states of mind have either dismissing or unresolved states of mind rather than preoccupied states of mind. As with CPS-referred parents, foster parents with dismissing states of mind often find the ABC intervention somewhat more challenging than do other parents.

The first component of the ABC intervention was developed with the challenges faced by foster parents specifically in mind. As discussed earlier, infants and young children placed with new caregivers often behave in ways that suggest they do not need nurturing care from their caregivers. In the first session of the intervention, we emphasize to foster parents that their children may be behaving in ways that suggest they're not needed, even though they very much *are* needed. This usually resonates with foster parents. Foster parents often see the videos of children turning away from their parents, or being inconsolable, and liken them to their own observations.

Jackie

Jackie, presented at the beginning of the chapter, was the foster mother of 8-month-old Raja. For Jackie, behaving in nurturing ways came naturally. Her own mother and grandmother had been nurturing, and she had found soothing her distressed children one of the most gratifying aspects of parenting when her own children were little. Placed at a young age, Raja turned to her quickly for nurturance, even though Raja's own mother had not been very nurturing to her.

Jackie "bought" Sessions 1 and 2, when the effects of babies pushing away caregivers was discussed. She could easily see how such behaviors would fail to elicit nurturing care from parents. She felt fortunate that Raja was making her job easy.

Following the lead also came easily to Jackie. Although she was initially somewhat "teachy," she readily understood how important following the lead was. She saw the effects on Raja immediately. Her play became easier, and Raja stayed engaged much longer than previously.

Just as we were beginning to wonder whether the intervention was necessary for Jackie, we observed a striking and concerning behavior—she behaved in ways that startled, or frightened, Raja at times. For example, she played a game where she was a tiger that crawled slowly toward Raja while making odd noises and then jumped at her with a roar. Raja smiled nervously at first and then sometimes laughed loudly, but she often jumped and pulled back from Jackie. We found other examples of this same kind of behavior when we did some probing. These intrusive and frightening behaviors can be rewarding to parents because they are so powerful in eliciting reactions from children.

The problem, though, is that such behaviors are fundamentally dysregulating to children. They disrupt the capacity to regulate physiology, emotions, and behaviors and the capacity to organize attachment.

Jackie was at first surprised when we suggested that these behaviors were frightening to Raja. She pointed out Raja's laughter and the fact that Raja sometimes appeared to ask for more. Videos of the behaviors did not convince her. What was convincing was a discussion of times when she had been overwhelmed by her father when she was a child. She could remember her father's overwhelming game of twirling her around as he said, "Oh no, you're going to spin out of control . . . here you go, here you go." She was petrified but often laughed uncontrollably.

This realization was critical in the work with Jackie. After recognizing what it felt like to her when she was a child to have a (sometimes) frightening parent and what it must feel like to Raja, she was able to see her behaviors differently. At times, she found herself still behaving in intrusive ways with Raja, but she could often stop and recognize what she was doing. She could then "override" her tendency to behave in such a way. For Jackie, the work of Sessions 5 (intrusive behavior), Session 6 (frightening behavior), and Sessions 7 and 8 (voices from the past) was relatively straightforward. The task of the parent coach was made easier because she could focus on just one of the targets (frightening behavior) given Jackie's strengths in other areas.

Jane and Trevor

Jane and Trevor's parent coach met them for the first time 3 months after Jimmy had been placed with them when Jimmy was 21 months old. Neither Jane nor Trevor was very nurturing of Jimmy at that point. When Jimmy was first placed with them, Jane had been embarrassed at times that Jimmy seemed to turn away from her. But Jane's own mother had been uncomfortable when Jane was upset as a child, so Jane was not predisposed to overcome this avoidance from the child. In fact, when Jimmy did signal that he was hurt or upset, Jane often tried to distract him quickly. In the first ABC session, Jane and Trevor left Jimmy alone with the parent coach while getting paperwork from another room. Even though Jimmy started crying, they did not return quickly. Upon her return, Jane laughed and said, "I wasn't gone long, silly. Why are you crying?"

Nurturing came more naturally to Trevor than to his wife. Raised by his maternal grandmother who was very nurturing, Trevor was comfortable responding to children's bids for reassurance, but Jane had discouraged him from doing so to some extent, worrying that he would spoil Jimmy. Given, however, that Jimmy had pushed them away for the most part, Trevor was not offering much nurturance, and Jimmy was not receiving much.

The focus of Sessions 1 and 2 on children pushing parents away resonated with both Trevor and Jane. They recalled times when Jimmy was first placed with them when they felt so unimportant to him. Trevor remembered one particular time when Jimmy fell off the porch and cut his forehead. Jimmy cried hard, but when Trevor picked him up, he turned his head away and would not look at Trevor. Trevor tried to stay engaged but recalled how powerful Jimmy was in pushing him away.

These two sessions were essentially all Trevor needed to license him to respond in nurturing ways. Jimmy had already started to come around some, and it didn't take the two of them long to change their dynamic. By Session 6 or 7, Jimmy approached Trevor directly when he was upset, and Trevor was consistently warm and nurturing.

Jane found Sessions 1 and 2 reassuring in normalizing her feelings about her reactions to Jimmy's pushing her away. Even with this reframing of his behavior, though, she did not find it easy to nurture him. Given her own discomfort with distress, she felt a compulsion to move through his distress as quickly as possible. Although her parent coach urged her to let Jimmy determine when he was okay rather than say, "You're OK" or "You're fine," she resisted. The parent coach emphasized that, while children who had not experienced adversity might not need comforting so much, Jimmy (and other children who had experienced adversity) did; in fact, nurturing was especially important for them. This allowed Jane to override her tendency to dismiss his distress at least sometimes during sessions. She gradually became more comfortable staying with his distress, and her own avoidance of such contexts lessened. Jimmy gradually started to look to Jane for reassurance when he was distressed.

Trevor and Jane, and even Jimmy, had made enormous strides by Session 7. Still, Sessions 7 and 8 helped to consolidate the gains. Jane could connect a very real voice from her past with her reaction to her child's distress. She could imagine her mother saying, "Now, you know you're too big to cry," when Jimmy fussed or cried. She recognized that this "voice" was a powerful influence on her behavior but that Jimmy in fact needed her to nurture him and not turn his attention away. Therefore, she began to practice recognizing what she was feeling when Jimmy was distressed, overriding her natural tendency to tell him he was OK, and to provide nurturing care. It was never "automatic" for her to respond in a nurturing way, and therefore there was often a slight delay; nonetheless, she usually nurtured Jimmy when he was distressed, and he came to expect it.

RESEARCH FINDINGS IN BRIEF

We have not followed foster parents as long as we have followed high-risk birth parents, and we are just now completing a randomized clinical trial. But so far, our findings are quite consistent with findings from our work with high-risk birth parents, and they suggest that ABC is a powerful intervention for this population. We have found that foster parents who receive ABC are more sensitive than foster parents in the control intervention (Bick & Dozier, 2013) and that children who receive the ABC intervention show more normative cortisol production and stronger impulse control and language skills than children in a control intervention (Bernard, Lee, & Dozier, 2017; Dozier, Peloso, Lewis, Laurenceau, & Levine, 2008; Lewis-Morrarty, Dozier, Bernard, Moore, & Terraciano, 2012; Lind, Raby, Caron, Roben, & Dozier, 2017). These effects are described in greater detail in Chapter 8.

CHAPTER 6

ABC for Parents
Adopting Internationally

Harvey and Alyssa had always thought they might someday adopt a child. After their second failed pregnancy, they decided to move forward with their adoption plans. In the early 2000s, international adoptions into the United States hovered around 20,000 annually, peaking in 2004 with nearly 23,000 international adoptions. Even then, navigating the system was challenging and could result in multiple trips to countries for preadoption arrangements and long waiting periods. By the time Harvey and Alyssa were ready to adopt a decade later, the numbers of children being adopted had plummeted, with only 5,647 children adopted into the United States internationally in 2015. This made the process of adopting substantially longer and more complicated than it was in earlier years. After several years and several failed attempts, Harvey and Alyssa adopted 26-month-old Grigory from Russia in 2012, one of the last years in which Russia allowed adoptions by Americans.

Grigory's birth mother left him at a baby home (an orphanage) when he was 2 months old. She was living in poverty in a small town outside St. Petersburg with two older children. She believed that Grigory would be better off in a baby home than living in poverty, a belief shared by many Russian parents. Like many children in baby homes, Grigory was not initially a "true" orphan. About a year later, though, his birth mother died of tuberculosis.

The baby home was staffed primarily by older women who worked shifts. Their work was difficult because there were many children to care for and few child-care workers. The rules and practices in this baby home had remained relatively unchanged over the last several decades, although reforms had come to some orphanages. Consistent schedules were set for children's feeding and changing, and children and staff interacted rarely outside of these caregiving routines. Bottles were typically propped up so that more babies could be fed at the same time, further reducing caregivers' time with babies.

Many of the children, including Grigory, were developmentally delayed. Grigory therefore seemed like a much younger child than his actual age of 26 months. His gross motor development was greatly delayed, and he was not yet talking. The exception to this bleak picture was that he had good fine motor coordination. Having been left for many hours in his crib, he had played with lint from a blanket as well as other bits of thread. He was able to grasp and manipulate things with his fingers in ways that were surprising given his other deficits.

Like many children in baby homes, Grigory was outgoing and friendly with strangers. When he first saw Harvey and Alyssa in the ward, he went immediately to them and tried to climb up into their arms. He showed no wariness about leaving the baby home with them a day later, even though they had spent little time together. Harvey and Alyssa felt so relieved—it seemed as if Grigory knew he was "their" child. In the airport and on the plane, though, he was as friendly with nearly everyone else as he had initially been with them. Harvey and Alyssa attributed it to Grigory being a very outgoing child but all the same felt a little unsettled by the behavior. By the time they got their luggage, they felt like he would have gone home with anyone.

THE CHANGING LANDSCAPE
OF INTERNATIONAL ADOPTION

International adoption has always been complicated, sometimes because of the factors leading parents to the point of adopting, such as infertility issues and often because of a host of challenges associated with the adoption itself. But whereas adopting was often difficult in the early 2000s, it is much more so today. The number of children adopted changed dramatically between 2005 and 2015, with numbers dropping substantially each year; the number of children adopted in 2015 was only 25% of what it had been at the peak in 2004. Thus, only one-quarter of the parents who might have adopted a decade ago successfully adopt today.

Some of the issues that led to the change were important ones to correct. In some countries, there was too little oversight of some adoption agencies and practices and foreign adoptions declined for political reasons, as is the case most notoriously for Russian adoptions. It seems that, in some cases, agencies persuaded parents to put their child up for adoption out of the belief that the child would have a better future elsewhere, and in some extreme cases, parents may have been paid to give their child up for adoption. Thus, reform was needed. However, many now agree that an overcorrection occurred. In 2008, the United States entered into the Hague Convention on the Protection of Children and Cooperation in Respect of Intercountry Adoption. The Hague Convention emphasized a child's rights to "preserve his or her identity, including nationality, name, and family relations." This essentially required countries to first consider within-country adoptions before considering international adoptions. Some countries fully stopped international adoptions, even though in some cases there were not enough families available within a country, and children therefore lived in orphanages.

The parents who today manage to adopt represent a select group. They are almost always highly motivated to provide the best for their children (however they define the best), and they have almost always been through a great deal to be where they are now.

CHILDREN ADOPTED FOLLOWING ORPHANAGE CARE

When children are placed into adoptive homes following orphanage care, rapid gains are seen in physical growth, followed by gains in cognitive and social development. Nonetheless, problems resulting from early deprivation persist for some children, especially with regard to disinhibited attachment, inattention, and regulation of physiology (e.g., Johnson, 2000; O'Connor, Rutter, Beckett, Keaveney, & Kreppner, 2000). The unremitting nature of these particular problems for some children has confounded parents and mental health professionals. There is very little in the way of evidence-based treatments for such children. This gap has been filled by extreme treatments, with little or no evidence of efficacy (e.g., Keck & Kupecky, 1995; Levy, 2000). The intervention strategies that are used most prominently for such children may have iatrogenic effects on physical and mental health (Lilienfeld, 2007; Pignotti & Mercer, 2007). These interventions, known as holding or attachment therapy, have been identified as "potentially harmful therapies" in Lilienfeld's (2007, p. 59) review. The use of such extreme treatments highlights the importance of developing evidence-based strategies that target this population. We have adapted ABC to target the specific needs of children adopted after living in institutional care.

Effects of Institutional Care on Development

Starkly depriving conditions are associated with the most pervasive effects on child functioning. Children in institutions are often delayed in physical growth. They show deficits in motor development, with many crawling and walking well behind schedule (Johnson, 2000). Extensive delays in cognitive functioning and language development are also seen (Carlson & Earls, 1997;

O'Connor et al., 2000). In addition to developmental delays, some children living in orphanages show highly anomalous behaviors, including stereotypies such as rocking, self-stimulating, and quasi-autistic behaviors. Social behaviors are sometimes odd and may include one of two extremes: some children are withdrawn and depressed in appearance, and others are indiscriminate in their attachment behaviors (Chisholm, 1998; Chisholm, Carter, Ames, & Morison, 1995; O'Connor et al., 2000).

Differences among Institutions

There are differences among, and even within, institutions in the care provided (Groark, Muhamedrahimov, Palmov, Nikiforova, & McCall, 2005; Gunnar, Bruce, & Grotevant, 2000; Smyke et al., 2007). Key variables include staff-to-child ratios and philosophies regarding staff interactions with children (Groark et al., 2005). Groark and colleagues (2005) in St. Petersburg, Russia, as well as Smyke and colleagues (2007) in Bucharest, Romania, found that conditions in institutions can be substantially improved, resulting in changes in child behavioral outcomes. These improvements were associated with reduced levels of indiscriminate sociability and aggression while children were still living in institutional care, but most of the gains were not sustained following adoption or foster care placement (McCall et al., 2016).

Even high-quality institutional care has deleterious effects on young children's development (Gunnar, van Dulmen, & the International Adoption Project Team, 2007; Rutter et al., 2007). As a rule, children miss the opportunity to develop selective attachment relationships to caregivers in institutions. Various factors operate to make caring for children in institutions perfunctory. Institutional care seems to have specific adverse effects on children that other depriving conditions do not.

Time Institutionalized

The length of time children are institutionalized has emerged as important in many studies. The specific length of time found to be important in predicting outcomes has varied from as little as 6 months institutionalized to 20 months or longer (Chisholm et al., 1995; Nelson et al., 2007; Rutter et al., 2007). van IJzendoorn and Juffer's (2006) meta-analytic results indicate that children adopted before 12 months of age develop secure attachments at about the same rate as children from intact dyads. This is in contrast to children adopted after 12 months who showed significantly higher rates of insecure and disorganized attachments. When considering these various findings, we may not be able to specify a particular age that robustly predicts a good versus poor prognosis. What is clear, though, is that the longer children stay in orphanage care, the more problematic the outcome.

Adoption of Children Who Have Experienced Early Institutional Care

Both human and nonhuman studies (e.g., Francis, Diorio, Plotsky, & Meaney, 2002; Rutter, 1998; van IJzendoorn, Bakermans-Kranenburg, & Juffer, 2007) suggest that there is rapid catch-up in physical and cognitive development following placement in enriched environments after even severe deprivation. Adoptive placement in itself appears to be a significant intervention with regard to physical and cognitive development catch-up (van IJzendoorn & Juffer, 2006).

Nonetheless, problems sometimes persist years after placement into adoptive homes. Kreppner and colleagues (2007) found that 61% of 6-year-olds who were raised in institutional care prior to adoption showed significant impairment. Nearly 25% showed impairment in one area, and 37% showed impairments in two or more areas. The areas that emerged as most problematic among 6-year-olds were cognitive impairment, inattention/overactivity, disinhibited attachment, and quasi-autistic behaviors (Kreppner et al., 2001, 2007; O'Connor et al., 2000). Other studies have also shown increased incidence of difficulties regulating behavior and physiology (Gunnar, Morison, Chisholm, & Schuder, 2001; Kreppner et al., 2007) and high incidence of disorganized attachment (van IJzendoorn & Juffer, 2006).

Attachment Quality

Conducting a meta-analysis of 10 studies of attachment quality among children adopted internationally, van den Dries, Juffer, van IJzendoorn, and Bakermans-Kranenburg (2009) found that children adopted internationally showed lower rates of secure attachment to their adoptive parents than did nonadopted children (47% and 67%, respectively). When disorganized attachment was included (in seven of the studies), children adopted internationally were found to be more likely to have disorganized attachments than nonadopted children (33% and 15%, respectively). In our sample of children adopted internationally, 52% had secure attachments and 39% disorganized attachments. Children adopted at older ages and/or those who spent more time in orphanage care are especially prone to developing disorganized attachments.

Indiscriminate Sociability

Indiscriminate sociability is seen at elevated rates among children who experienced institutional care (Chisholm et al., 1995; O'Connor et al., 2000; Zeanah, Smyke, & Dumitrescu, 2002; Zeanah et al., 2005). These behaviors have been variously referred to as indiscriminate friendliness, indiscriminate sociability, and disinhibited attachment and are included in the *Diagnostic and Statistical Manual of Mental Disorders* (DSM-5) among behaviors described as Disinhibited Social Engagement Disorder (American Psychiatric Association, 2013), previously referred to as the disinhibited subtype of reactive attachment disorder (DSM-IV-TR; American Psychiatric Association, 2000). Descriptively, these behaviors involve children approaching strangers in ways that are usually reserved for attachment figures.

Disinhibited attachment represents a clinically significant problem that is persistent for some children many years after adoption (Chisholm et al., 1995; Rutter et al., 2007; Zeanah & Smyke, 2005). In the Bucharest Early Intervention Project, Zeanah and Smyke (2005) found that behaviors characteristic of disinhibited attachment were still seen 18 months after previously institutionalized children were moved to foster care. Rutter and colleagues (2007) found that of children between the ages of 6 and 11, disinhibited attachment was seen at high rates among those who had been institutionalized. The behaviors were relatively stable across this time period. In particular, the severe behaviors, seen almost exclusively among previously institutionalized children, were the most stable over time, whereas behaviors that were only moderate in severity were relatively unstable over time (Rutter et al., 2007). Although reactive attachment disorder/inhibited type (characterized by withdrawn behaviors toward an attachment figure) was seen at increased rates among previously institutionalized children shortly after placement in foster care, these behaviors abated rather quickly and were not overrepresented at 18 months postplacement (Zeanah & Smyke, 2005).

Problems with Inattention

Children who have lived in institutional settings appear to be especially at risk for problems with inattention and inhibitory control (Gunnar et al., 2007; Kreppner et al., 2001, 2007). Gunnar and colleagues (2007) found that problems with inattention/overactivity were more pronounced among children who had experienced early institutional care than among children who were adopted internationally without early institutional care. Kreppner and colleagues (2007) found that many children who had been adopted following institutional care showed problems with inattention/overactivity, but that such problems were usually seen in combination with reactive attachment disorder, quasi-autistic behaviors, or severe cognitive impairment.

The evidence regarding conduct problems among previously institutionalized children is more mixed than the evidence regarding problems with inattention. Several studies have found that children adopted after institutional care show higher rates of externalizing behaviors (e.g., getting in fights, drinking alcohol) years after adoption than do comparison children (e.g., Fisher, Ames, Chisholm, & Savole, 1997; Kreppner et al., 2007; MacLean, 2003). Fisher and colleagues (1997) found that institutionalized children showed elevated rates of externalizing behaviors several years after placement despite not showing such elevations early in placement. Gunnar and colleagues (2007) found that previously institutionalized children showed elevated levels of externalizing behaviors relative to the general population, but not when compared with adopted children who had not experienced institutional care. This failure to find differences in externalizing behaviors in several studies has led some researchers (e.g., Gunnar et al., 2007; Kreppner et al., 2001) to suggest that inattention/overactivity, and not externalizing behaviors more broadly, is specifically related to early institutional care.

Quasi-Autistic Behaviors

Rutter and colleagues (1999) found the incidence of quasi-autistic behaviors disproportionately high among children who had lived in orphanage care. Of the 111 children studied who had experienced early institutional care, 6% met diagnostic criteria for autism spectrum disorder (ASD) and an additional 6% showed isolated symptoms of autism. Given the prevalence of ASD in the general community of 1.46% (Centers for Disease Control and Prevention, 2014), this rate is striking. Rutter and colleagues studied the similarities between these children and other children diagnosed with ASD without histories of institutionalization. In terms of symptomatology, the groups were fairly similar. One key difference was that previously institutionalized children were less likely to show stability over time in meeting diagnostic criteria, suggesting greater plasticity among this group. As Rutter and colleagues pointed out, the lack of stability suggests the possibility that the diagnosis of ASD for such children may not be appropriate. The term "quasi-autistic behaviors" has therefore been used to describe such behaviors, given that their meaning isn't entirely clear.

ADAPTATIONS OF ABC FOR PARENTS
ADOPTING INTERNATIONALLY

Given that children adopted internationally have particular problems with disorganized attachment and attentional issues, ABC is well suited to the parents of these children. In addition to these issues that are shared with other children who have experienced adversity, children adopted internationally are more likely to show indiscriminate sociability and quasi-autistic symptoms than are other children. Therefore, ABC for children adopted internationally represents only a relatively minor adaptation of the ABC model. Primary attention is paid to helping parents nurture their children and follow their lead, as is the case with ABC for CPS-referred parents and foster parents. Differences include the omission of consideration of frightening behavior (unless such behavior is observed) and attention to indiscriminately sociable behavior and quasi-autistic behavior as needed. Indiscriminate sociability is addressed at the point in the intervention when frightening behavior would otherwise be addressed. In the rare case that quasi-autistic behaviors are observed or described, attention is directed toward them in Session 5.

Attachment State of Mind

Parents adopting internationally are unusual in some key ways that affect how they respond to the intervention. As shown in Chapter 2, 75% of those in our sample of parents adopting internationally have autonomous states of mind, as contrasted with 56% of low-risk parents. Only 11% of our sample of parents adopting internationally have unresolved states of mind. Given the challenges associated with adoption (e.g., the lengthy process with stops and starts, sometimes following unsuccessful attempts to get pregnant and/or miscarriages), we had anticipated that adoptive parents might have rates of unresolved states of mind higher than the general population. One of the wonderful things about data is that they can disabuse us of incorrect assumptions.

Consistent with the high rates of autonomous states of mind, parents adopting internationally tended to interact with their children in sensitive ways prior to the intervention. However, concerns about cognitive delays sometimes led parents to be intrusive or controlling in play interactions rather than to sensitively follow children's lead.

ABC with Harvey, Alyssa, and Grigory

Alyssa and Harvey, worried by the 1-month postadoption point, reached out to their adoption clinic for help. Alyssa in particular was concerned that Grigory was delayed cognitively. Both were worried that Grigory would approach any stranger anywhere as if the person were a trusted attachment figure.

Both Alyssa and Harvey had always valued education, and they wondered whether Grigory would be able to excel academically. Alyssa spent many of her waking hours thinking about how to provide challenges that would accelerate his development. Harvey and Alyssa's parent coach came to their house for the first time at the 6-week postadoption point to help ease a minor power struggle that had developed between Grigory and Alyssa. Alyssa could often be heard saying, "Use your words, Grigory," when he signaled that he wanted to be picked up, that he was hungry, and other such things. Harvey had not bought fully into the idea that they needed to push Grigory and so was more responsive to cues than Alyssa was. Grigory found Harvey much more engaging than his mother and preferred going to Harvey when he was hurt or worried and when he wanted a play partner.

The challenge for the parent coach was to help Alyssa and Harvey follow Grigory's lead and nurture him when he was distressed, even though they were concerned about cognitive catch-up. Both parents were highly motivated, but Alyssa in particular was convinced that she was on the right track. Sessions 1 and 2 focus on nurturing the distressed child even when he doesn't signal the need for nurturance. In Session 1, Grigory began crying when a fly, buzzing around his head, frightened him. Alyssa said right away, "Use your words, Grigory. What do you need?" The parent coach was able to refer to that example later in the session and the next as she talked about children not showing their needs clearly, even though the primary issue here was Alyssa not responding to the child's signals. The parent coach talked about how important it was for Grigory to be nurtured even though he was not able to come to Alyssa or Harvey directly. The fact that Alyssa did not behave in a nurturing way was not addressed at that point. In those first several sessions, Harvey was nurturing several times when Grigory was upset. The parent coach commented on his nurturance, remarking how important it was, especially because Grigory had experienced some challenges in his life. She commented that, even though trying to get him to use his words at such times might seem important, taking advantage of any opportunities for nurturing him so that he could learn to show his needs clearly was even more important. Harvey was comfortable nurturing Grigory, and so Grigory learned to go to his father when he needed him quickly. The transition for Alyssa came between the fifth and sixth sessions. She reported a time when Grigory banged his head and just sat on the floor stunned. She sat beside him on the floor and patted his head, talking softly to him. After a minute, he nestled in close to her and let her put her arm around him. It was a rewarding moment for her and the beginning of a shift in their relationship.

Not surprisingly, given her concerns about Grigory's developmental delays, Alyssa also struggled to follow Grigory's lead. Although she started to respond in more nurturing ways after the first few sessions, Alyssa still tried to turn other moments, including play time as well as routine activities, into opportunities to teach. She often corrected Grigory's words or insisted that he answer questions. Here is an example of Alyssa's failing to follow the lead: When Grigory was "reading" a book, Alyssa pointed to a picture of a cat and said, "What's that?" When Grigory said, "ruff ruff," Alyssa corrected him, saying "No, that's a cat." Even though it might seem minor, little moments like this took the lead away from Grigory, requiring him to shift in response to Alyssa's agenda rather than being the one in control of interactions.

An additional influence also shaped Alyssa's approach to interacting with Grigory. Alyssa had initiated occupational therapy services. Parents adopting internationally, concerned about their children's motor and cognitive delays, often use occupational and physical therapy services. Occupational therapy goals are sometimes at odds with ABC goals in that they may suggest not responding to the child's signals unless the child communicates in a specified way (e.g., using words, speaking in full sentences).

What we emphasized with Alyssa (and with many parents adopting internationally) is that, however counterintuitive it might seem, her son's language would improve most if she were very responsive to him—that is, if she followed Grigory's lead in language. For example, we suggested that instead of saying "Use your words," Alyssa should say, "Oh, you want me to pick you up?" Instead of saying "What color is that one?," Alyssa should say, "You have a blue one. I'm going to find a blue one too." Through such interactions, Grigory would have the experience of a responsive parent and would gain experience with language that would help him build the ability to communicate effectively. Indeed, we have found that ABC enhances children's language skills and does so through its effects on parents' sensitivity (Raby, Freedman, Yarger, Lind, & Dozier, in press).

Initially, Alyssa asked whether she might make Grigory "use her words" some of the time and she could follow his lead at other times. Even though her parent coach discouraged that idea, she could see Alyssa going back and forth between the approaches. Gradually, however, Alyssa recognized that Grigory was much more responsive to her when she interacted sensitively, which provided some motivation. Despite notable shifts in her behavior, Alyssa continued to vacillate between providing nurturing and responsive interactions at some times and not at others.

Indiscriminate sociability represented a significant problem for Grigory. When the parent coach came into the home the first time, Grigory greeted her as if he knew her well, running to her and hugging her legs. After the parent coach sat down on the sofa with her laptop, Grigory climbed up on her lap. In subsequent sessions, the parent coach tried a number of strategies to discourage

Grigory from close contact, such as sitting on the floor and pulling her knees up to her chest so that he could not access her lap and handing Grigory back to his mother. Grigory was often insistent, however. For example, he brought toys to the parent coach and put his face right in her line of sight, inches from her face.

During the early sessions, indiscriminate sociability is approached indirectly, with the parent coach serving as the example of an uninteresting, disengaged stranger. In Session 4, this issue is dealt with directly, which involves talking with parents about indiscriminately sociable behaviors (that parents have likely observed and been uncomfortable with), the impact of the behaviors on parents, and strategies for dealing with the behaviors. A key component is helping parents recognize and acknowledge the effects of their child's indiscriminate behavior on them; it's easy to feel rejected when children do not reserve close contact for parents but instead approach everyone as if they are attachment figures. As a result of feeling rejected themselves, parents may become somewhat rejecting—or at least disinterested—in response. However, if parents can recognize what's going on, they can avoid getting into this pattern. Continuing to be nurturing when the child is distressed and to follow the child's lead (issues worked on in Sessions 1–3), even when the child does not seem to need or want it, is critical.

We also help parents develop strategies that directly target these behaviors, including limiting the number of adults the child has contact with in the first months, discouraging others from being responsive to the child's friendly overtures, and redirecting the child if he (or she) engages with strangers. If parents are comfortable doing so, such strategies involve talking with others about the need for them to not respond to the child's overtures.

Sessions 7 and 8 (voices from the past) were compelling for both Alyssa and Harvey. Alyssa had always been a high achiever, knowing that was something that had made her special in her parents' eyes. She recalled in Session 7 how much her parents had emphasized achievement—and being good—above all else. Although it was not immediate, she soon acknowledged that this had come with real costs. She recalled times when she had been worried as a child about something (e.g., her best friend of 3 years found a new best friend) and was unwilling to talk about it with her mother because her mother had always valued her toughness. Through remembering this incident and others, Alyssa was able to recognize that she wanted to have a relationship with Grigory where he would come to her no matter what.

For Harvey, the biggest challenge was feeling rejected by Grigory. He had seen Grigory come to rely on him more and more in the several months of their relationship. But when Grigory approached a stranger with the same enthusiasm with which he approached Harvey, he sometimes felt like he was being kicked in the stomach. This feeling of "not mattering" took him back to times as a child when his mother, who was raising 10 children, treated the children as if none of them were special. Although Harvey had talked about the powerful feeling that he was being rejected by Grigory in earlier sessions, it was useful for him to recall times from his early years when he had experienced similar feelings.

By Session 10, Grigory's habit of approaching strangers with indiscriminate friendliness seemed to be abating. Clearly, his parents had a special place for him, and he consistently went to them when he was frightened or upset and not to strangers. The video montage shown in Session 10 highlighted the many times across the 10 visits that Alyssa and Harvey had provided nurturance to Grigory when he was upset, followed his lead, and delighted in him. What stood out to Alyssa and Harvey as they watched the video was that Grigory seemed so comfortable in their arms and engaged during their play.

INTERVENTION EFFECTIVENESS FOR CHILDREN ADOPTED INTERNATIONALLY

We had wondered if ABC would have measurable effects on parents adopting internationally because they represent such an unusual group and adoption is such a powerful intervention.

We have been heartened to find that parents adopting internationally become more sensitive in their interactions with their children following the intervention than parents assigned to a different intervention—and that changes in sensitivity are sustained several years after the intervention (Yarger, Bernard, Caron, Wallin, & Dozier, in press). The children of these parents in the ABC condition show gains in several ways. First, they exhibit lower levels of disorganized behavior (scored on a continuum) than children in the control condition (Raby, Carlson, & Dozier, 2018). They also show better ability to regulate attention and behavior than children whose parents did not receive the ABC intervention (Lind et al., 2017). Parents report fewer behavior problems among children in the ABC condition than those in the control condition, and we see fewer behavior problems in challenging tasks among ABC than among control children (Raby et al., 2018). At the anecdotal level, we have seen changes in indiscriminate sociability, similar to those described in Grigory's case; however, the base rate of these behaviors is so low that we have not been able to examine intervention effects statistically. We are still coding behavioral data from this study and will have more results in the next several years. We describe intervention effects in greater detail in Chapter 8.

CHAPTER 7

ABC for Parents of Toddlers

Three-year-old David saw his mother's ChapStick and reached for it, saying, "I want put ChapStick on." His mother, Sarah, said, "I'll put it on for you." He said, "I want to put on," pulling it away. His mother said, "You can have it, but I have to put it on for you." And thus the struggle began. After David became more and more distraught and frustrated, he began flailing about. Sarah warned him that he would be put in time-out if he could not settle down, and when he kicked his legs out, she said angrily, "Now you're in time-out." David flailed and cried and struggled.

Two months later, the situation began similarly. David had become very upset when his brother left for soccer practice and David couldn't go. He was angry and hit at his mother. She backed up and said, "I know you're angry, honey."

David's mother, Sarah, was working with a parent coach implementing ABC for Toddlers. The parent coach's goal throughout ABC for Toddlers was to help Sarah stay physically and emotionally available to David when he became overwrought. By Session 10, Sarah was well equipped to hang in with David, reminding him that she understood his frustration and was there for him.

Watching David and Sarah struggle was painful early on— and Sarah hated the struggles as much as David did. She had read about time-out and was convinced that she should be firm in her interactions with David.

Toddlers (2- to 4-year-olds) face several critical developmental tasks: establishing attachment relationships with caregivers, using attachment relationships to help them co-regulate difficult emotions (i.e., with their parents' help), and developing strategies to become increasingly independent in regulating their emotions (Cassidy, 1994; Cole et al., 2011). The task of developing independent self-regulatory strategies is especially difficult for toddlers who have experienced early adversity (Bernard et al., 2010; Bruce et al., 2009), which can make parenting toddlers in foster care quite challenging. In particular, these children often struggle with dysregulation and may have difficulty clearly signaling their need for support (Dozier & Bick, 2007).

Attachment and Biobehavioral Catch-Up for Toddlers (ABC-T) was adapted from our infant intervention. Similar to ABC, ABC-T was designed to help foster parents behave in sensitive and nurturing ways to promote the development of secure attachment relationships and to support children's physiological and behavioral regulation. In addition, ABC-T encourages parents to use the attachment relationship to help toddlers calm down effectively when they are frustrated or overwrought.

Unlike interventions that aim to enhance children's behavioral regulation using strategies with strong self-regulatory demands (e.g., time-out), ABC-T focuses on helping the parent stay physically and psychologically available to the child when the child is upset. We make the assumption that children who have experienced adversity need support when they are most distressed. Positive experiences in which parents serve as co-regulators are seen as critical from an attachment perspective because they provide the young child with experiences of an available parent when he or she is struggling with potentially overwhelming emotions. The parent's support can help the child manage strong emotions and gives the child confidence in the parent's availability. Over time and with continued support, the child can begin to learn to manage strong feelings. Given the emphasis on enhancing children's regulatory capabilities in the ABC-T intervention, we expected the intervention to promote foster children's executive functioning—an important predictor of later success in handling challenges in academic and peer contexts (Allan, Hume, Allan, Farrington, & Lonigan, 2014). Executive functioning refers to higher mental processes, such as planning, inhibiting a dominant response, and holding multiple pieces of information in mind.

Toddlers and parents must balance toddlers' growing need to use independent regulation strategies, even while children are still largely reliant on their parents for help with regulating their emotions and behaviors. Toddlers are often frustrated by this process and become dysregulated, displaying intense negative affect and oppositional, defiant behavior (Shaw, Bell, & Gilliom, 2000). These behaviors can elicit strong emotional reactions from parents that may lead to ineffective co-regulatory strategies, such as minimizing or dismissing negative emotion and punitive responses (Fabes, Leonard, Kupanoff, & Martin, 2001). Parents need to override their own strong emotional reactions if they are to serve as effective co-regulators for their children.

ABC-T was developed to address the emerging regulatory difficulties faced by children who have experienced early adversity and the challenges faced by parents caring for them. Specifically, ABC-T seeks to enhance children's regulatory capabilities by (1) increasing parents' nurturing behaviors in response to children's distress, (2) increasing parents' responsiveness to children's non-distress signals (i.e., following the lead), and (3) encouraging parents to serve as co-regulators for their children under challenging conditions. Two of the three primary intervention targets (nurturance and following the lead) were shared across the infant and toddler intervention, although they were adapted for older children in ABC-T. These parenting targets were retained because, as core components of ABC, they are effective in enhancing physiological regulation (Bernard et al., 2015) as well as cognitive self-regulation (Lewis-Morrarty et al., 2012). These core components of ABC have also been proven effective in promoting the secure, organized attachment relationships in which co-regulatory strategies can be rooted (Bernard et al., 2012; Dozier et al., 2009).

In addition to these parenting strategies included in ABC, ABC-T focuses on helping parents learn strategies for serving as co-regulators for their children when children become overwhelmed. Opportunities for parental nurturance (a core target in both ABC and ABC-T) are distinguished from opportunities for parental co-regulating or calming (a target in ABC-T only) based on the specific child emotions that trigger the parental response. Parental nurturance opportunities include times when children are sad, hurt, scared, or worried, whereas parental calming opportunities include times when the child is frustrated, irritated, angry, or otherwise overwhelmed by emotions. ABC-T helps parents recognize these as co-regulation opportunities, understand the importance of remaining psychologically available to their children rather than minimizing their children's emotions, and implement behaviors that soothe and calm their children effectively. Parent coaches also discuss the importance of avoiding behaviors that can lead to or exacerbate child dysregulation, such as tickling, yelling, lecturing, and unnecessary arguing or butting heads.

ABC FOR TODDLERS

ABC-T Sessions

The first two sessions of ABC-T have the same content as ABC. In Sessions 1 and 2, the focus is on providing nurturing care even when the child does not elicit nurturance. This can be more challenging for parents of toddlers who have experienced adversity because toddlers have a more entrenched expectation that parents will not be nurturing than do infants.

Session 3 helps parents learn to follow their children's lead, again as in the infant version of ABC. Session 4 continues the emphasis on following the lead of children's everyday behaviors and introduces the idea of avoiding power struggles. Often, parents think in terms of praising children only when children do things considered "good," and they do not think that everyday or ordinary behaviors should receive attention. This inattention to everyday behaviors often results in children (especially children with emerging behavioral problems) receiving most attention when they behave in ways that parents consider undesirable. Parents may also get into power struggles with their children when they either could be following their children's lead or helping their children calm down. Often, when parents engage in power struggles, it leads to children becoming more rather than less dysregulated. This session focuses on parents attending to and following children's "ordinary" behaviors and avoiding getting into power struggles when possible. The parent coach emphasizes that these behaviors lay the foundation for calming skills, which are needed when children become dysregulated. It is critical that parents consistently follow children's lead before they move on to learning about calming skills in Session 5.

Sessions 5 and 6 highlight how to support children when they are dysregulated and need help calming down. Parents are helped to consider how their own negative emotions (e.g., anger, frustration) may lead them to behave in ways—yelling, lecturing, threatening—that can exacerbate child dysregulation. In order to serve as effective co-regulators of children's difficult emotions, parents must stay calm themselves. Parent coaches offer several recommendations to help children calm down when they are becoming dysregulated, including labeling the child's emotion, making the environment easier to manage, and providing comfort both verbally and physically. The importance of following the lead of everyday child behaviors, while avoiding power struggles, is reviewed and stressed.

To make room for the focus on helping parents to serve as co-regulators when children become overwrought, intrusive and frightening parental behaviors are not explicitly addressed. Given that intrusive and frightening behaviors may still be problematic, however, attention is directed to these behaviors in the remaining sessions as needed.

Sessions 7 and 8 focus on parents' voices from the past in ABC-T as in ABC. Given that many parents have the greatest difficulty with avoiding power struggles, it is often these struggles that are emphasized.

Again, there is much to consolidate in Sessions 9 and 10 for parents. We want parents to be able to provide nurturing care, follow their child's lead, and serve as co-regulators to the distressed toddler.

ABC-T is a more difficult intervention to implement than the infant version of ABC (for a full list comparing ABC and ABC-T session topics, see Table 7.1). For both parent coaches and parents, there is more to master—often under more difficult conditions than for the infant intervention. Although we emphasize in the infant intervention that the child may make the parent's task difficult, it is unmistakably the case with the toddler intervention. Indeed, part of what the intervention targets is helping the parent provide effective care when the child pushes her or his own buttons. Several examples are provided that illustrate the challenges and successes of the ABC-T intervention.

Flying Ninja Kicks

Artis had been a foster parent for several years and had come to pride herself on having well-behaved children. Three-year-old Robbie had recently been placed in her care. Robbie was a boisterous, energetic child who challenged Artis's need for order. For example, Robbie loved to do "flying ninja kicks" in the living

TABLE 7.1. ABC and ABC-T Session Topics		
Session	ABC	ABC-T
1	Target 1: Nurturance	Same as ABC
2		
3	Target 2: Following the lead	Same as ABC
4		Avoiding power struggles
5	Target 3: Frightening behavior	Calming
6		
7	Voices from the past	Same as ABC
8		
9	Practice and consolidation	Same as ABC
10		

room, running across the living room and kicking up one leg. Artis fussed and Robbie giggled. The relationship between Robbie and Artis became increasingly contentious. Artis was negative much of the time, fussing at Robbie for one thing or another. Robbie did not seem beaten down by the criticism, but he also was not very responsive to Artis.

Through ABC-T, we urged Artis to embrace and delight in Robbie's energetic ways. The parent coach suggested first that Artis just notice and comment on little things that Robbie was doing. Artis was puzzled, unsure what she could comment on in a positive way. Her parent coach suggested that she comment on how well Robbie was driving the (pretend) tractor or on how many blocks he had put together in a single pile. Artis commented, but her comments were sometimes coupled with a warning (e.g., "You've got a big pile of blocks, but it's gonna fall over"). The parent coach urged her to make the comments entirely positive, with no criticism or suggestion allowed. With practice, Artis's comments improved. She said, "Robbie, you're driving that tractor so well!" Robbie grinned and said, "Look, Mommy, I'm driving it up the hill!"

Interestingly, Artis began to appreciate Robbie's energetic nature rather than feeling annoyed by it. The parent coach helped Artis to expand the behaviors she was willing to accept in her house. As a parent-coach supervisor, I (M. D.) remember supervisees suggesting that the limit was somewhere before flying ninja kicks. I asked them, if he wasn't at risk of kicking anyone or the TV or other objects, why couldn't ninja kicks be among the things that he could do—and among the things that we'd hope Artis could delight in? Indeed, over time, we encouraged Artis to allow and to take delight in Robbie's flying ninja kicks. This was important because this active, energetic little boy could feel appreciated for something that was so "him"—and power struggles were avoided.

Robbie and Artis developed a close, caring relationship. Robbie felt appreciated and Artis took joy in him. His energetic nature was not always appreciated by others and sometimes got him into trouble, but Artis was able to become a support to him.

Opioid Addiction

Flo was a 27-year-old mother with two children: 2-year-old Davey and 4-year-old Drake. Flo had become addicted to an opioid (oxycodone) in her early 20s following a car accident. When her doctor became reluctant to continue writing prescriptions for her, Flo first drove around to various clinics for prescription refills. Eventually, the clinics closed down, and Flo found that she could access heroin more easily than prescription opioids.

Much of Flo's attention had been directed toward finding access to drugs since her children were born. She was intermittently attentive to them, but it was hard for her to sustain attention.

Her children, though, were difficult to ignore. Both were intensely demanding. As Flo grew fidgety and restless, being increasingly in need of a fix, her children's disruptive behavior escalated. Often, even when Flo was relaxed and attentive, they spiraled out of control. For example, Drake took Davey's truck and ran around the house with it. Davey yelled for his mother to get the truck and then tore after Drake screaming. Flo yelled at both of them that they would get whippings if they did not stop right that minute.

Flo's parent coach had experience working with a range of clients, but she nonetheless found work with Flo and her children challenging. Flo often had difficulty staying "tuned in" to the sessions and was highly variable from one session to another. For example, in Session 3, she seemed to "get" the importance of nurturance and following the lead, and the parent coach was optimistic that change had occurred. However, in the next session, Flo was distracted and not following her children's lead. Her children's behaviors tracked her own behaviors, with the children frazzled and out of control when Flo was inattentive. Progress was bumpy but gains were seen overall. To our surprise, her sensitivity ratings were in the acceptable range at the end of the 10 sessions, and more surprising, Davey was classified as having a secure attachment to her.

ABC-T EFFECTIVENESS

As with our study regarding children adopted internationally, we are now finishing data collection for our toddler study and have limited findings at this point. Still, thus far, our findings indicate that ABC-T is an effective intervention for toddlers. We have found that the intervention improves parental sensitivity and that children's language abilities and executive functioning are enhanced (Lind, Raby, Caron, Roben, & Dozier, 2017; Raby et al., in press).

CHAPTER 8

The Evidence Base for ABC

U ntil recently, decisions about which interventions to use with vulnerable children and families were based on familiarity, anecdote, and case examples but not on strong research evidence. The move toward using research evidence to decide which interventions to use is exciting.

TYPES OF STUDIES

The randomized clinical trial design is considered the "gold standard" in assessing the efficacy of interventions. Randomized clinical trials involve randomly assigning parents (or families or children) to one of two or more intervention groups. Sometimes the control group involves another intervention, and sometimes it involves a wait list or "treatment as usual." In our research, the control intervention has been of the same duration (an hour each session), frequency (weekly), and setting (families' homes) as ABC. We have chosen this approach because it offers a rigorous comparison—parents have similar expectations and experiences in the two groups, and we therefore have the greatest confidence that differences between groups result from what is unique about ABC.

Many studies of intervention effectiveness compare groups that were not randomly assigned or examine change in pre–postintervention designs. These designs do not provide as clear a picture of intervention effects as randomized clinical trials. In the case of comparison of groups without random assignment, the groups may be different for a variety of reasons unrelated to the intervention. For example, assume that one agency, Children First, had its staff trained to deliver an experimental intervention and that a second agency, First Families, did not. The researchers then found that outcomes were better for children who received the intervention (all from Children First) than for children who did not receive the intervention (all from First Families); the intervention children were classified as having secure attachments more often and were referred for maltreatment less often than children who did not get the intervention. But what you would—or should—worry about is that there may be a number of differences between the agencies and the families served besides their having received the intervention or not. Perhaps case planners at Children First engage in more professional development activities related to trauma than case planners at First Families; or perhaps parents at Children First tend to be younger on average than First Families parents. Any of these systematic differences between the groups might explain why children who received the intervention looked different on key outcomes than children who did not receive the intervention.

In the case of pre–postintervention designs, it is not usually possible to know how much children or parents would have changed without the intervention. Especially within the first several years of life, children are changing rapidly. Even after 3 or 4 months, children may look quite different than before the intervention began. Consider an 8-month-old who has experienced neglect early in life. He doesn't crawl or scoot around the floor, he shows little emotion when interacting with his mother, and he has only recently started to babble and play with toys within reach. By 12 months and after 10 sessions of an intervention, he is very actively exploring his world, smiling and clapping in response to his mother, and showing sustained interest while playing with toys. Can we attribute these changes to the intervention? Maybe. Or maybe they simply reflect normal developmental changes or changes that would have occurred anyway because a grandparent became more involved in his care or because his mother was able to give up her second job and spend more time with him. With a pre–postintervention design (with no control group), we cannot know. With a randomized clinical trial, however, particularly one that involves an active treatment-control group, we can.

We have now conducted four different randomized clinical trials of the efficacy of ABC. We have used the same research design in each trial, contrasting the ABC intervention with an intervention that we have called Developmental Education for Families (DEF). We have examined whether the ABC intervention has effects on key parenting behaviors and on expected child outcomes.

TYPES OF DATA COLLECTED

An important issue is whether parent reports or more objective observational measures are used to assess change. Parents' reports of outcomes are susceptible to a number of influences, and it is usually difficult to disentangle these other influences from the issue that is reported on. For example, consider some of the influences affecting parents' reports of their children's behavior problems. We know that depressed parents tend to overreport their children's problem behaviors (Boyle & Pickles, 1997; Chilcoat & Breslau, 1997; Najman et al., 2000). Think about Crystal, introduced in Chapter 4. You could imagine that her current challenging circumstances could color her report of every aspect of her functioning as well as her child's. Indeed, a global reporting bias emerges among parents, with parents typically reporting in a consistent way across domains (Stokes et al., 2011). Furthermore, parents are often concerned about how their responses will be used. For example, foster parents tend to overreport problem behaviors, whereas birth parents underreport (e.g., McLaughlin et al., 2011). Birth parents may worry that their children's problem behavior will reflect poorly on them as parents, whereas foster parents may be signaling that their job as foster parents is a difficult one.

Other issues can systematically affect parents' responses, such as the desire to support their parent coach by indicating that they experienced positive outcomes or their expectation that they have changed because they participated in treatment (known as the Rosenthal effect). What we worry most about when the parent report is the primary outcome is that parents' perceptions may change, but their own behavior or their children's behavior may not.

For these reasons, in our work we rely primarily on behavioral and biological indicators of change rather than parent or child reports. These behavioral and biological measures are often time consuming, both to collect and to code. But we consider the investment very worthwhile.

ABC CHILD OUTCOMES

The primary targets of the ABC intervention were attachment quality and child physiological, emotional, and behavioral regulation. Over time we have added to these outcomes as it has become clear what pervasive effects the intervention could have.

Attachment

Attachment in Infancy

Prior to the intervention, when James fell and bumped his head, he sat on the floor and cried loudly but did not move toward his mother. Sonya, who had been involved in several abusive relationships, sometimes reacted to James angrily and sometimes in nurturing ways. Throughout ABC, Sonya's parent coach focused on supporting Sonya's providing nurturance to James whenever he needed it. He sometimes just came over and snuggled against her, and even though he was not showing signs of distress, Sonya was encouraged for putting her arm around him or patting his hand tenderly at such times. By the end of the intervention, when James was hurt or scared, he moved immediately to Sonya, and she reassured him consistently.

Because we knew that children who have experienced adversity are at elevated risk for disorganized attachment unless parents behave in nurturing ways, the ABC intervention sought to help parents behave in nurturing ways so that children developed secure, organized attachments.

We assessed attachment through the Strange Situation, the lab-based measure of attachment quality. The Strange Situation was designed to "ratchet up" the child's attachment system through a series of separations and reunions (Ainsworth et al., 1978). Of particular relevance for coding is the child's behavior upon reunion. These reunion behaviors reveal how the child responds when distressed and in the parent's presence.

James's behavior in the Strange Situation paralleled what we had seen in the home. During reunion episodes, when the parent reenters the room, children with secure attachments typically behave in ways that show that they expect their parent to be there for them. If distressed, children with secure attachments usually approach their parents (e.g., walking toward them, reaching out their arms) and maintain proximity (e.g., clinging, staying on parent's lap) until settled. They tend to settle easily upon the parent's return. When James's mother returned following each separation, he greeted her enthusiastically. It took him somewhat longer to get down from her lap in the second reunion than in the first, but he was happily engaged with the toys within 30 seconds of his mother's return each time. These behaviors are prototypical secure behaviors—James was classified as having a secure attachment (B3, which is the most prototypical of the secure subcategories). Like James, slightly more than half of the children whose parents received the ABC intervention had secure attachments. This is in contrast with 33% of the children whose parents received the control (DEF) intervention. The percentage of children with secure attachments was significantly larger in the ABC than in the control group.

Jenny, whose mother received the control intervention, fell prone on the floor when her mother returned in the first reunion. When her mother called to her, she continued to lie flat, crying hard. These behaviors are prototypical disorganized behaviors. Her mother picked her up and asked her what was wrong. For the rest of the reunion, Jenny behaved in ways characteristic of a secure child, returning to play and showing her mother toys. In the second reunion, Jenny sat on the floor and cried inconsolably, not moving toward her mother. When her mother approached, Jenny continued crying. Her mother did not pick her up, and Jenny continued crying hard but without moving toward her mother. She remained distraught. After about 60 seconds, her mother went to pick her up, and Jenny gradually calmed down. Again, the behavior of becoming upset but with no move toward the parent is characteristic of disorganized attachment, reflecting a collapse in the attachment strategy. Slightly more than half (57%) of the children in the control group had disorganized attachments as contrasted with only 32% of children in the ABC group, a significant difference (Bernard et al., 2012).

These findings regarding changes in attachment quality can be seen in Table 8.1 and are striking when one considers that the intervention does not seek to change families' living conditions, parents' use of substances, or their mental health problems. Rather, it seeks to change only three primary parental behaviors. Families are probably as likely to live in motel rooms or shelters after the intervention as before and probably as likely to have

TABLE 8.1. Effects of ABC on Children's Attachment Classifications		
	ABC	**Control**
Attachment disorganization		
Organized	68%	43%
Disorganized	32%	57%
Attachment security		
Secure	52%	33%
Insecure	48%	67%

problems with addictions after the intervention as before. What typically changes is that parents become sensitive, nurturing, and nonfrightening—and as a result, children are more likely to develop secure and organized attachments than they would have otherwise.

We consider the reductions in attachment disorganization especially exciting because disorganized attachment is associated with so many problematic long-term outcomes. As discussed in detail earlier, children with disorganized attachments are at risk for externalizing problems such as oppositional defiant disorder or conduct disorder and dissociative symptoms such as spacing out.

Among children adopted internationally, the rates of secure attachment are strikingly high regardless of treatment condition, but we nonetheless see lower levels of disorganized attachment among ABC children who experienced high levels of adversity prior to adoption than among children in the control condition (Raby, Zajac, & Dozier, 2018).

Attachment in Middle Childhood

By the time children are of middle childhood age (8–10 years), it's possible to ask them to reflect on their relationships with their parents. Kathryn Kerns developed a self-report inventory called the Security Scale (Kerns, Aspelmeier, Gentzler, & Grabill, 2001) that asks children to respond to 15 questions about their relationships with their parents. Children are asked to indicate which one of two statements best describes them, such as "Some kids find it easy to trust their mom" or "Other kids are not sure they can trust their mom," and then to indicate if the statement they choose is "really like you" or "sort of like you." Children with whom we had intervened in infancy were asked to complete this questionnaire at age 9. We found that children whose parents received the ABC intervention reported that they felt greater security in their relationships with their parents ($M = 3.49$, $SD = 0.38$) than children whose parents received the control intervention ($M = 3.28$, $SD = $

0.47). These differences are striking when considering that the 10-session intervention was completed 7 or more years before the assessment.

Self-Regulation

Children who experience adversity are often dysregulated physiologically, emotionally, and behaviorally. Because more responsive parents are more likely to have children with better self-regulation than less responsive parents (e.g., Raver, 1996), we designed the intervention to encourage parents to follow their children's lead, with the expectation that this would enhance children's self-regulatory capabilities. Self-regulation can be seen in children's regulation of their biological/physiological systems (such as the HPA axis), regulation of emotions, and regulation of behavior.

Child HPA Axis Regulation

We have focused our assessments of HPA axis regulation on children's diurnal production of cortisol. From early in development, healthy children typically show a diurnal pattern, with high morning values and low evening values of cortisol. The high morning values help a person to get up and be alert in the morning, and low evening levels help one to wind down and sleep well at night. When these values are thrown off, for example, because of travel across time zones, changing sleeping patterns, or stress, there are consequences for both physical and mental health (Adam et al., 2017). The effects of adversity, such as living in a chaotic environment and exposure to maltreatment, are seen in a blunted cortisol pattern across the day. It was our goal to normalize this diurnal production of cortisol.

In order to assess the diurnal pattern of cortisol, we asked parents to collect saliva samples from their children when they woke up in the morning and before they went to bed at night for 3 days in a row. Parents held one end of a cotton swab and put the other end in the child's mouth to soak it with saliva. They then stored these samples in their freezer until a research assistant picked the samples up and brought them back to our lab. In the lab, the saliva was extracted from the cotton swab, and the saliva was analyzed for levels of cortisol.

As we had hoped, the ABC intervention helped normalize children's patterns of cortisol production. Children who received the ABC intervention showed higher morning values and a steeper downward slope across the day than children who received the control (DEF) intervention. These effects could be seen immediately after the intervention (Bernard, Dozier et al., 2015) and also 3 years later, when the children were 5 years old (Bernard, Hostinar, & Dozier, 2015) (see Figure 8.1).

We expected that these changes in children's cortisol rhythms were likely due to parents becoming more responsive co-regulators as a result of ABC. When children were 8–10 years old, we collected saliva samples again and tested whether changes in parental sensitivity mediated the link between participation in the ABC intervention and children's cortisol patterns in middle childhood. ABC parents showed higher sensitivity (following

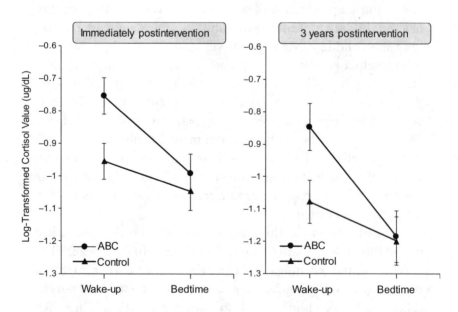

FIGURE 8.1. Effects of ABC on diurnal cortisol rhythms.

their child's lead) when children were toddlers, which, in turn, predicted steeper declines in cortisol from morning to evening when children were 8 years old (Garnett, Bernard, Zajac, & Dozier, 2018). These results identify parental sensitivity as a key mechanism of change; by enhancing parental sensitivity, ABC had long-term effects on children's HPA axis regulation into middle childhood.

Autonomic Nervous System Activity

The autonomic nervous system controls bodily processes, such as heart and breathing rates, digestion, and metabolism. Whereas the sympathetic division of the autonomic nervous system prepares the body for a "fight-or-flight" response to an acute stressor, the parasympathetic division regulates processes under nonstressed conditions. Respiratory sinus arrhythmia (RSA), an index of parasympathetic nervous system activation, refers to the variation in heart rate during the respiratory cycle. RSA levels while at rest provide an index of an individual's capacity to respond flexibly to environmental demands and are associated with adaptive emotion regulation skills and social competence (Beauchaine, 2001; Grossman & Taylor, 2007).

To assess whether children in the ABC intervention showed better regulated autonomic nervous system activity, we had 9-year-old children engage in a challenging discussion with their parents that was designed to elicit negative emotions. Research assistants helped children select a recent event or situation that upset them, such as getting into a fight with a friend. Then, physiological data were recorded from sensors that monitored heart rate and breathing, first while children were at rest, then as they discussed the distressing event with the parent, and then while having a positive discussion. Children in the ABC group showed higher levels of RSA, reflecting better regulation of their autonomic nervous system, than children in the control group (Tabachnick, Raby, Goldstein, Zajac, & Dozier, 2018). Again, these differences at the physiological level, seen many years after the intervention, suggest impressive, long-term changes.

Child Negative Emotion Expression

Early in childhood, children are learning to express and regulate their emotions appropriately. When children get to preschool, they are constantly challenged with potentially frustrating situations—for example, a peer taking their toy without permission, a puzzle being too challenging, or a teacher setting limits. In order to make and keep friends, persist and succeed in the face of difficult tasks, and comply with rules, children must develop the capacity to regulate negative emotions. By observing how toddlers *express* negative emotions in potentially challenging tasks, we can get a glimpse of their ability to tolerate and regulate feelings, such as anger, disappointment, and frustration.

When children were about 2 years old, we administered the Tool Task (Matas, Arend, & Sroufe, 1978), which had been used in the Minnesota Longitudinal Project to assess parenting and children's socioemotional competence in a challenging context. During the Tool Task, toddlers were presented with three problem-solving tasks that were too challenging for them. First, they were given a clear tube with a ball stuck in the middle and a wooden stick. They needed to use the stick to push the ball out of the tube. Second, they were given the same tube with a ball stuck in the middle, but this time the stick was in two pieces; so, they needed to put the two sticks together in order to push the ball out of the tube. Third, they were shown a clear box with a car toy inside; in order to retrieve the toy, they needed to follow multiple steps, such as putting weighted blocks on a lever to lift the car to a hole on the top of the box. The researcher presented each task in sequence, telling the parent (who remained in the room), "These tasks are too hard for most children at this age. You can let him (or her) try it, then give any help you think is needed."

During the Tool Task, we saw great variability in how children approached the task, how long they persisted, the extent to which they sought and used the parent, and the frequency and intensity of their expressions of negative affect. Some children became frustrated and angry after barely attempting the first task; for example, Amir immediately approached the clear tube and stuck his arm in one side, trying to reach the ball. After realizing that his arm wouldn't fit, he picked up the stick and banged it on the tube; then he picked up the tube and slammed it on the floor. To his dismay, none of these strategies worked to get the ball out of the tube. He started to whine and grabbed his mother's hand to pull her closer. His mom said, "No, you try." Amir said, "No, you!" When she leaned back to look at the magazine in her lap, Amir yelled, "You!" He picked up the stick and swung it at his mom, who caught it with her hand and pulled it away from him. He then flung himself on the floor and yelled in a piercing tone. Not surprisingly, his frustration only escalated further when presented with more difficult tasks. Amir scored high on the scales of negative emotion expression: anger expression, anger directed at parent, and global sadness/negative affect.

James similarly found the tasks challenging. He approached the first tube with interest, picked it up, and shook it multiple times. When the ball did not fall out, he lay on his stomach and peered through the hole of the tube. He looked at his mother, Sonya, for help; similar to Amir's mom, Sonya urged him to keep trying. James picked up the stick and banged it against the tube; he smiled, seemingly entertained by the banging noise. He tried reaching his arm in the tube and fussed slightly when it got stuck. His mother suggested, "Try the stick, not your arm. Put the stick in the tube," as she pointed. Fumbling several times, James eventually fit the stick into the tube and successfully pushed the ball out the other side. James scored low on the scales of negative affect expression. He seemed as perplexed by the problem as Amir but was visibly less distressed and more competent in his efforts.

We found that children who received ABC scored lower on anger expression, anger directed at their caregivers, and global sadness/negative affect during the Tool Task than children in the control group (Lind, Bernard, Ross, & Dozier, 2014). When we consider what this means for development, we find that Amir and James are likely to handle the typical challenges of preschool quite differently. Imagine the different responses from the boys when they are playing kickball and another child hits them with the ball. James might be disappointed, but he responds by muttering something quietly to himself, for example. Amir, however, is likely to blow up, yelling that the ball was thrown too hard or saying that the game just wasn't fair. Similarly, in the classroom, James is able to deal more effectively with the challenge of math problems that he doesn't understand, keeping his frustration under control, compared with Amir. James's ability to stay calm under such circumstances will allow him to persevere and help him stay in the teacher's good graces. This ability to regulate negative emotions is critical to children navigating their social and academic worlds (Kim, Nordling, Yoon, Boldt, & Kochanska, 2013; Panlilio, Jones Harden, & Harring, 2017; Penela, Walker, Degnan, Fox, & Henderson, 2015). When children cannot regulate negative affect effectively, in addition to experiencing more challenging social and academic worlds, they are at increased risk for later problems with internalizing disorders, such as anxiety and depression (Zeman, Shipman, & Suveg, 2002). Given that children who have experienced early adversity are already at increased risk for such disorders (Green et al., 2010; Infurna et al., 2016), this added risk is of particular concern.

Child Executive Functioning: Inhibitory Control

Executive functioning is the "boss" of the brain. As mentioned earlier, executive functions refer to the ability to plan and organize, shift from one task to another, inhibit behavior, and execute plans, among other things.

One of the most important qualities for children to have when they enter school is the ability to sit and attend to their teacher and not jump up and look out the window at children running by. More important than knowing their letters or numbers is having adequate "inhibitory control"—that is, the ability to inhibit a dominant response in favor of engaging in the more socially appropriate alternative behavior, or in the words of Robert Sapolsky, making "the right decision when it is the harder decision to make" (2017, p. 63).

Walter Mischel's famous "marshmallow test"—telling children they can have one marshmallow now, or several if they can wait—requires a number of related executive functions, including inhibitory control and delay of gratification. This test has proven to be powerful in predicting long-term outcomes. Preschool children who waited longer to eat the marshmallow had higher SAT scores and better social and cognitive functioning in adolescence than children who did not wait as long (Mischel, 2014). Furthermore, waiting longer to eat the marshmallow predicted lower body mass index 30 years later than eating the marshmallow quickly (Schlam, Wilson, Shoda, Mischel, & Ayduk, 2013). Similar findings have been obtained in other large-scale longitudinal studies that link self-control in childhood to later outcomes. In the Dunedin Multidisciplinary Health and Development Study, a birth cohort of 1,037 New Zealand children was followed from birth to 32 years. In this study, self-control was assessed in terms of a composite of observer ratings and parent, teacher, and self-reports on lack of persistence, inattention, hyperactivity, and impulsivity multiple times before children turned 10 years old. Controlling for childhood socioeconomic status and IQ, adults who had stronger self-control as children had better physical health (e.g., cardiovascular health, weight), reported higher income and fewer financial difficulties, and were less likely to have been convicted of a crime than adults who had weaker self-control as children (Moffitt et al., 2011). Similarly, in the Environmental-Risk Longitudinal Twin Study (E-Risk), level of self-control at age 5 distinguished siblings on a number of outcomes at age 12 that are expected to predict adulthood well-being. Controlling for differences in IQ, the sibling with higher self-control at age 5 was less likely to begin smoking, performed better in school, and engaged less in antisocial behaviors at age 12 than the sibling with lower self-control (Moffitt et al., 2011).

We used a task similar to the marshmallow test with our children. At preschool age, we presented children with a shelf of exciting toys—a Mr. Potato Head with many colorful pieces, an electronic cash register toy with grocery items and pretend money, and a miniature gumball machine filled with candy. This task is taken from the Disruptive Behavior Diagnostic Observation Schedule (DB-DOS; Wakschlag et al., 2008), an observational procedure that challenges children's behavior and emotion regulation abilities. For 5 minutes, parents were instructed to fill out a questionnaire while their child was allowed to read a book. The only rule was that children were not allowed to touch the toys on the shelf. Reading a book is of course boring in comparison with playing with an array of exciting new toys. The challenge for children was therefore great.

From the 5-minute segment of video, we marked all of the times that the child touched the forbidden toys. This allowed us to see whether or not the child touched the toys and, for children who did touch the toys, to compute the latency to touch (how long the child waited to first touch the toys) and the total amount of time that the child spent touching the toys.

James looked quizzically at his mother when she handed him the book and started filling out the questionnaire; he glanced at the toys on the back shelf, and his mother reminded him that he was not allowed to play with them yet. He then looked at the book and managed not to look at the toys again for the duration of the episode. After about 30 seconds, he said to his mother, "I'm finished." When she said she still had work she needed to complete, he continued looking at the book. This strategy of turning attention away from the tempting object is an effective one that worked well for James.

Amir, however, reached for the toys immediately when his mother started filling out her questionnaire. He began pushing buttons on the cash register, which resulted in loud dinging noises. His mother reminded him that he couldn't play with the toys, and he immediately began fiddling with the gumball machine. She then said, "Amir, stop! No touching!" The remainder of the 5 minutes was characterized by Amir continuing to play with the forbidden toys and his mother continuing to fuss at him.

Like James, more of the children in the ABC intervention than in the control intervention were successful in not touching the toys (Lind et al., in press). Only 34% of the ABC children touched the toys, as contrasted with 53% of the children in the control group. Even among just the children who touched the toys, the length of time before they touched them was longer for the ABC children (180 seconds) than for the control children (125 seconds). Furthermore, we found that parental sensitivity—following the child's lead (coded from a video-recorded parent–child play observation conducted approximately 1 month after the ABC intervention or control intervention)—partially mediated the effect of the ABC intervention on children's latency to touch the toys. Specifically, ABC parents were more sensitive than control parents following the intervention, with higher parental sensitivity in turn predicting longer latency to touch the toys. This finding held when controlling for parental sensitivity during the assessment of inhibitory control, suggesting that it was not simply differences in parental behavior during the challenging task that were responsible for the group differences. Such evidence of mediation provides support for the hypothesis that parent sensitivity is one key mechanism through which ABC has its effect on child outcomes.

Set Shifting

Shifting sets—that is, being able to change from adding to subtracting, from adding 2 to adding 4, from snack time to working on spelling—is an important skill. The Dimensional Change Card Sort (DCCS; Zelazo, Frye, & Rapus, 1996) is a widely used task that has proven powerful as an index of children's ability to shift sets. In this task, children are shown two images that vary on two dimensions: shape and color. Specifically, there is a picture of a blue rabbit and a red boat, each attached to boxes for sorting cards. By the age of 3, children can learn one rule and apply it consistently. For example, children can learn a "shape rule," for which all of the rabbits go in the box with the rabbit picture, and pictures of boats go in the box with the boat picture. What is difficult, though, is learning to apply a new rule—in this case, when children are then asked to use a "color rule," putting all the red pictures in the red pile and all the blue pictures in the blue pile. At the age of 3, most children cannot apply a new rule after having learned and applied a previous rule; they stay stuck in following the first rule. Children are often able to state the new rule, but then when given cards to sort, they continue to use the previous (shape) rule. Even when reminded of the new rule on each trial ("Remember, in the color game, all of the red ones go here, and all of the blue ones go here") and told what category the test card falls in ("Here's a blue one, where does it go?"), children will still stay stuck and continue sorting based on the original rule they learned. By the age of 4, some children can learn and apply the new rule and some cannot. By 5 years of age, most children can shift to the new rule. Given that shifting sets requires flexibility in applying rules, this skill is sometimes referred to as "cognitive flexibility."

As you would expect, children's ability to shift sets is highly correlated with other executive functioning skills, such as working memory and inhibitory control. Taken together, these executive functioning skills have been linked with gains in early academic skills, such as math achievement and literacy (Blair, Ursache, Greenberg, Vernon-Feagans, & Family Life Project Investigators, 2015; Fuhs, Nesbitt, Farran, & Dong, 2014), suggesting that executive functioning skills, such as shifting sets, are critical for school readiness.

We used the DCCS to examine our ABC and control-group children. Although many of the results we have presented are with CPS-involved children living with their birth parents, these results are with children in foster care. On this card-sorting task, both ABC children and control-group (DEF) children performed well when asked to follow the first rule, sorting by shape—that is, children were able to place pictures of rabbits in the box with the rabbit picture and pictures of boats in the box with the boat picture. Where children differed was when they were asked to shift to a new rule, sorting by color instead of shape. As can be seen in Figure 8.2, children in the ABC group performed well on this task, showing their ability to shift effectively to the new rule, nearly as well as low-risk (nonfoster) children. In contrast, the control-group children did not shift to the new rule effectively.

We first found these effects on set shifting in our sample of foster children who received ABC as infants (Lewis-Morrarty et al., 2012). In our more recent study of ABC-T, for toddlers in foster

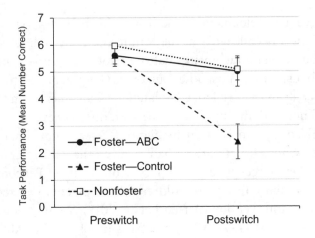

FIGURE 8.2. Effects of ABC on set shifting.

care, we found similar effects using a graded version of the card-sorting task (Beck, Schaefer, Pang, & Carlson, 2011). Children whose parents received ABC-T performed better than children whose parents received the control intervention and similar to the nonfoster comparison group (Lind et al., 2017). Thus, the original version of ABC for infants, as well as ABC-T, led to enhanced cognitive flexibility in early childhood.

Language

Twenty-plus years ago, I (M. D.) remember Alan Sroufe talking about what attachment quality and parental sensitivity should predict and not predict. Sroufe made the point that not "all good things" should be predicted by attachment. That is, attachment and sensitivity should be expected to predict such outcomes as relationship quality, self-efficacy, and self-regulation, but not outcomes that were more academically oriented, such as achievement, language, or academic functioning (Sroufe, 2016). Buying that perspective, we did not expect to see outcomes for variables such as children's language. We had extended further into cognitive domains related to executive functioning than we might have first expected but had stopped short of expecting differences in language development. Nonetheless, in the last several years, Sroufe and his colleagues at the Minnesota Longitudinal Project have found that attachment quality predicts cognitive outcomes more robustly than most other outcomes (Raby et al., 2015). It was for this reason that we looked at language outcomes, even though we had not initially expected to see such differences.

Indeed, as can be seen in Figure 8.3, we found that foster children whose foster parents had received the ABC intervention showed better receptive vocabulary scores on the Peabody Picture Vocabulary Test than children whose parents had received the control intervention (Bernard et al., 2017). We first noted this finding in our study of ABC for infants in foster care. ABC children had a mean standard score of 98.1 (scoring at the 45th percentile), and children who received the control intervention had a mean standard score of 88.1 (scoring at the 28th percentile).

We recently replicated and extended these findings in the randomized clinical trial of ABC for toddlers in foster care (Raby et al., in press). Similar to the previous findings, foster children in the ABC-T group had a mean of 99.4 (almost exactly the

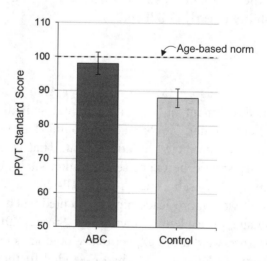

FIGURE 8.3. Effects of ABC on foster children's receptive language.

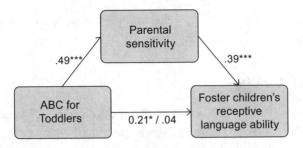

FIGURE 8.4. Effects of ABC-T on foster children's receptive language: Mediation by parental sensitivity.

population mean), whereas children in the control group had a mean nearly 0.5 standard deviation lower (92.3). This effect was fully mediated by parental sensitivity (see Figure 8.4). That is, the intervention's effect on children's language development is *through* parental sensitivity.

Although we had not originally anticipated such an effect, it makes sense to us when we think about how the intervention—and sensitivity—work. Parents are helped to follow their children's lead (i.e., to be sensitive) behaviorally and verbally through talking about what their children are doing. Language researchers have found that poor children often do not hear as many words as do other children, which has been referred to as the 30 million word gap (Hart & Risley, 1995). However, recent scholars (e.g., Golinkoff et al., 2015; Tamis-Lemonda, Kuchirko, & Song, 2014) have emphasized the importance, not so much of the number of words that children hear, but of how responsive and contingent parents' speech is to children and their behaviors. When parents' vocalizations are responsive, children become engaged in the language.

James's mother's verbalizations are highly contingent on his behavior. For example, she comments, "James, that truck is zooming along," while he plays with his truck and car. When he puts the horse in the barn, she says, "You put that horsey in the barn, sweetie?" Her language is of great interest to him because it tracks his behavior. He attends to the language and learns new words and new ways of expressing himself.

Neural Activity

As the cerebral cortex becomes more developed and specialized, brain wave activity changes. More specifically, slower wave (e.g., theta) activity is reduced and faster wave (e.g., beta and alpha) activity increases (Bell, 1998). Such changes are theorized to serve as markers of cortical differentiation and efficiency. To examine differences in brain wave activity, electrodes are placed on the child's head in various locations, with the electrical activity recorded by electroencephalogram (EEG).

In the Bucharest Early Intervention Project, children who were placed out of orphanage care into foster care at younger ages showed the positive effects of the intervention on increased alpha activity (oscillatory activity between 7 and 12 Hz) during middle childhood. These effects were not seen for children in the control group or for older children placed into foster care (Vanderwert, Marshall, Nelson, Zeanah, & Fox, 2010). We looked to see if we could replicate these findings among our children. We were aware that a 10-session intervention is a "light touch" relative to moving children out of orphanage care. Nonetheless, we found similar effects, with children in the ABC group showing greater high-frequency beta activity (oscillatory activity between 12 and 20 Hz) than children in the control group (Bick, Palmwood, Zajac, Simons, & Dozier, 2018).

We also examined children's brain activation through functional magnetic resonance imaging (fMRI) in each of two tasks when children were between 8 and 11 years old. In one task, children viewed photos of neutral and fearful faces. The children with histories of CPS involvement showed more occipital cortex and fusiform gyrus activation than a group of low-risk children, regardless of whether they were in the ABC or control group (Valadez, Tottenham, & Dozier, 2018). This finding suggests that, regardless of whether their parents received the ABC intervention, high-risk children showed more attention to threat at the level of brain activation. What was exciting, though, was that the ABC group showed more prefrontal cortex and insula activation than children from the control intervention. This suggests that even though ABC children are as threat-sensitive as control children, what differentiates ABC children is their greater prefrontal cortex involvement, and thus their greater regulation, during threat. This finding is consistent with better cognitive and behavioral regulation seen in behavioral tasks among ABC than control children. Although ABC cannot protect children from becoming threat-sensitive as the result of living challenging lives, it can help them control their reactions to this threat.

In a second fMRI task, children viewed photographs of their own mothers and other women with both neutral and smiling faces. Children in the ABC group showed greater activation of the posterior cingulate gyrus and middle/inferior temporal gyrus, brain regions involved in face processing and attention, when viewing photographs of their own mothers than strangers relative to children in the control group (Valadez et al., 2018). These results are consistent with their mothers having a special and salient place for children.

ABC PARENTING OUTCOMES

Parental Sensitivity

When her parent coach first met her, Sonya had trouble responding sensitively to James. Her many challenges (including the end of her relationship with her sometimes abusive boyfriend and her move to a motel) weighed her down, and she had little energy for noticing the little things he did. She periodically tried to engage with James but quickly took over control and led the interaction. For example, when he was stacking blocks, she began directing him, suggesting that he use all blocks of one color—an instruction that baffled him.

At the end of the intervention, Sonya was remarkable in her ability to follow James's lead. When he approached her—which he often did because Sonya had become so rewarding—she usually turned her full attention to him. For example, while greeting the parent coach upon her arrival, James crawled on all fours meowing like a cat, and Sonya said enthusiastically, "A cat!" This "following the child's lead" is what we mean by sensitivity.

Consistent with these anecdotes, we have found that parents who have completed the ABC intervention are more sensitive than parents who have completed the control intervention. We assess sensitivity by observing parents playing with their children, with instructions to "play as you usually would," using a developmentally appropriate set of toys that we provide. We found that foster parents who completed the ABC intervention were more sensitive than parents who completed the control intervention (Bick & Dozier, 2013). Approximately 3 years after ABC, we administered the Three Boxes Task, borrowed from the National Institute of Child Health and Human Development (NICHD) Study of Early Child Care (NICHD Early Child Care Research Network, 1999, 2003; Vandell, 1979), to assess sensitivity. In the first box was a set of Duplo blocks; in the second box, a cash register, pretend food items, and dress-up clothes; in the third box, construction paper, markers, and stickers. Parents were instructed to play with their child as they normally would, but to play with the toys in each of the boxes, going through the boxes in order. Coding parental behavior in this task, we found differences in sensitivity among CPS-referred mothers at approximately 3 years postintervention (see Figure 8.5). CPS-referred mothers who received ABC showed higher sensitivity (following the lead), higher positive regard (delight), lower detachment, and lower intrusiveness than CPS-referred mothers who received the control intervention. Furthermore, ABC mothers looked nearly indistinguishable from a low-risk comparison group of mothers.

Similarly, we found changes in parenting behavior among internationally adoptive parents (Yarger et al., in press). We see increases in parental sensitivity and reductions in parental intrusiveness from baseline to postintervention, with changes sustained more than 2 years after the intervention. We note that these parents adopting internationally start high in sensitivity. We consider sensitivity ratings above the midpoint of this 5-point scale

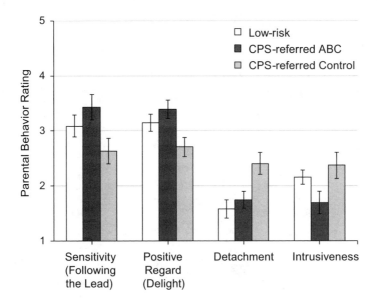

FIGURE 8.5. Effects of ABC on parental behavior among CPS-referred mothers (3 years postintervention).

(i.e., above 3) to reflect adequate levels of sensitivity. Looking at Figure 8.6, you can see that parents adopting internationally on average were rated about 3.4. Given that parents were interacting with their infants in relatively sensitive ways before the intervention, it was possible that the intervention might not result in changes in sensitivity—and indeed that the intervention might not result in changes for children. But, as you can see, that is not what we found. Parents' level of sensitivity improved more for the parents receiving ABC than for parents in the control group, and these changes were sustained across the period studied.

These sustained changes in parenting behavior seen across samples are key to changes in children's outcomes.

Parental Secure Base Script Knowledge

Given that the ABC intervention works to help parents behave in more nurturing ways, we considered it possible that ABC would also change the way parents think about scenarios that involve

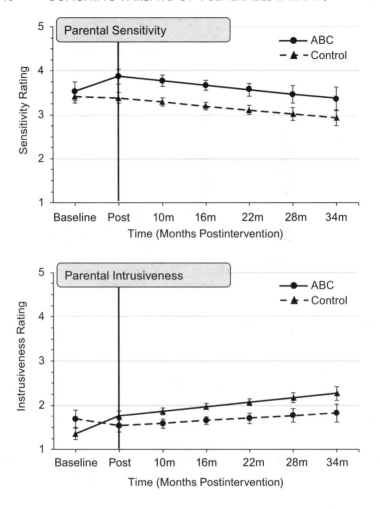

FIGURE 8.6. Longitudinal change in parenting behaviors among adoptive parents.

the need for nurturance. Harriet and Everett Waters (2006) proposed that individuals' histories of experiences with attachment figures are consolidated and represented in memory as a "secure base script," consisting of temporal–causal elements that characterize secure base interactions. To assess knowledge about the secure base script, Harriet Waters developed the Attachment Script Assessment (ASA; Waters & Rodrigues-Doolabh, 2001), which presents participants with four prompt-word outlines (two about parent–child dyads and two about romantic couples) of 12 words each and asks them to tell a story using the words. To a participant with a consolidated and accessible secure base script, the words imply secure base script interactions. An example of a prompt-word outline, "Doctor's Office," is shown in Figure 8.7.

When asked to tell a story using these words, Sonya came up with the following narrative:

> "'Mommy, Mommy, Mommy!' Tommy cried as he ran through the front door. Mother hurried down the steps into the kitchen where she saw Tommy holding his arm in a funny position. Mother said, 'Oh honey, that looks like it hurts! What happened?' 'I fell off my bike,' he said. She didn't want to worry Tommy, so she hurriedly grabbed the phone and called the doctor's office. Mother was trying to comfort Tommy and talk to the nurse on the other line who said for them to come in to the office. Once they got to the doctor's office, Tommy was still crying, and his mother tried to hold his hand and comfort him. 'Mommy, I gonna have to get a shot?,' Tommy asked. 'Don't worry, Tommy. If you do need a shot, I'll be right here for you.' The doctor had Tommy go ahead and get an X-ray. Sure enough, as suspected, he had fractured his elbow. When it was all over, Tommy looked at his mother with tears in his eyes. 'Mommy, I did okay. Didn't I?' 'Tommy, I think you did great. I think you did so great we should stop and get ice cream on the way home.' Smiling, Tommy went with his mother out to the bus stop, and off to the ice cream store they went."

What we see in Sonya's story are clear elements of a secure base script. The child in her story seeks out his mother when he

Tommy	hurry	mother
bike	doctor	toy
hurt	cry	stop
mother	shot	hold

FIGURE 8.7. ASA prompt-word outline: "Doctor's Office."

is hurt, and his mother takes several steps to comfort him while at home and in the doctor's office. The mother's help is effective in supporting the child through his distress, allowing the child to return to exploration by the end. ASA narratives are scored on a scale from 1 to 9. At the high end of the scale, participants tell a story that shows extensive secure base script organization and elaboration on the sequence of events consistent with the secure base script, much like Sonya's.

In contrast, at the low end of the scale, participants may tell a story that lists events in a way that lacks any key elements of the script or in which the story describes events inconsistent with secure base script support (e.g., the parent in the story fails to respond to the child's distress). Another parent told quite a different story than Sonya when given the same set of words:

> "Tommy was riding his bike outside and he fell. He got hurt pretty bad. Mom had to take him to the doctor. He was crying really loud because he thought the pain was so bad and he thought he had to get a shot. The mother was scared; she didn't know what to think because you know how a mother is when it comes to her child. You just don't know what to expect. And she was all hysterical. When she got to the doctor's office, the doctor said, 'It's not as bad as what it seemed; he'll be all right. He'll live.' Mom said to him, 'Tommy, you shouldn't have been biking fast so that you got hurt. That's what happens when you don't follow the rules.'"

In contrast to Sonya's story, this second story is lacking several core components of the secure base sequence. There was no clear bid for support from the mother when the child got hurt. The mother also failed to offer support to the child to comfort him and was instead consumed by her own feelings of anxiety. When the problem was solved, the mother fussed at the child, attributing his distress to his own misbehavior.

If parents experienced nurturing care themselves, with their own attachment figures available and effective in responding to secure base support needs, they are likely to learn the secure base script. In contrast, if individuals experience insensitive parenting, with their parents unavailable, inconsistent, or ineffective when secure base support is needed, the script is not learned. Although many of the CPS-referred parents with whom we worked experienced inconsistent or ineffective secure base support in their own childhoods, likely resulting in low secure base script knowledge, we wondered whether the ABC intervention might change their knowledge of or access to the secure base script. Perhaps frequent in-the-moment commenting about secure base script elements (e.g., "He cried [bid for help], and you picked him up [bid for help is detected and help is offered]. Look how quickly he calmed in your arms [help is effective]!") could help parents learn the secure base script. Or perhaps frequent experiences of serving as an effective secure base figure for their own child could help parents develop and consolidate the script.

Indeed, we found that parents assigned to the ABC intervention showed higher secure base script knowledge than parents assigned to the control intervention. Parents in the control group were significantly lower in secure base script knowledge than a low-risk comparison group; the ABC and low-risk groups did not differ significantly (Raby et al., 2018; see Figure 8.8). Furthermore, parents' secure base script knowledge scores were positively

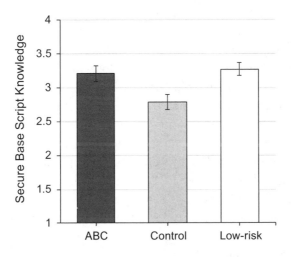

FIGURE 8.8. Effects of ABC on mothers' secure base script knowledge.

correlated with parental sensitivity scores during parent–child interaction tasks.

Parental Brain Activity

Seeing changes in parental sensitivity over time suggested to us that there must surely be changes in parents' brain activity as well. A growing body of research has examined parents' neurobiological responses when they view infant pictures, such as photos of their own baby or of a crying baby, or hear infant sounds, such as infant crying. Together, these studies provide evidence that a number of brain regions implicated in emotion perception, reward processing, executive functioning, and other cognitive and affective processes are activated in parents in response to infant stimuli. One way to look at brain processes is by measuring event-related potentials (ERPs). ERPs assess changes in the brain's electrical activity in response to a specific "event" or stimulus, such as seeing a picture or hearing a noise. They are extracted from the ongoing EEG signals by averaging electrical activity across a large number of trials. With this approach, any random brain activity is canceled out, and what is left is a waveform that has a number of positive and negative peaks called "components." ERP components can be quantified in terms of latency (when the brain response occurs after a stimulus is presented), amplitude (how big the brain response is), and location on the scalp (where it occurs).

Using ERP methodology, María José Rodrigo and her colleagues (2011) compared the brain responses of neglecting mothers and control mothers when they viewed pictures of babies with varying emotion expressions—crying, neutral, and laughing faces. As mothers viewed pictures, they were asked to categorize them according to each baby's emotional expression.

Consistent with other ERP studies of parents, Rodrigo and colleagues (2011) found that comparison mothers showed different patterns of brain activity for different expressions of emotion at various components along the waveform. Early in the waveform is a component called the N170—a negative-going peak that occurs approximately 170 milliseconds after the stimulus (in this case, a child's face) is presented. A number of studies have found that the amplitude of the N170 is different for different emotional expressions, with people typically showing larger N170 peaks to emotional faces than neutral faces. Indeed, Rodrigo and colleagues found that mothers had larger N170 responses to crying baby faces than to neutral or laughing baby faces. Later in the waveform is a positive-going component called the late positive potential (LPP). The LPP typically begins at around 300 milliseconds and extends to 1,000 milliseconds or longer. This prolonged positivity is thought to reflect attentional control and stimulus evaluation and is especially responsive to stimuli that are emotionally salient and biologically relevant (Hajcak, Jackson, Ferri, & Weinberg, 2016). It makes sense, then, that parents' LPP responses would be sensitive to baby stimuli. Similar to what they found for the early N170 component, Rodrigo and colleagues found that mothers showed a larger LPP to crying baby faces than to neutral faces. Importantly, neglecting mothers could see the differences in the faces of crying, neutral, and laughing babies; they were just as accurate as comparison mothers in differentiating between the types of faces. However, neglecting mothers' patterns of brain activity suggested that they were processing the images differently than comparison mothers. The N170 of neglecting mothers failed to differentiate between crying, laughing, and neutral baby faces—the amplitude of neglecting mothers' N170 responses was similar regardless of the facial expression. Furthermore, neglecting mothers showed blunted LPP responses compared with control mothers.

Given that parents' sensitive behaviors changed following the intervention and that the changes were sustained over time, we expected that changes should also be seen in brain activity. So we tested whether the ABC intervention affected the response of neglecting mothers to babies' faces. We assessed brain activity among CPS-referred ABC mothers, CPS-referred control (DEF) mothers, and low-risk comparison mothers (with no history of CPS involvement) while they viewed and categorized pictures of babies with crying, smiling, and neutral facial expressions (for the results, see Figure 8.9). Whereas low-risk comparison mothers showed larger N170 responses to emotional faces than to neutral faces, CPS-referred mothers who received the control intervention failed to differentiate between babies' emotional expressions. ABC mothers, however, showed larger N170 responses to emotional faces than to neutral faces, similar to comparison mothers. Similar group differences were seen in the LPP, with ABC mothers and comparison mothers showing larger responses to emotional faces than to neutral faces, and DEF mothers showing no difference between expressions (Bernard et al., 2015).

We also tested associations between ERP responses and maternal sensitivity. Mothers who showed larger differences between ERP responses to emotional faces and neutral faces were more sensitive during their interactions with their children than mothers who showed smaller differences. These changes in maternal brain activity and behavior were observed approximately 3 years after parents participated in ABC. The sustained changes in parents clarify why we would see some of the changes in children's behaviors years after the intervention. The ABC intervention appears to change parental behavior and biology in lasting ways—which likely supports child behavioral and biological changes over time.

SUMMARY

We consider these results very exciting evidence for the effectiveness of the ABC intervention. Parents who received the ABC intervention are more sensitive than parents who received the control intervention, and these effects are sustained several years postintervention. These ABC parents also show differences in brain activity. Indeed, changes in neural activity may be one of the mechanisms for intervention effects over time. The intervention components targeting nurturance and frightening behavior were developed with the goal of increasing the chances that children would develop secure, organized attachments. As expected,

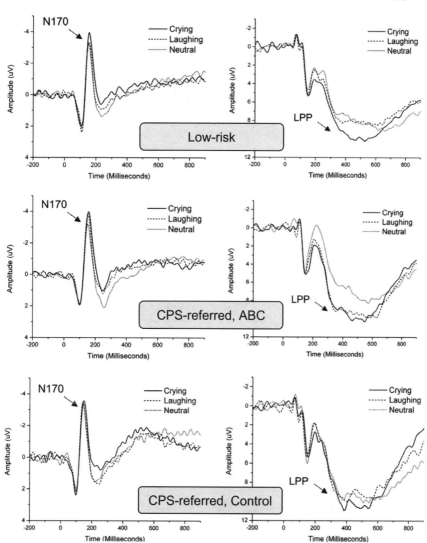

FIGURE 8.9. Effects of ABC on brain activity among CPS-referred mothers.

children are more likely to develop secure and organized attachments, show more normative cortisol production, exhibit stronger vocabulary capabilities, have stronger executive functioning, and display fewer behavioral problems if their parents received the ABC rather than a control intervention. The effects are evident in high-risk birth children, foster children, and internationally adopted children.

CHAPTER 9

Intervention Fidelity

Regardless of how effective an intervention is, if it cannot be implemented by others with fidelity—that is, with clinicians implementing it as intended—then the intervention will be of limited usefulness. It is critical to define the key ingredients of the intervention in ways that are clear and measurable, and then ensure that those components are delivered when the intervention is implemented in the community. This issue of model fidelity is a large and thorny one that contributes to the fact that interventions often fail to show effects in the community similar to the effects seen in randomized clinical trials. Fidelity to the model is often not maintained when the intervention is rolled out into the community. In one study where community providers claimed they were implementing evidence-based treatments, only 8% were judged as meeting the threshold for adequate fidelity to an evidence-based model (Santa Ana et al., 2008).

Steps toward implementing an intervention with fidelity in the community include knowing very clearly what outcomes the intervention is targeting, the mechanism for achieving those outcomes (i.e., what one must do to achieve those outcomes), and the critical ingredients (or elements) of the intervention. We had clearly articulated some of these issues but not others.

We knew exactly what we wanted to change in terms of child outcomes—child attachment and child behavioral, emotional, and physiological regulation. We were also clear about how to achieve changes in these child outcomes—or the mechanism by which the intervention would have its effects on child outcomes. Theory and the previous findings of others as well as our own provided compelling evidence that enhancing parental sensitivity (the composite of following the lead, nurturing, and avoiding parental frightening behavior) was the key to these child outcomes. Enhancing intervention fidelity was the intervention mechanism. But we needed to work to define the critical elements of the intervention.

In a recent call for proposals, the National Institute of Mental Health differentiated fidelity from adherence. *Adherence* was defined as ensuring that specific elements that are part of the intervention are implemented and that elements that are not included in the intervention are not implemented, whereas *fidelity* was defined as ensuring that the intervention is implemented competently or effectively. Ensuring adherence is clearly the easier and more straightforward of the two. Many models assess adherence through checklists of things the clinician should do in implementing the intervention (prescribed) and things the clinician should not do (proscribed).

INTERVENTION ADHERENCE

Manualized Content

We have developed a manual (Dozier & Attachment and Biobehavioral Catch-up Lab, 2015) that guides discussion of the targeted parenting issues. Some of these things are prescribed—that is, things we expect parent coaches to do (such as covering material in the manual and discussing particular research studies)—and some are proscribed—that is, things we expect parent coaches not to do (such as not addressing comments to the child, not reading from the manual, not talking too much).

The manual provides an overview of the session's objectives, followed by specific suggestions for how and what to present in the session.

Use of Videos

The ABC intervention uses videos in two ways, and both are assessed in adherence ratings. These include videos of other parents engaged in activities and videos of themselves engaged in the activities. Watching videos of other parents enhances the likelihood that parents will have successful experiences when they engage in the tasks. For example, before being asked to play with blocks with their child, parents watch a mother who followed her child's lead very effectively while playing with blocks. When the child picked up a block, she commented on it, for example. When the child put a block on the tower and waited for the mother to put on a block, she asked, "You want me to put one on?" and then proceeded to place a block on the tower. In the second video, the same mother failed to follow her child's lead, suggesting to him that he build a big tower (rather than following what he was doing), providing instruction on how to place the blocks, and asking questions about the color of the blocks. Prior to the parents' beginning the task themselves, the parent coach and parents carefully dissect each video, talking about how the mother was or was not following the lead in very specific terms. These examples provide scaffolding such that parents will be more likely to be successful in following their child's lead when they are then video-recorded. We want parents to experience the feeling of being successful and of seeing themselves be successful.

Parents are asked to engage in the activity with their child. As parents are playing with their child, the parent coach makes frequent comments that again scaffold the interaction. The parent coach is particularly attentive to any instance in which parents follow the child's lead, describing it specifically. Often this results in a cascade of behaviors in which parents follow the child's lead. The parent coach continues to make comments, describing the behaviors and relating them to positive child outcomes. The following week, brief clips of parents are shown to highlight how they engaged in the targeted behaviors. These clips are typically about 2–5 seconds in length. For example, consider Cassie who struggled with following her child's lead. A 4-second clip was shown to her in which Brian held up his block before putting it on his building, and Cassie said, "You got a block, Brian?" She was shown the video several times, with the parent coach pointing out that she was following Brian's lead by commenting on exactly what he was doing. The parent coach went on to say, "You didn't ask him what color it was, you didn't tell him where to put the block—you just followed his lead. That may not seem like a big deal, but that's the kind of thing that will help him be able to pay attention when he gets to school."

Measuring Adherence

An adherence checklist is completed for each session. The parent coach and supervisor mark whether each of the indicated activities was completed. For example, for Sessions 1 and 2, the adherence assessment for prescribed behaviors includes whether the parent coach:

- Considers common ideas about parenting
- Describes Mary Ainsworth study accurately
- Describes study of security predicting independence
- Describes child behavior in three videos
- Describes the Sroufe avoidance and heart rate study
- Describes the diary study showing that parents respond to children "in kind"

Proscribed behaviors include:

- Talks to child
- Makes negative comment to parent (positive comments only until Session 3)
- Talks for more than 1 minute consecutively

INTERVENTION FIDELITY

In-the-Moment Commenting

In a category by itself in terms of importance are the parent coaches' in-the-moment comments about the relevant parenting behaviors they observe. These comments provide parents with frequent feedback that describes their behavior (e.g., "He cried and you picked him up"), links their behavior to intervention targets ("That's such a good example of your nurturing him"), and ties their behavior to long-term child outcomes ("That will let him know he can trust that you'll be there for him").

In-the-moment comments are important for a host of reasons. First, they provide parents practice and feedback in the intervention targets. Given that we expect parent coaches to make comments at least once each minute, that means that parents receive feedback about intervention-related behaviors at least 60 times in an hour's session. Parents will have heard that they followed their child's lead, or nurtured their child, or delighted in their child 60 times at the end of the session. That's powerful in changing behavior (Bakermans-Kranenburg et al., 2003).

Over the years, we increasingly incorporated in-the-moment comments as a key aspect of the intervention. But we found that some parent coaches struggled with making comments. For some it came almost naturally, whereas others only gradually learned how to make comments over time, and some never mastered it. Consider two examples.

Johanna

Johanna was one of several parent coaches who rather naturally made comments in the moment. It was partly from watching her on video and seeing the powerful effects of her comments that we began to incorporate making in-the-moment comments a formal part of the ABC intervention. She was comfortable and at ease making such comments. One striking example was a time when a child was crying loudly and the parent was asking about scheduling the next session. Johanna said, "Remember, we were talking about nurturance. This is one of those times when she needs you to pick her up." The mother then picked the child up, and Johanna commented, "That is so nurturing. She was crying and you picked her right up." Another time when the child was fussing, Johanna said, "You just want your mom, right?" Since that time, we have refined a number of aspects of commenting, such as waiting until at least Session 3 before making a negative comment (such as "This is one of those times . . .") and not speaking directly to the child. But even in its unrefined form, these comments were observed to be powerful for the parent.

Ann

Ann was a parent coach for whom making comments did not come naturally. She joined our team after we had established that we wanted parents to make comments (but before we had incorporated the components described later that make it easier to learn to make comments). Each week in supervision, we watched her sessions and suggested places where she could make comments. At various times, Ann said that she feared she would seem condescending to the parent or that she was not sure what to say. Her supervisor made suggestions for comments, and Ann indicated that the suggestions seemed reasonable. But in the following session, nothing had changed—she had again made few comments throughout the session.

Making comments can be difficult for many reasons. In sessions, parent coaches are asked to keep two agendas in mind: they need to cover the manualized content while paying attention to every interaction between the parent and child. This task is challenging, requiring parent coaches to know the manual well enough that they can flexibly move in and out of the content while attending to the parent–child interaction. Although we consider covering the manualized content secondary to making in-the-moment comments, parent coaches are often concerned that the manualized content should take precedence over in-the-moment comments. Making comments can feel difficult for parent coaches, who express fear that parents will feel patronized if they make comments, that their comments will sound repetitive, that they will interrupt the parent–child interaction, or that they will interrupt the parent talking to the parent coach.

Nevertheless, since we had observed anecdotally that in-the-moment commenting mattered, we persisted. After developing a tool for measuring in-the-moment commenting (described next), we found that the parent coach's in-the-moment comments were associated with change in parent sensitivity (Caron, Bernard, & Dozier, 2016); that is, the more often parent coaches made in-the-moment comments, the more sensitive parents became. This finding provided us with empirical evidence that making comments was a key ingredient.

Given that making in-the-moment comments wasn't easy but was critical to intervention effectiveness, we realized that this was where we needed to focus our attention. We needed to recruit potential parent coaches who would be able to make these comments, we needed to focus our training and supervision on making these comments, and we needed to track feedback based on progress in relation to the capacity to make comments. Our progress in developing an effective strategy was iterative. It took us years to come up with a solution that worked for ABC, but we are now quite proud of our definition and assessment of fidelity.

Developing a Fidelity Protocol

Telling parent coaches to make comments in the moment was not enough. As exemplified by Ann, even with supervision and support, we sometimes saw little progress. It occurred to us that we needed a quantitative system that provided frequent feedback to parent coaches. Building this system took time, but we developed and refined one. The system, as we describe next, codes whether parent coaches make comments when they have the opportunity, and it also codes critical aspects of the comments (e.g., whether comments are on target and the nature or quality of the comments).

Consider the following example. James falls down and bumps his head, looks distressed, and Sonya says, "Oh sweetie, I know that hurt!" This presents an *opportunity* for a parent-coach comment because James presented his mother with a chance to nurture him. If the parent coach says, "He looked upset and you said 'Oh sweetie' right away. That is such wonderful nurturance," then the parent coach has made an in-the-moment comment regarding nurturance. Her comment is coded as occurring (hit vs. miss), relating to a particular target (nurturance vs. following the lead), and providing information about two of three possible components (description of the mother's behavior and labeling of the intervention target). This information about the quality of comments is precisely what our fidelity monitoring system captures.

For coding, we use an Excel spreadsheet that automatically calculates critical metrics based on the data we enter. On this spreadsheet (shown in Figure 9.1), the parent's behavior is described (e.g., child bumps head, and mother says, "Oh sweetie, I know that hurt" [see 1a of Figure 9.1]); this maternal behavior is identified as related to one of the targets (in this case, it is coded for nurturance [1b]). Second, the parent coach's behavior is described (e.g., she said, "He looked upset and you said 'Oh sweetie.' That's such wonderful nurturance" [1c]); the parent coach's comment is then coded for two things. The first is the target—in this case, nurturance (1d). Second is the number of "components" or pieces of information that the comment contained. In this case, the comment included a description of the behavior and link to the target, and it is therefore coded as including two components (1e).

Let's consider another example (2a–2e in Figure 9.1), going step by step through the coding procedure. First, the coder asks, did the parent have an opportunity to follow the lead or nurture the child? If so, the time is noted and the behavior is described. In the second example in Figure 9.1 (2a), the child said, "Momma," and the mother looked up and said, "Yes, what's up, honey?" Second, the coder asks, what was the target of the parent's behavior? In this case, the parent followed the child's lead (2b) by responding to the child's verbal bid. Then, did the parent-coach comment on the parent's behavior? If so, the coder transcribes the comment (2d): "Wow, you just followed his lead again. He said 'Momma' and you looked at him and said, 'What's up, honey?'" Next, what was the target of the parent coach's comment? In this example,

(Time) Parent's Behavior	Behavior Target	(Time) Parent Coach's Response	Response Target	Number of Components
(1a) (3:34) Child gets hurt; Mom says, "Oh sweetie, I know that hurt!"	(1b) Nurturance	(1c) (3:40) "He looked upset and you said, 'Oh sweetie.' That's such wonderful nurturance."	(1d) Nurturance	(1e) 2
(2a) (4:25) Child says, "Momma." Mom looks up and says, "Yes, what's up, honey?"	(2b) Following the lead	(2c) (4:30) "Wow, you just followed his lead again. He said, 'Momma,' and you looked at him and said, 'What's up, honey?'"	(2d) Following the lead	(2e) 2
(3a) (5:00) Child knocks over blocks; Mom laughs and smiles.	(3b) Delight	(3c) No comment	(3d) N/A	(3e) N/A
(4a) (5:20) Child fusses and Mom picks him up.	(4b) Nurturance	(4c) (5:30) "That was great following his lead."	(4d) Following the lead	(4e) N/A

FIGURE 9.1. Sample ABC fidelity coding sheet.

157

the parent coach's comment was related to following the lead (2d). Finally, the coder asks, how many components were included in the comment? In this example, similar to the first, the comment both described the behavior and labeled the target; therefore, the number of components is coded as 2 (2e).

As can be seen in the third row of the sample coding spreadsheet, parent behaviors are coded even when the coach does not make a comment. For example, at 5 minutes into this video clip, the child knocked over blocks and the mother laughed and smiled in response (3a). This represents an expression of delight in the child (3b) and presents an opportunity for the parent coach to comment. The parent coach did not comment, however. So, the parent coach's lack of response (3c: No comment) would count as a missed opportunity. Similarly, off-target comments are captured when the target of the parent's behavior (e.g., 4b: Nurturance) does not match the target of the parent coach's comment (e.g., 4d: Following the lead). In this example, the child fussed and the mother picked him up, representing an opportunity to comment on nurturance. The parent coach commented but incorrectly labeled the behavior as following the lead. Thus, this comment would count as "off-target."

Coding takes time, so it is not feasible to code full sessions. We elected to code a 5-minute segment from just one of each parent coach's sessions each week even if the parent coach has multiple sessions. Trained coders can complete coding for a 5-minute clip in about 30 minutes; providing feedback on one clip weekly is realistic, but doing much more would be unwieldy. Although we have more work to do to demonstrate that 5 minutes is the optimal period of time to code, preliminary evidence indicates that it is enough time to provide reliable data on comments regarding following the lead. The 5-minute clip is randomly selected from sessions, so that parent coaches and supervisors do not influence whether clips are taken from especially difficult or easy sessions.

When we initiated this system, supervisors provided feedback to parent coaches during a video-conferenced supervision meeting. Parent coaches were provided with information regarding their rate of commenting (how many comments were made per minute) and percent of comments that were on-target, the number of missed opportunities, the average number of components included in comments, and so on (see Figure 9.2).

When we got to this point, we thought we had what we needed for an effective fidelity monitoring and supervision tool. It worked for fidelity monitoring. We were able to define our expectations for fidelity criteria—that coaches have a rate of at least one comment per minute or fewer than 50% missed opportunities; that at least 80% of comments be on-target, correctly labeling nurturance, following the lead, or delight; and that, on average, comments include at least one component. With the fidelity monitoring system, we were able to tell which parent coaches were meeting these expectations. Yet surprisingly, we found that parent coaches still often failed to make comments. They continued to raise a host of concerns—that the comments might seem condescending to parents, that they might say the wrong thing, that they were focused on the manual content, that they didn't want to interrupt the parent–child interaction. These were all reasonable concerns, but we could counter each with evidence to the contrary. The bottom line was that they did not make more comments—even when faced with quantitative evidence that they were not reaching criteria, and even with our arguments that they would be more effective parent coaches if they did.

Fidelity Monitoring Metric	Score	Criteria
Total Number of Opportunities	18	
Total Number of Comments	5	
Number of On-Target Comments	5	
Percent of On-Target Comments	100%	≥ 80%
Number of Missed Opportunities	13	
Percent of Missed Opportunities	72%	< 50%
On-Target Comments per Minute (Rate)	1.0	≥ 1.0
Average Comment Level (Number of Components)	1.0	≥ 1.0

or

FIGURE 9.2. Weekly summary of fidelity coding.

It occurred to us that it might be more powerful if parent coaches coded their own sessions. We trained our first parent coach "in-house" to code her own sessions. Voila! What we found was that after months of making minimal progress in increasing in-the-moment comments, this parent coach's progress increased significantly after she began her own coding (Meade, Dozier, & Bernard, 2014). As we tried this with other parent coaches, we noticed the same thing.

What seemed to be happening is that parent coaches were becoming their own critics. In coding themselves, parent coaches become aware of—exquisitely aware of—times that they could have commented or that they could have made more precise or useful comments. They began self-correcting and coding themselves implicitly during sessions. They started coding family members and people they saw in the grocery store! Self-coding was powerful.

This concept of coding one's own behaviors during sessions was not so foreign to our postdoctoral fellows, staff, and graduate students who were implementing the intervention as part of our randomized clinical trial. But it was definitely foreign to many of those outside of the university setting. The first time we introduced coding to new parent coaches during training was in Hawaii, and I (M. D.) noticed parent coaches' eyes glaze over as I presented it. I'm sure that I was presenting the task with too much trepidation of my own. In addition, the system had been developed for feedback and for research purposes, but not for self-coding, so it needed to be simplified. But even with this rough start, it represented a turning point for us: These parent coaches learned to implement the intervention with fidelity, and 9 years later many are still using the intervention and are coding one another to ensure they are maintaining fidelity.

Nuances of In-the-Moment Commenting

Positive Comments for the First Two Sessions

During the first two sessions, parent coaches are expected to make only positive comments. If a parent fails to pick up her child or fails to follow her child's lead, the parent coach does not comment in those moments. The parent coach looks for an opportunity, even if it is fleeting, to comment on the parent following the child's lead or nurturing the child. Consider the example of a child who banged his head when he fell and is crying. His father fusses at him for climbing onto the table and says that it served him right that he fell. At some point, his father looks at him and says, "Hey bud, you OK?" It is *then* that the parent coach makes a comment. For example, she might say, "We've been talking about how hard it is for some children to show what they need directly, but you were able to see that he needed you then. This is a great example of your providing him nurturance. And that's the kind of thing that will let him know you're there for him."

In this example, if the father had never made any vaguely nurturing comment, the parent coach would not make a negative comment (or even a comment suggesting that the parent pick the child up). It is critical in these early sessions that the parent feel supported and that a good working relationship is built between the parent coach and the parent. Often parent coaches feel an urgency to comment on behaviors they see that are not in line with targets. Although a sense of urgency is useful (10 sessions is not a long time), parents need to value the relationship with the parent coach if they are to make the significant changes in parenting we are asking them to make. Even in cases where the parent behaves in a frightening way with the child (e.g., fussing loudly, roaring like an animal), we ask parent coaches to refrain from addressing the issue. There will be time for addressing it later, and at that point, parents will hopefully be receptive.

Negative Comments

Although we expect parent coaches to continue to have a high ratio of positive to negative comments, beginning in Session 3, they are allowed to make gentle and careful comments suggesting that parents are not engaging in the desired behaviors.

Parents have almost always heard lots of critical feedback, and they likely have effective ways to distance themselves from it or, alternatively and at least as bad, to feel that they deserve criticism.

At the gentlest level, parent coaches make comments that "highlight the good" when a parent is not engaging in a desired behavior. Highlighting-the-good comments are intended to reinforce approximations of a target behavior. These comments have a positive tone and highlight the most positive aspects of a negative behavior. They describe parental behaviors that are closest to the targets within a negative sequence of behavior. For example, Clara picked up her child after the child fell off the sofa and fussed at her for not being more careful. The parent coach highlighted one aspect of this only: Clara's picking her child up and saying, "She fell and you picked her up. It's so important that she knows that you're there for her when she needs you."

Similar to highlighting the good is the elaboration of comments when a parent engages in a behavior that is rare for her, pointing out other ways that she might have responded. Take the example of Jackie, who was often "teachy" with her child. Raja picked up a pull-out piece (which was a ladybug) from a book and said "circle." Jackie said, "You got a circle?" The parent coach said, "Wow, she pulled out the piece and you said, 'circle.' You looked right at her and said 'circle'; you didn't correct her, or ask her what it was, or ask what color it was. You followed right along, even though it might have been hard. Oddly enough, following her lead like that is exactly the kind of thing that will help her develop her vocabulary." Analogously, Clara's daughter Eloise bumped her head, and Clara asked if she was okay. Given that she was rarely nurturing, her parent coach made an elaborated comment, saying "She bumped her head, and you said, 'Are you okay?' You didn't fuss at her for running into the table, you didn't tell her she wasn't really hurt, you didn't tell her to be a big girl. Nurturing the way you did is so important in helping her trust that you'll be there. It seems little, but this is the kind of thing that will help her know she can come talk to you when she's worried about something later on, when she's a 6-year-old or a 10-year-old." This elaboration allows extended attention to a behavior that the parent needs work on.

At an intermediate level on the gentleness continuum, parent coaches can make comments that are suggestions. These comments make it clear that the parent is not engaging in the desired behavior, and it is therefore important that these comments be used sparingly. Consider the example of James who was crying and reaching for Sonya, but Sonya kept talking to the parent coach without acknowledging him. Suggested comments include, "What do you think he needs right now?" or "I'm sorry—I'm taking all your attention. Don't let me keep you from paying attention to James when he needs you." Either of these comments brings the parent's attention to the child's need and suggests that the mother respond.

At the extreme end of the continuum, the parent coach might tell the parent that she should not engage in the behavior she is engaging in or indicate that she engage in a different behavior. Using the example of Sonya above, the parent coach might say, "It looks like he needs you to pick him up now" or "Try picking him up and see what happens." However, given that we want to increase the mother's sense of efficacy rather than enhance her sense that the parent coach knows what the child needs, we avoid being any more prescriptive than necessary.

Although it is important to limit the frequency of these negative comments relative to positive comments, we also know that they can be powerful. One parent coach made positive comments at a very high rate but never made negative comments—something that we could discern from her weekly coding sheets. Her overall rate was high, her missed opportunities were low, and she included multiple components in most comments. But given that she failed to make negative comments meant that parents weren't getting the refined feedback—the corrective feedback—that they would have received from other parent coaches. We have not yet examined the effect of negative comments on parent behavioral change, but we suspect it is important.

SUMMARY

The importance of developing a reliable and valid system for monitoring fidelity cannot be overemphasized. Without such a system, one never knows what is being implemented. We have worked hard to develop observational procedures for assessing fidelity. The use of this system provides parent coaches with regular feedback about whether they are implementing with fidelity and provides us with assurance that ABC is being implemented with fidelity. It allows us to sleep at night.

CHAPTER 10

Disseminating ABC

When the first strong evidence emerged regarding ABC's effectiveness, we were asked to make the intervention available to agencies in a nearby city through foundation funding. Had we known what we now know, we would never have said yes. It was too early, and we had many things to learn before the intervention could be implemented with fidelity in other communities. In retrospect, it seems that we did nearly everything wrong. But the mistakes we made in this first attempt, as well as in the next several tries, helped us to rethink things and to recognize the tasks we still needed to accomplish. No one should be discouraged, though, as we describe these first experiences. We have developed practices at this point that we think set us apart, including most especially a fidelity monitoring system that allows us to have confidence that the intervention is being implemented with fidelity.

We describe the things that went wrong from that first experience because it provides such a clear example of how challenging dissemination efforts can be.

WHAT WENT WRONG

Selection of Sites

Sites from the community were recruited by the foundation that had contacted us. These sites made applications to the foundation and were awarded funding that paid training and supervision costs. From the perspective of the sites, this arrangement was attractive; they saw it as giving them some prestige and, at the same time, allowing them a training opportunity for no cost. This arrangement is not unique to this foundation; for example, federal contracts often have funding that works in similar ways. Agencies are invited to receive training that is made possible by the funding received by a central entity.

The downside of this arrangement is that, because the agencies were not required to fund the training and supervision themselves, they did not have to demonstrate at a concrete level that they were "buying in" or that they were committed.

Buy-in Is Critical

Supervisors and administrators need to know and be able to accommodate the time required for learning a new intervention and for preparing for supervision and for sessions. In our example, clinicians in some sites where jobs were already overwhelming were being asked to learn and implement ABC in addition to other demands. There were no changes in their other responsibilities. At the extreme end, we found that parent coaches came to supervision sessions totally unprepared for supervision or even missed supervision sessions altogether, and we occasionally saw parent coaches read from their manual during intervention sessions. No intervention could be implemented effectively under such conditions.

Selection of Clinicians

Different interventions have different requirements for clinicians. Some require a specific degree (e.g., master's or PhD) or licensure or a particular length of time working with families. Based on our previous experience, we did not believe that a specific degree or length of time was what would differentiate clinicians who would become effective coaches from those who would not, so these were not useful criteria for us. However, given that we did not set criteria, we essentially got all comers—some who had the capacity to learn to implement ABC effectively and some who did not. This meant that, even if we had an effective training and supervision system (which we did not), there would be some parent coaches who did not succeed.

Training

Our initial training sessions were too long and too didactic. The training took 5 days—consisting mostly of overview of session material and presentation of case material. Parent coaches in attendance must surely have faded in and out during the week. We have since learned that we should give prospective parent coaches what they need to get started but that the important learning will occur through supervision—after they have picked up cases.

Supervision and Fidelity Monitoring

To monitor fidelity, it is necessary to have a clear sense of what parent coaches need to be doing. We held supervision weekly through video-conferencing (and we continue to supervise through video-conferencing). But early on, we provided very different feedback than we do now—the feedback was exclusively qualitative. For example, supervisors suggested to parent coaches that they do more or less of something, but we did not have a system for providing quantitative feedback with regard to whether parent coaches were improving over time. We found that clinicians, sites, and the foundation were baffled when they heard that clinicians were not implementing the intervention as intended. Administrators at the sites, as well as the foundation directors, became frustrated with us.

As is apparent, we made mistakes at nearly every level. We did not have the agency buy-in, and, as a result, we could not expect agencies to provide the time, support, and resources needed to implement the intervention successfully. We had not defined critical criteria for screening successful parent coaches, and we were therefore training and supervising clinicians who were not always likely to succeed. And finally, we did not have a system for clearly monitoring the progress of each parent coach over time.

DOING IT RIGHT (OR BETTER)

When reading of our struggles, it may be no surprise to hear that many others have faced challenges as they have moved interventions from university-based clinical trials to community models. Interventions often show much smaller effects—or even no effectiveness—when implemented in the community than shown through efficacy trials (Durlak & DuPre, 2008; Weisz, Jensen-Doss, & Hawley, 2006). A number of factors influence this difference.

Selection of Sites

When we are approached by agencies interested in implementing ABC, we emphasize the time required for parent coaches to learn the intervention and for ongoing supervision even after the initial training process.

For ABC, time is needed to go to parents' homes for visits, to prepare for sessions (looking over notes from the previous session and planning the focus of the session, clipping videos to show the parent), to code for fidelity assessment, and to participate in two types of supervision. Administrators at sites need to know what is involved and to provide enough time and support for parent coaches to implement.

How much time is required? Given that ABC is a home-visiting model, parent coaches travel to and from parents' homes, which adds to the time required per parent seen. We estimate that a parent coach working full time can see about 10 families on average per week, although we are aware that if visitation occurs in a small neighborhood (e.g., Brownsville in Brooklyn, as seen by our colleagues at Power of Two), more families could be seen in a day.

Two types of supervision per week are provided: (1) clinical supervision for 60–90 minutes by a PhD-level supervisor with small groups of two or three parent coaches and (2) fidelity supervision individually by a staff member for 30 minutes.

When parent coaches are first mastering the intervention, they need time to study the intervention manual before implementing the intervention with families. Study involves becoming very familiar with the manual content so that it's "second nature," allowing parent coaches to move easily between the manualized content and making in-the-moment comments. In addition, they need time to complete fidelity coding. Throughout the year of supervision, parent coaches need about 30 minutes per week to complete their fidelity coding, with somewhat more time required initially.

We find that when agencies implement the ABC intervention as part of a grant (e.g., through federal or foundation funding), it's critical to ensure that the agency has fully bought in—that administrators are aware of the time commitment and that appropriate cases will be available.

Screening Potential Parent Coaches

Whereas we did not think that academic degree or years of experience were critical in determining who would become good parent coaches, being willing and able to make comments was critical. We recognized that making comments was very natural for some, challenging yet doable for others, and next to impossible for others. This was the basis for our first screening tool.

In this first screening tool, potential parent coaches are shown videos of parent coaches making strong and appropriate comments regarding nurturance and following the lead. They are then shown videos (of a parent nurturing her child in the first video and following the child's lead in the second) in which the parent coach fails to make comments; they are asked to make an appropriate comment themselves. Some potential parent coaches readily make comments that are similar to the model videos shown, whereas others seem stumped by the request. We assign a score that reflects the comfort of potential parent coaches in making the comment as well as the appropriateness of the comment (whether it identifies the correct target, etc.) from the audio-recorded assessment.

The second screening tool is designed to assess openness and comfort with nurturance. For some parent coaches, the idea of picking up a crying baby is natural; they do not need to be convinced of the importance of it. Accompanying this natural ability, as attachment theory would suggest, is an attitude of openness and nondefensiveness. These individuals "get" the intervention targets easily and are open and receptive to feedback from supervisors.

For others, providing nurturance is not natural. They struggle with their competing feeling that picking up the baby would spoil the child. Accompanying this feeling is often a defensiveness—a "push-back" against supervisors who made suggestions.

We observed anecdotally that we were often unsuccessful in training parent coaches who did not believe in picking up a crying baby and those who were prototypically dismissing. Even if they became comfortable with intervention targets when they were with us, they did not hold up well when a dismissing parent resisted the intervention. They were quick in some instances to accept the parent's claim, for example, that a child was not "really" upset. Therefore, we wanted to screen out such parent coaches.

In conducting this screening, we use several questions from the Adult Attachment Interview (George et al., 1985). We do not attempt to assess attachment state of mind from the screener, but the questions do allow us to see the extent to which potential parent coaches are open and reflective, as opposed to defensive, about their own attachment experiences and appear to value versus devalue attachment. We ask potential parent coaches to generate adjectives for their mothers and recall specific memories that support the adjectives, as well as to recollect specific memories of being upset, separated, and rejected as young children.

Potential parent coaches are scored on 5-point scales on both of the screening tools. For the in-the-moment commenting screening tool, a score of 5 is given to a potential parent coach who differentiates the nurturing and following-the-lead clips accurately and makes a comfortable comment regarding each as if she is addressing the parent. A score of 1 or 2 is given to a potential parent coach who is not able to act as if she is addressing the parent and/or does not differentiate between nurturance and following the lead. For the mini-AAI, the potential coach is given a score of 5 for providing clear memories supporting the adjectives chosen, and clear and contained memories of being upset as a child. Scores of 1 and 2 are given when memories cannot be provided.

We typically accept applicants for training when they score 3 or above on both measures. Although relatively few parent coaches are excluded using this screening tool (up to 25%), when agencies send us larger numbers to select from, we can identify those we think will be strongest based on responses to the screening tool. Most important, we are able to screen out those who fall below a threshold. Combined with other improvements, our rate of success in certifying parent coaches has soared. Whereas roughly 20% of the first group we trained became certified parent coaches (or the equivalent, given that we did not have defined certification criteria), now close to 100% of those who complete the year of supervision become certified.

The screening tools predict in-session fidelity. Following more than 42 parent coaches over nearly 200 sessions, we found that parent coaches who scored higher on these two screening tools made more in-the-moment comments in their actual sessions than parent coaches who scored lower (Caron, Roben, Yarger, & Dozier, 2018).

Training

Whereas in our first attempts we spent most of the training time on manual content, our current training focuses more on training parent coaches to make in-the-moment comments and to code comments than on session content. Over time, we have moved from a 5-day to a 2-day training session. During the very first afternoon of the 2-day training, we introduce parent coaches to coding in-the-moment comments. Parent coaches begin to dissect ongoing dialogue between parent, parent coach, and child for opportunities for comments and practice coding. Parent coaches can then use this emerging skill as they are introduced to intervention content on day 2 of training. On the second day, the training staff walks parent coaches through the 10 sessions, with some practice of in-the-moment commenting and some case examples.

This means we're doing a lot and doing it fast. What we tell trainees is that they will learn how to implement the intervention through working with families and through supervision. Just as we do not believe we can tell parents what is important about parenting (rather, we need to observe interactions and provide coaching), we cannot tell parent coaches what to do and expect that to "take." We can set them up so that they can start, but the important work will occur through supervision.

Supervision and Fidelity Monitoring

Two types of supervision, both on a weekly basis, are provided. The first is the more traditional supervision with a PhD-level supervisor, and the second is fidelity-focused supervision with a staff supervisor.

Clinical Supervision

Clinical supervisors meet with small groups of clinicians through video-conferencing each week for an hour to an hour and a half. The groups usually consist of two or three parent coaches. When possible, parent coaches from a single agency meet together, but when necessary, parent coaches from multiple agencies or cities are combined. Case conceptualization through clinical supervision is not unlike previous supervision experiences that parent coaches have often had for other programs, although many note that the regular and focused use of video is new or emphasized more in ABC supervision than in prior work. Each week, parent coaches upload videos to Health Insurance Portability and

Accountability Act (HIPAA)–compliant, encrypted software, and clinical supervisors review session videos with the group during the weekly meetings. The goals are to provide direct feedback to the parent coach about content delivery and in-the-moment commenting, but also expose the other group supervisees to other cases, contexts, and implementation styles and challenges. Supervision time is limited, and parent coaches often have multiple cases at any one time, therefore limiting the amount of time that can be devoted to any one case. Supervisors typically sample from various cases and focus on those that are most challenging.

When watching and discussing each case, supervisors and coaches focus on the parent's primary strengths and weaknesses related to intervention targets. This focus on conceptualizing each case in terms of the ABC targets is critical in keeping parent coaches focused on the targets of change. Evidence is presented regarding the extent to which the parent is nurturing, follows the lead, and engages in frightening behavior, with plans to address each issue discussed.

Given that the intervention is time-limited, parent coaches are encouraged to feel a sense of urgency when parents are not making progress toward intervention goals after several sessions. The ongoing case conceptualization, focusing on the ABC targets, becomes especially important as parent coaches approach Sessions 7 and 8, when we discuss voices from the past. We expect the parent coach to have clearly identified the targets that the parent struggles with before Session 7, so that she can structure the discussion around those targets. Recall Maria, who showed frightening behavior toward her children, such as deepening her voice and roughly grabbing them. If left up to her, she might have identified her voices from the past as her parents failing to nurture her when she was upset. Although this was likely the case based on what we learned from her AAI, we had also seen her respond in nurturing ways to her own children's distress many times throughout the early ABC sessions. Thus, it seemed that Maria was already convinced of the importance of being nurturing and was able to respond sensitively to her children's distress, despite not receiving this type of care herself.

In supervision, then, the parent coach was helped to consider how she would identify frightening behavior as Maria's voice from the past, assuming that Maria was not aware of it yet herself. The parent coach brought clips to supervision of Maria responding in frightening ways and other clips when her behavior was not frightening. The supervisor and other supervisees generated ideas for how to approach the conversation sensitively, suggesting language such as, "Now this clip looks a little bit different," "It's such a strength that you can recognize how your voice startled him there," and "Of course you will be frightening sometimes; that's what you received from your parents. It's a strength that you know that." Although the parent coach went into Session 7 well prepared for the discussion, she was surprised to find that Maria was unable to see how her behavior was frightening. When she watched the clips, Maria could not hear that her tone of voice was threatening or see that the way in which she grabbed Dominic startled him. She was very open to the feedback, though, likely given that the language suggested in supervision was gentle, yet direct, and that she felt so strongly supported by her parent coach. By showing similar clips repeatedly over the next several sessions, as recommended by her supervisor, the parent coach was able to help Maria recognize when her tone of voice and behavior shifted into being scary for her children. If the parent coach had not thoroughly prepared for these challenging conversations through supervision, she might have avoided targeting frightening behavior directly, leaving Maria unaware of her behavior and the children at increased risk for disorganized attachment.

Fidelity-Focused Supervision

The second type of supervision focuses on coding and is conducted on an individual basis by an expert coder. As with clinical supervision, fidelity-focused supervision is conducted through the video conference. The supervisor selects a 5-minute clip from one of the parent coach's sessions and asks the parent coach to code this segment prior to supervision. In the 30-minute supervision session, coding is reviewed to ensure that the parent coach can "see" and code behaviors in the same way as the supervisor.

Early on, parent coaches often miss many behaviors when coding. In a given 5-minute clip, there are often 10–20 (or more) behaviors that can be coded when the parent nurtured her child (or did not nurture), followed the lead (or did not follow the lead), showed delight, or behaved in a way that was frightening. When comparing their coding sheets, then, coding supervisors have often coded more behaviors than parent coaches have coded. Thus, early supervision sessions often focus on identifying behaviors and correctly labeling the targets. The supervisor often plays the video during supervision, pausing after any codable parent behavior, so that the trainee can practice observing and coding each behavior. This practice is important because it enhances the ability of parent coaches to observe behaviors as they occur during sessions.

In addition to reviewing the coding of parent behaviors, the coding supervisor reviews the coaches' rate and accuracy, as well as the number of components included in comments. Early on, supervisors focus primarily on the coaches' rate of commenting. In their first several weeks, it is not unusual for parent coaches to fail to make any comments in a 5-minute period. However, providing specific feedback regarding missed opportunities and practicing commenting typically lead to quick changes. Parent coaches are first encouraged to make comments without worrying about the quality of the comments. After they have success at simply making comments, supervisors can then focus on enhancing the quality of commenting by focusing on each of the three components (describing the behavior, linking to intervention target, and linking to child outcome).

Other issues addressed through in-the-moment supervision include working on helping the parent coach vary the wording so that comments do not sound redundant, helping them clarify ambiguous comments (e.g., "Nice job!") and helping them include different components. For example, one parent coach seemed repetitive in her comments, saying, "Good job following his lead" and "He picked up the toy and then you picked it up, nice following his lead," over and over in ways that sounded rote when we observed the video. The supervisor worked with her to consider ways she could make the comments at the same rate but vary them more so that they seemed natural and spontaneous.

DISSEMINATING

We are now disseminating the ABC intervention in 18 states in the United States and in eight other countries. Although we got ahead of ourselves early in implementation, as described, we now have a system that works very well to ensure that we are selecting parent coaches who are likely to be successful, that we have an effective training and supervision system, and that we can monitor fidelity quantitatively. In Chapter 12, we describe Power of Two in New York City as an example of successful implementation.

Effectiveness of ABC in Dissemination Sites: Pre- to Postintervention Assessments

When we train parent coaches in other places, we ask them to conduct assessments of sensitivity with their parents before and after the intervention. Parents are instructed to "play as you normally would" for a period of 9 minutes (2 minutes interacting at a distance and 7 minutes close) with a specified set of developmentally appropriate toys. Parent coaches set up video cameras but otherwise try to be engaged with other things so as not to affect parent behavior more than necessary. We code these interactions for sensitivity and provide the data for agencies to use (typically to demonstrate to funders and others that the intervention is effective). We use the de-identified data to allow us to assess the effectiveness of ABC in the field. What we find is that the effect size for sensitivity is as large as the one we see in randomized clinical trials. In particular, we find an average effect size across agencies of 0.72, ranging from 0.35 to 1.15. When we omit the site that included parents who are not appropriate for ABC, the lower bound is 0.70, and the average is 1.01. These are large effects (Cohen, 1992).

Finding an effect size that is as large in community settings as in randomized clinical trials is not in line with what is often seen in dissemination research. Interventions are typically much less effective when implemented in the community than in the lab, with effects sometimes negligible (Durlak & DuPre, 2008). We raise several issues with regard to this observation. First, on the one hand, we are indeed proud that the intervention appears to be effective when implemented under "usual" conditions by community clinicians. To the extent that this is the case, we think it is at least in part because we have specified so clearly what we want parent coaches to do in session and that the fidelity assessment tool allows us to quantify this intention. We are comfortable that we know when parent coaches are implementing with fidelity. We have also developed many other powerful procedures, including expectations for agencies, selection criteria, and supervision guidelines.

Second, on the other hand, we are aware of the problems that may arise in relying on pre- and postintervention data to draw conclusions. Among the problems are that parents could have made changes without any intervention, and parents may learn what is expected of them and behave accordingly during the video (or during sessions) only. Without a control group, conclusions should be tentative. Several ongoing randomized clinical trials conducted at intervention sites suggest that our strong findings will be borne out. For example, Lisa Berlin and Brenda Jones Harden implemented ABC through a randomized clinical trial with Early Head Start parents. ABC parents were more sensitive in their interactions with their children following the intervention than were parents assigned to a "Book-of-the-Week" condition (Berlin, Martoccio, & Jones Harden, 2018). These results from an effectiveness trial conducted outside of our own lab offer strong support that we are moving ABC into the community successfully.

CHAPTER 11

Other Interventions Targeting Sensitive Parenting

ABC is in good company. A number of other interventions, also primarily informed by attachment theory, target parenting in infancy and early childhood (see Steele & Steele, 2018). Although these interventions vary in many important ways, they offer strong evidence when considered together that sensitive parenting and attachment quality in early childhood can be changed.

A meta-analysis conducted by Marian Bakermans-Kranenburg and colleagues in 2003 provides a useful framework for considering some of the key differences among programs. In their review of over 80 studies, Bakermans-Kranenburg and colleagues categorized interventions in terms of a number of dimensions. First, programs vary widely in their *duration*. Whereas some programs are relatively short term, similar to ABC, others span 1–2 years, with 50 or more sessions. Second, programs vary in their *focus*. Some programs, like ABC, focus nearly exclusively on changing sensitive parenting behavior. Others focus on changing parents' mental representations, which could mean changing parents' internal working models of their own attachment-related experiences, processing past or current traumatic experiences that influence their relationship with their child, or enhancing reflective functioning skills. The programs that focus on changing representations tend to be longer than those that focus on changing behavior. Other programs focus on providing parents with more general support or resources, such as helping them access community resources or providing mental health services. Finally, some programs incorporate multiple foci. Additional dimensions on which programs vary include the *setting* in which they are implemented (home vs. clinic) and the *approach* used to promote change (such as whether or not video-feedback is used). Some of these dimensions emerged as important in distinguishing more from less effective interventions. We return later to a discussion of these findings.

From among a large number of attachment-based interventions, we have selected only a few to discuss in some depth here, with the purpose of offering examples of programs that vary in the dimensions mentioned above. We describe three examples that have a substantial evidence base: (1) Video-Feedback to Promote Positive Parenting, a short-term intervention that, like ABC, aims specifically to change parenting behaviors; (2) child–parent psychotherapy, an intervention that primarily aims to change parenting by targeting parents' representations; and (3) Nurse–Family Partnership, a home-visiting program that provides first-time mothers with comprehensive support beyond children's attachment needs.

A FOCUS ON BEHAVIOR: VIDEO-FEEDBACK TO PROMOTE POSITIVE PARENTING

Video-Feedback to Promote Positive Parenting (VIPP; Juffer, Bakermans-Kranenburg, & van IJzendoorn, 2008) is a brief intervention of four to six sessions. The original version of VIPP, designed for parents during the first year of their infants' lives, focused specifically on helping parents respond sensitively to their children during times of distress and exploration. An adapted version of VIPP for toddlers and preschoolers, called Video-Feedback to Promote Positive Parenting and Sensitive Discipline (VIPP-SD), integrates principles from attachment theory (Bowlby, 1969/1982) and coercion theory (Patterson, 1982). In addition to the first target of helping parents respond sensitively to children, VIPP-SD includes a second target of helping parents apply behavioral principles to manage challenging child behavior. In VIPP-SD, sensitive discipline skills include parenting strategies such as positive reinforcement, redirection, and sensitive procedures for time-out. Similar to ABC, VIPP and VIPP-SD are examples of programs that target change at the behavioral rather than representational level.

VIPP is implemented in parents' homes or child-care settings. The main approach used in VIPP is providing individualized video-feedback to the parent. During each session, the intervener films the parent and child interacting during typical activities, such as playing together or mealtimes. Between sessions, the intervener selects moments of the video that highlight relevant examples of the session themes, such as exploration versus attachment behavior (a theme for the sensitive parenting target) or positive reinforcement (a theme for the sensitive discipline target). The intervener develops a script of feedback to provide to the parent in the next session. While reviewing the video with the parent during the session, the intervener, following the script, connects observations from the video to the core themes, paying particular attention to positive examples of parent–child interaction. This video-feedback is the central approach of VIPP; it is through the tailored feedback that the session content is individualized to the parent. Other attachment-based interventions also use personalized video-feedback, such as Circle of Security (COS; Powell, Cooper, Hoffman, & Marvin, 2016) and Group Attachment-Based Intervention (GABI; Steele, Steele, Bonuck, Meissner, & Murphy, 2018).

VIPP and VIPP-SD have been tested in multiple randomized clinical trials and have a strong evidence base. Meta-analytic evidence (of 12 randomized clinical trials involving 1,116 parents) showed that the intervention enhanced parental sensitivity, with effects seen consistently across samples characterized by parental risk factors, such as insecure attachment and low income, and child risk factors, such as autism and externalizing behavior (Juffer, Bakermans-Kranenburg, & van IJzendoorn, 2018). Furthermore, positive effects on child behavior have been found, including reduced rates of disorganized attachment (Juffer, Bakermans-Kranenburg, & van IJzendoorn, 2005) and behavior problems (Velderman et al., 2006).

INTERVENING AT THE REPRESENTATIONAL LEVEL: CHILD–PARENT PSYCHOTHERAPY

Child–parent psychotherapy (CPP) was developed by Alicia Lieberman and Patricia Van Horn (Lieberman, Ghosh Ippen, & Van Horn, 2006). It was designed for children from birth to age 5 who have been exposed to trauma. Based on the assumption that trauma undermines the protective role of parents, a primary aim of CPP is to provide a corrective attachment experience for the child. Specifically, the goals of CPP are to enhance the child's sense of safety in the parent–child relationship and environment, increase the parent's sensitive responding to the child's emotional needs, support the parent in balancing her own needs and the child's needs, and shape the parent's perceptions of the child and attachment representations more generally (Toth, Michl-Petzing, Guild, & Lieberman, 2018). Given its origins in psychoanalytic principles (Fraiberg, 1980), much of the work of CPP focuses on the representational level. CPP seeks to change parents' processing of their own traumatic histories as a key to changing their response to their children's experience of trauma. With the targets of CPP spanning both representation and behavior, it is not surprising that this is one of the longer interventions. The work of CPP extends over the period of about a year, with 52 weekly sessions recommended.

CPP sessions are conducted in a variety of settings—homes or clinics—and typically involve both the parent and child, though individual parent sessions are sometimes conducted. CPP therapists aim to create a supportive therapeutic environment to allow parents to work through traumatic experiences and explore how their own experiences growing up may have influenced their parenting. During sessions, interactions between parents and child provide opportunities to identify maladaptive perceptions of the child or maladaptive patterns of interaction. These observations then allow further working through of previous trauma at a representational level. Other approaches that focus on the representational level include Parenting (or Mothering) from the Inside Out (Suchman, Ordway, de las Heras, & McMahon, 2016) and Minding the Baby (Sadler et al., 2013; Sadler, Slade, & Mayes, 2006). A common theory of change among these approaches is that behavioral change will follow from changes in parents' representations.

In randomized clinical trials conducted by Lieberman and her colleagues (Lieberman et al., 2006) and Cicchetti, Toth, and colleagues (Cicchetti, Rogosch, & Toth, 2000; Cicchetti, Toth, & Rogosch, 1999; Toth, Rogosch, Manly, & Cicchetti, 2006), CPP has been shown to have a main effect or a moderating effect on attachment quality. In a randomized clinical trial comparing CPP to a psychoeducational parenting intervention and community care as usual, both CPP and the psychoeducational parenting intervention led to increases in secure attachment among maltreated children (Toth et al., 2006). A follow-up study of the same sample found that, at 1-year postintervention, children who received CPP showed higher rates of secure attachment and lower rates of disorganized attachment than children who received either the psychoeducational parenting intervention or the care-as-usual group (Stronach, Toth, Rogosch, & Cicchetti, 2013). Thus, although both CPP and the comparison intervention showed effects on attachment soon after the interventions, effects were sustained only among children who received CPP.

The effectiveness of CPP on maltreated children's diurnal cortisol regulation has also been examined. Whereas maltreated children in the care-as-usual group showed low levels of morning cortisol, children who received CPP or the psychoeducational parenting intervention showed levels comparable to a nonmaltreated comparison group (Cicchetti, Rogosch, Toth, & Sturge-Apple, 2011). Although the effectiveness of the control (psychoeducational) intervention as well as CPP makes it hard to know what aspects of CPP predicted positive outcomes (e.g., targeting parents' attachment representations versus providing long-term support), the results offer evidence that CPP contributes to changes at the behavioral and biological levels.

SUPPORTING MOTHERS BEYOND PARENTING: NURSE–FAMILY PARTNERSHIP

David Olds and colleagues developed Nurse–Family Partnership (NFP), a home-visiting program for low-income first-time mothers (Donelan-McCall & Olds, 2018; Olds, 2002). In addition to attachment theory, NFP is based on principles of social ecology theory (Bronfenbrenner, 1979) and self-efficacy theory (Bandura, 1977). Social ecology theory suggests that parent–child dyads are influenced by multiple social ecologies, including families, households, and communities. Thus, improving children's development requires understanding the context in which children develop. Unlike ABC, for which parent coaches are narrowly focused on changing parenting behaviors, NFP takes a multidisciplinary approach, offering support to the mother that extends beyond the relationship with her baby.

NFP aims to modify risk and protective factors during pregnancy and early childhood that are linked empirically with poor outcomes in adolescence and adulthood, such as antisocial behavior and substance abuse. The proximal targets for change include prenatal health behaviors, such as substance use and other behaviors that increase risk for preterm delivery or low birthweight; sensitive and safe parenting; and mothers' own risk factors, including lack of economic stability, social support, and access to resources.

Mothers enroll in NFP during their third trimester of pregnancy, with the program extending through the child's second year, making it the longest in duration of the programs we discuss here. The NFP nurse typically visits the mother every 2 weeks for approximately 75–90 minutes per visit, but visits tend to be more frequent around the time of delivery and less frequent as the child approaches 2 years old. Each visit focuses on the proximal targets of prenatal health, sensitive parenting, and the mother's own life course. These targets are addressed in multiple ways. Prenatal health, for example, is targeted by providing information to the mother about healthy practices, tracking diet information and weight gain, facilitating compliance with treatment, and coordinating health care. After the child is born, the nurse provides support to the mother in caring for the child's physical health by teaching her how to notice signs of illness and seek medical care as needed. The target of enhancing sensitive parenting also follows a psychoeducational approach, helping the mother read and interpret her infant's signals and learn appropriate responses. Activities are sometimes used to demonstrate ways that the mother may promote early cognitive and language development as well. Throughout the program, issues related to the mother's own life course are discussed. The nurse helps the mother engage in decision making that is consistent with her future goals when considering issues related to education, employment, and living circumstances.

NFP has been evaluated in several large-scale randomized clinical trials in Elmira, New York; Memphis, Tennessee; and Denver, Colorado. Across the trials, mothers who participated in NFP showed differences in parenting behaviors compared to control mothers, with some of these changes specific to sensitive and responsive interactions (Olds, 2002) and others reflecting differences in cognitive stimulation, safety in the home, and punishment (Kitzman et al., 1997; Olds, Henderson, Chamberlin, & Tatelbaum, 1986). Nurse-visited mothers were less likely to be reported for child maltreatment during their infants' first 2 years than control mothers (Olds et al., 1986, 1997). Given evidence of improvements in sensitive parenting and reductions in child abuse and neglect, we might expect to see changes in children's attachment security and disorganization, but attachment quality was not assessed as an outcome of NFP in these trials. As predicted, NFP led to improved prenatal health behaviors and delivery outcomes (Olds et al., 1986) and changes to the mothers' life course more broadly, such as reductions in subsequent pregnancies, less time receiving public assistance, and fewer arrests relative to control mothers (Olds, Henderson, Tatelbaum, & Chamberlain, 1988, 1997, 2004). NFP has effects on child outcomes, including enhanced cognitive functioning and reduced behavioral problems at age 6 (Olds et al., 2004), increased achievement scores at ages 9 and 12 (Kitzman et al., 2010; Olds et al., 2007), and fewer arrests at age 15 (Olds et al., 1997) when compared to outcomes for children in a control intervention.

DISTILLING THE EVIDENCE

Meta-Analytic Findings

Meta-analyses, which aggregate effect sizes across studies, offer a useful approach for distilling the evidence for the effectiveness of parenting interventions. As introduced earlier, Bakermans-Kranenburg and colleagues conducted a meta-analysis in 2003 that examined the effectiveness of preventive interventions in enhancing sensitive parenting and attachment security. Results from 51 studies that used a randomized design, which included a total of 6,282 mothers and their children, demonstrated a significant and moderate effect of parenting interventions in enhancing maternal sensitivity (Bakermans-Kranenburg et al., 2003). The combined effect of 29 intervention studies and 1,503 families on enhancing attachment security was also significant, albeit relatively small. Although a 2005 meta-analysis found that interventions, overall, were *not* effective in changing disorganized attachment (Bakermans-Kranenburg, van IJzendoorn, & Juffer, 2005), an updated meta-analysis (Facompre, Bernard, & Waters, 2018) demonstrated a significant, moderate effect of interventions on reducing disorganized attachment.

Perhaps even more informative than providing aggregate effect sizes, meta-analyses allow for the examination of factors that influence the magnitude of the effects observed—such as the extent to which differences among interventions (in their length, focus, approach, etc.) contribute to variability in parent and child outcomes. A few notable findings with regard to such moderators of intervention effectiveness emerged from the Bakermans-Kranenburg and colleagues meta-analysis in 2003. First, interventions that were shorter in duration (defined as fewer than 16 sessions) were *more effective* than longer interventions. Second, interventions that had an exclusively behavioral focus on changing sensitivity were *more effective* than those that focused on changing parental representations, offering support, or targeting multiple foci (such as representation plus support). Taken together, as highlighted by the title of their meta-analysis "Less Is More," these findings suggested that a targeted approach, with a behavioral focus and limited number of sessions, may be most effective. Even for multirisk families, such as those served by ABC and the other interventions reviewed, short-term, behaviorally focused interventions were found to be most effective. However, Facompre and colleagues (2018), in their meta-analysis of intervention effects on disorganized attachment specifically, did not replicate these findings; duration and intervention focus did not significantly moderate the effectiveness of interventions.

Resources for Evaluating Program Effectiveness

Because individual agencies and clinicians may have difficulty distilling the literature, even with the availability of meta-analyses and review papers, it is fortunate that a number of clearinghouses or registries of interventions have emerged (e.g., California Evidence-Based Clearinghouse for Child Welfare). Also, the federal government provides funding to states for provision of home visitation services, through the Maternal, Infant, and Early Childhood Home Visiting Program (MIECHV) under the Health Resources and Services Administration (HRSA). To ensure that all programs funded have evidence of effectiveness, programs are evaluated by Home Visiting Evidence of Effectiveness (HomVEE), a review initiative launched by the U.S. Department of Health and Human Services. HomVEE assessed the quality of research evidence of home-visiting programs across domains of child and family well-being, such as child development and school readiness, maternal health, child maltreatment, positive parenting practices, and family violence. In order to meet HomVEE standards for an evidence-based home-visiting program, research studies must meet methodological standards and show significant intervention effects on two or more domains of child and family well-being. Two resources for evaluating programs' evidence of effectiveness are the MIECHV (*https://mchb.hrsa.gov/maternal-child-health-initiatives/home-visiting-overview*) and the California Evidence-Based Clearinghouse for Child Welfare (CEBC; *www.cebc4cw.org*). Each of these rates ABC as having a strong evidence base. It is one of about 20 programs listed as eligible for MIECHV funding. ABC received the highest rating of 1 (well supported by research evidence) by the CEBC.

CHAPTER 12

Power of Two

FROM PARENT TO PARENT COACH: LENIXIA

Lenixia entered Charlene's apartment for Session 1, where twins Sebastian and Synia were on the floor. As she started to set up her camera, feeling a little bit nervous as a new parent coach, Lenixia noticed Sebastian fuss and crawl toward his mother. Charlene picked him up and said, "It's OK, Seb, this is Lenixia; she's here to play with us." Lenixia, taking a deep breath, said, "That was so nurturing how you picked him up when he fussed and came to you." This was Lenixia's first in-the-moment comment as a parent coach.

When Lenixia (who is now a parent coach) first heard about ABC, she was living in a shelter at the border of East New York and Brownsville, neighborhoods in Brooklyn, New York, with high rates of poverty, crime, and homelessness. Her daughter was 9 years old and her son, Shafique, was an infant. She never imagined that she would be in a shelter—she and her husband had always had steady employment and were always able to provide for their family. But when Lenixia was pregnant with Shafique, she had complications during her pregnancy that left her unable to work. During that time, she and her husband struggled financially, unable to keep up with their rent and other bills. After being evicted from their apartment, Lenixia and her family entered the family shelter system and were placed at Women in Need (WIN).

Shelters are tough places to live in, especially for families. Lenixia saw other mothers at the shelter really struggling; they were depressed, stressed, and hopeless; many were at their lowest point. And she saw this affect their parenting—some reacting in overly harsh ways to their children and others seeming to withdraw. Lenixia met other mothers with active Administration for Children's Services (ACS) cases who were at risk of having their children removed or whose children were indeed removed and placed in foster care.

Lenixia attended a community meeting at WIN, at which parent coaches from Power of Two were giving a presentation about ABC. Power of Two was a new organization based in Brownsville that was bringing ABC to New York City. The parent coaches explained that ABC was a home-visiting program that aimed to support parents in building a strong foundation for children that would support their happy and healthy development. Lenixia thought she was a good parent, but she was stressed and wanted to make sure she was doing everything she could for her kids.

Lenixia was born in Dominica, an island in the Caribbean, and moved to St. Martin when she was 8 years old. She grew up with both of her parents, an older brother, and sisters who were 10 years younger than she was. Lenixia recalls her parents always being there for her, but she felt especially close to her father, who provided a model for protective and nurturing care. Before starting ABC, Lenixia answered questions from the AAI about her own experiences growing up. When asked about her choice of the word "caring" to describe her father, Lenixia recalled a fight she got into on the school bus: "He didn't judge me, he heard the whole situation before he did anything. I was thinking he would really be pissed. But the way he handled it, you know, it made me feel . . . protected. Made me feel it was OK." Lenixia didn't feel as comfortable seeking support from her mother, even though her mother always provided for her basic needs: "I just never felt she understood me the way my dad understood me . . . I don't think she like really listened to hear what I said before she judged. Like one time, the teacher said something to me, and I didn't want to tell my mom, but the teacher ended up calling my parents. My dad wanted to ask me what happened, but my mom, the minute she heard, she snapped. So I just felt more comfortable going to my dad, even if I knew he might be upset."

Lenixia's parent coach came weekly to her unit in the shelter to meet with her and Shafique for ABC. From the start, Lenixia showed strengths in being nurturing when Shafique was distressed—when he fell down, she picked him up and cuddled him; when he was fussy, she gently rubbed his back and said, "OK, I know." Nurturance came naturally to her. This was consistent with her responses on the AAI, for which she had recalled vivid examples of times when her father responded to her distress with comfort and protection and openly reflected on times when she missed out on such experiences with her mother.

In the first ABC session, the parent coach quickly began commenting on the many moments when Lenixia was nurturing to Shafique or followed his lead. Two minutes in, Shafique looked up at Lenixia as the parent coach was introducing what to expect in ABC. "Look at him smiling at you, and you're delighting in him, smiling back!" the coach interrupted herself briefly, and then returned to what she was saying. A minute later, Shafique held up a pretend piece of cheese and Lenixia pretended to eat it, smacking her lips. "And that's great," said her parent coach, "he held up the cheese and you pretended to eat it. That's what we call 'following the lead,' which we'll talk about in a couple weeks. You're already in Session 3, and we're only on Session 1!" Lenixia acknowledged the comment but quickly turned her attention back toward Shafique, who started banging a plastic spoon on a bowl of pretend cereal.

Following Shafique's lead with delight was more challenging for Lenixia than being nurturing. She found it hard at times to just enjoy being with Shafique, especially during this stressful time in her life. When the parent coach showed up for Session 3, Lenixia was having a particularly difficult day; she was overwhelmed and broke down crying. Although it could have been tempting for her parent coach to offer to postpone the session and address Lenixia's current stressors, the parent coach suggested that they start the session. After a few minutes had passed, Lenixia was laughing with Shafique as she followed his lead, seemingly pulled out of her depressed mood. Although Lenixia found the comments from her parent coach reassuring, what was most rewarding for her was the reaction she got from Shafique. In a subsequent session, Lenixia's husband and daughter were home, and they all tried to follow Shafique's lead together. Shafique clapped, then looked at Lenixia, and she clapped. Then, Shafique turned to his father who clapped and then to his sister as she clapped. This beautiful moment of following the lead with delight was featured in the montage that Lenixia received at the end of ABC, and offered evidence to Lenixia that she was giving Shafique her best, even in challenging circumstances that felt out of her control.

As Lenixia was approaching Session 10, her parent coach let her know that Power of Two was hiring outreach liaisons—program graduates who would talk to other parents about ABC. Lenixia submitted her resume, interviewed soon after, and was hired for this part-time position. As an outreach worker, Lenixia's job was to talk to other parents in Brownsville about the program. Using her own story, she was quickly able to engage other parents, ease discomfort about having someone come to the home, address hesitations about being video-recorded, and reduce feelings that parents would be judged. Lenixia frequently showed other parents the video montage she received from her parent coach at Session 10. A few months into her position as an outreach liaison, Lenixia and her family moved out of the shelter and into an apartment in Bedford-Stuyvesant in Brooklyn.

A month later, Lenixia had the opportunity to interview for a parent-coach position with Power of Two. During the screening interview, Lenixia was presented the video clips drawn from sessions of other parents—showing moments when parents followed their child's lead and moments when parents were nurturing. After seeing example clips of in-the-moment commenting, Lenixia was asked to try commenting on the videos herself. Typically, we show these clips twice, allowing potential parent coaches time to observe the interaction and plan the comment they want to make, before seeing the video a second time. Lenixia didn't wait for the second time. As the first clip of nurturance was playing, she said,

"That is such a nice way to be nurturing. When he fell down, you picked him up and held him." Her other comments expertly labeled the targets as well, sounding genuine, yet precise.

Lenixia was hired to be a parent coach at Power of Two, a role that she describes as her "dream job." She truly enjoys parent coaching and seeing other parents light up when playing with their children in sessions. She feels like she is giving back what she received. She has a caseload of about 10 families, mostly living in the Brownsville community. She has found it easy to connect with families, especially through in-the-moment commenting. Knowing how the comments felt to her—how they helped lift her out of difficult times and reassure her that she was doing a good job—she tries to make comments often. However, Lenixia has also found challenges in the parent-coach role. In particular, she struggled to comment on negative behaviors—times when parents were not nurturing, did not follow their children's lead, or behaved in ways that were intrusive or frightening. Although we try to limit the frequency of these negative comments so that parents hear more positive than negative comments, we consider it important to gently scaffold and shape parents' behaviors when they are inconsistent with the ABC targets. Lenixia worried that parents would feel judged by these negative comments. Noticing her reluctance, Lenixia's supervisor discussed her hesitation and practiced this commenting style, reassuring her that parents were comfortable with her and would not be offended by her feedback. Indeed, when Lenixia started making these gentle scaffolding comments, parents received them well. She saw changes in their behavior right in that moment that further highlighted to her the power of her commenting.

Lenixia will tell you that ABC and Power of Two changed her life—that "ABC is forever in [her] bones."

FOUNDING POWER OF TWO

Lenixia is one of over 1,000 parents who has received ABC through Power of Two, a nonprofit organization whose mission is to support parents in providing their children with the foundation needed for happy and healthy development.

After overseeing the family shelter system in New York City, Anne Heller became keenly aware of intergenerational patterns of poverty and trauma. The data she reviewed about families using New York City's shelter system suggested that most families who came into the shelter system did so once and not again. However, there was a subset of families—10% or so—that returned to the shelter system time and time again. Not surprisingly, these families were often also involved with the child welfare system and had many other stressors beyond homelessness—problems such as depression, domestic violence, unemployment, and lack of support. Anne wondered how she could have an impact on these most vulnerable families. She started reading about research on "toxic stress" and adverse childhood experiences (ACEs), which collectively showed that trauma and adversity could have lasting and devastating effects on mental and physical health when experienced during childhood (Anda et al., 2008; Felitti et al., 1998). She learned about the importance of sensitive parenting and attachment relationships for protecting children from the negative consequences of early life stress, primarily through Harvard's Center for the Developing Child (*https://developingchild.harvard. edu*). Furthermore, she was struck by economist James Heckman's (2012) findings that early childhood programs delivered a 13% rate of return on investment, considering the longitudinal effects on graduation rates, adult employment and income, and physical health outcomes.

Anne was already familiar with some other programs available in New York City that aimed to support parents when children were young, such as Nurse–Family Partnership and Healthy Families America. Despite the compelling evidence for the effectiveness of these programs, she worried that the most vulnerable families would have trouble committing to programs that lasted 2 years or longer. She wondered whether there were any short-term programs that also had a strong evidence base. Anne reasoned that short-term programs, in addition to being accessible and appealing to families, would be easier to bring to scale than long-term programs, as they would be less expensive to deliver. She came across ABC, and as she read about it, she was struck by the evidence showing that just 10 sessions of targeted coaching could create lasting changes in parenting and in children's physiological well-being. Furthermore, she thought ABC would fill a gap in New York City.

Anne reached out to Mary in order to learn more about ABC and to consider how she might bring it to New York City. At the time, I (K. B.) had just started a faculty position at Stony Brook University, located on Long Island, not far from New York City. Mary put Anne in touch with me, and we quickly started planning for how to bring ABC to children and families in New York. In 2015, Power of Two was founded.

SERVING BROWNSVILLE

With the goal of bringing ABC to the six neighborhoods in New York City with a child poverty rate above 50%, Power of Two launched in Brownsville. Brownsville is the one neighborhood in Brooklyn with a child poverty rate above 50%. The Children's Committee for Children (CCC) in New York maintains a comprehensive database, tracking information about children's well-being across New York City's five boroughs and 59 community districts. Based on CCC's Community Risk Ranking, which aggregates data related to child poverty and family homelessness, infant mortality rates, violence and crime, and achievement scores, Brownsville is one of the worst of the 59 community districts in terms of risk to children's well-being. Brownsville is a densely populated community, with over 61,000 residents in just over one square mile. More than half of the families in Brownsville live in public housing, and it has among the highest number of families entering homeless shelters of all communities in Brooklyn; there are 15 homeless shelters in Brownsville and its surrounding area. The majority (over 75%) of Brownsville residents are black, and approximately 20% are Latino. Approximately one-tenth of the residents are under the age of 5, which is significantly higher than Brooklyn as a whole. In 2015, 2,576 children under 5 years old were subjects of reports of child abuse and neglect allegations in Brownsville and neighboring East New York, reflecting 11.4% of the total population of children.

According to a recent CCC report, "Against this backdrop, it is incredibly challenging to ensure that children and families in Brownsville have the opportunities they need and deserve to realize their full potential. The large child population in Brownsville—including very young children—provides an opportunity for the city to implement strategies to improve outcomes in Brownsville at the earliest stages of a child's development" (2017, p. 9).

Anne estimated that making ABC available to the 700 infants born into poverty each year in Brownsville (out of 1,400 total births) would require about 18 parent coaches, each serving about 40 families per year. With funding from several private foundations, Power of Two hired three parent coaches to serve the Brownsville community in their first year.

Monique and Xavier

One of the first families served by Power of Two was Monique and her son, Xavier. Early in Session 1, Xavier, who was about 10 months old, toppled backward on the bed, where he sat with his mother. Monique caught him as he startled and started crying and lifted him back up. Seemingly frantic, she placed her hand over his face, pulled him toward her, kissed his head, and then quickly said, "You're OK. No, no, no—you're OK. You can't be jumping around like that, just sit still. Look, here, have a banana." Her parent coach said, "You rubbed his head and kissed him," noting to herself that Monique's response also including non-nurturing behaviors, like distracting him with food, verbally minimizing his distress, and being intrusive. "That's it, that's all they need," Monique said, agreeing with her parent coach.

Prior to starting ABC, when asked during the AAI about a time when she was physically hurt, Monique described a time when she got bullied by a girl on the playground who called her names and pushed her off her bike. "How did your aunt [her primary caregiver] respond that time?" the parent coach asked. "My aunt literally said that I probably deserved it. That's what she said. I was just a little kid. And her response totally blamed me for getting bullied. It was like she didn't even care." In addition to these memories of her aunt dismissing her distress, Monique angrily recalled threatening and abusive experiences with her uncle—experiences that left her terrified of being alone with him. "Where the hell was ACS then? I would've preferred to have stayed with my mom, even though she was probably too messed up to take care of me anyway." Given Monique's history of neglect and abuse, it was not surprising that she struggled to be nurturing at the start of ABC.

A FOCUS ON FIDELITY

Monique's parent coach maintained a high rate of commenting throughout her sessions. In Session 4, the parent coach commented, "That's great that you asked him 'What's the matter?' as he fussed." Monique responded, "But I know what's the matter—he doesn't feel good." "Yeah, but it's great that you ask him because that's checking in with him and letting him know you're paying attention. That's how he learns—when you hold him like that, when he's distressed—that's how he learns that he can always count on you to help him." The parent coach, noticing that Monique struggled in particular with nurturance, often elaborated on any examples of nurturance, making sure that her comments included all three components (i.e., description of behavior, link to intervention target, and link to child outcome). A few minutes later in the same session, Xavier fell backward on the kitchen floor and bumped his head on the refrigerator. Monique quickly scooped him up, appearing alarmed herself, as her parent coach said, "That's such a nice job of nurturing him. You're hugging him and letting him know you're there for him. That's excellent nurturing, and it's so hard. See, that hug already helped him feel better." Monique pretty quickly put him down, ready to show him the pudding activity, but Xavier started to fuss. "Oh, it looks like he might not be ready yet"; this was the parent coach's gentle comment on Monique's non-nurturing behavior of distracting him while he was still upset. Monique picked Xavier up again, and the parent coach commented, "There you go again being nurturing." This time, Monique waited until Xavier started smiling and pointing before she put him down. "That was great following his lead as he signaled to get down, and you imitated him when he made a noise." Monique's parent coach expertly supported her in being nurturing and following the lead through her frequent on-target comments.

When evidence-based interventions are adopted, organizations have varying degrees of commitment to ensuring model fidelity, as we described earlier. Power of Two's organizational structure is designed to promote model fidelity. Every full-time parent coach holds caseloads of 10–15 families, with time allotted in their weekly schedules for clinical supervision, fidelity-focused supervision, coding, and other session preparation, such as video review and video editing. In addition, Power of Two has its own fidelity supervisors on site, who are reliable coders of in-the-moment commenting. Thus, although parent coaches at all dissemination sites receive a year of clinical and fidelity-focused supervision with the team at the University of Delaware, Power of Two has a built-in capacity to continue to monitor fidelity after the coaches meet certification criteria.

All Power of Two parent coaches have met certification criteria in their first year, similar to the success rates for ABC parent coaches at other dissemination sites. We have examined changes in parent coaches' fidelity across their first year of delivering ABC at Power of Two. Across 730 coded sessions, conducted by 20 parent coaches, we found that, on average, parent coaches started at a commenting rate of 1.1 comments per minute, with significant variability between coaches. Parent coaches showed significant growth across the year, with an average of 1.8 comments per minute by the end of their first year (Bernard et al., 2017).

EVALUATING POWER
OF TWO'S EFFECTIVENESS

After ABC, Monique brought Xavier to Power of Two's office for a postintervention research visit. During this visit, Monique and Xavier participated in the Strange Situation procedure. During the third episode, the stranger entered the room and sat quietly in the chair. Xavier, who had been playing with a stacking ring toy on the floor, scooted backward toward his mom. "Mama," he said, and Monique responded, "Hey, honey," following his lead. Xavier stood up, put his hand on her knee, and looked cautiously at the stranger. As his mom started talking to the stranger, Xavier returned to playing on the floor. Monique soon heard a knock on the one-way mirror, cueing her to leave the room. As she left, Xavier burst into a cry, crawling after her. When Xavier failed to settle with the stranger, Monique was sent back into the room for the first reunion. She knocked, called his name, and entered with her arms reached out. Xavier reached out his arms, still being supported by the stranger given that he wasn't yet a sturdy walker. Monique picked him up, kissed his cheek, and he settled quickly in her arms. As she sat down with him on the floor, he briefly fussed and then reached for the ring-stacking toy, handing a ring to his mom. Monique sat behind Xavier as he banged the rings together. After 3 minutes, Monique was cued to leave again for the second separation, this time leaving Xavier in the room alone. He cried loudly until the stranger returned and continued to fuss in the stranger's arms, settling only for a few seconds at a time when she showed him toys. When Monique entered for the second reunion, Xavier quickly crawled toward her across the room, pushing away toys in his way, crying loudly, and clinging to her leg when he reached her. Monique picked him up and sat down in the chair with Xavier on her lap. He settled immediately but fussed again when she put him down. Monique picked him up, wrapped one arm around his belly and pulled his head in close to her chest, and rocked him back and forth. Although she still showed some intrusive behaviors—bouncing Xavier vigorously on her knee, poking his stomach, and abruptly changing positions—Xavier's responses during the reunions showed that he had developed the expectation and confidence that his mom would respond to his distress. He had developed a secure attachment.

Monique was participating in Power of Two's effectiveness trial of ABC in the Brownsville community. As opposed to efficacy research, which tests an intervention under ideal conditions (with the focus on fidelity and highly trained clinicians), effectiveness research involves evaluating an intervention under "real-world" conditions. Brownsville families who consent to research are randomly assigned to receive ABC immediately or after a waiting period. Although a waitlist design has its limitations, such designs are common in effectiveness research. Similar to the efficacy trials, Power of Two is collecting data on parent sensitivity (coded from a standardized parent–child play interaction), child attachment quality (coded from the Strange Situation), and child physiological regulation (assessed through diurnal rhythms of cortisol, assayed from saliva samples).

Such a study can replicate and extend the evidence for ABC's effectiveness, while also providing data regarding its effectiveness in Brownsville in particular. Furthermore, results from such a study can inform Power of Two's practices for the provision of ABC. For example, baseline parent sensitivity data suggest that approximately 12% of parents in Brownsville are already scoring high on sensitivity (a 4 or 5 on a 5-point scale). It is unlikely that such parents need ABC. These data can be used to inform practices for screening parents and selecting which families are most in need and will benefit most from ABC.

Similar to sensitivity data collected at other dissemination sites, preliminary data from the effectiveness trial in Brownsville demonstrate that ABC leads to significantly higher levels of parent sensitivity at postintervention than the waitlist condition. Additionally, preliminary results from approximately 60 children show that children who received ABC have more normative (higher) cortisol levels at wake-up than children in the control group. Finally, we have also seen evidence of intervention effects on parents' report of depression. Only 27% of parents report clinically elevated depressive symptoms after ABC, compared to 47% of control parents (Dash, Rodriguez, Imrisek, & Bernard, 2018). Although these results are preliminary, they offer promising evidence of ABC's effectiveness as it is moved into community settings.

EXPANDING TO SERVE CHILDREN
IN FOSTER CARE

As Power of Two's plans were developing to serve families in Brownsville, ACS, which oversees the child welfare system in New York City, was developing a proposal for Title IV-E Foster Care Waiver funding from the federal government. The Title IV-E Foster Care Waiver program allows child welfare agencies to use federal dollars to support and evaluate innovative child welfare policies designed to increase permanency, reduce child maltreatment, and promote child well-being. ACS became interested in ABC as one approach to targeting these issues.

Along with Anne, we were involved in discussions with the ACS Division of Policy, Planning, and Measurement about how to best implement and scale ABC, with one major question being whether staff at foster care agencies should be trained in ABC or whether ABC should be implemented by a team of parent coaches at Power of Two. Although the former (training staff at individual agencies) was the approach taken in many other dissemination sites, we were excited about the potential benefits of having Power of Two deliver ABC. Centralizing the effort at Power of Two seemed like an ideal way to scale ABC, while ensuring fidelity and optimizing effectiveness.

Thus, with Title IV-E Waiver funding, ACS launched Strong Families NYC, which involved four innovative practices based on evidence: comprehensive trauma screening, reduced caseloads and increased supervision for case planners, increased collaboration between mental health clinicians and foster care case planners (through a program called Partnering for Success), and delivery of ABC through Power of Two. Collectively, these initiatives highlight an exciting focus on addressing the needs of vulnerable children in evidence-based and trauma-informed ways.

Vanessa and Her Grandson

Vanessa was feeling desperate, overwhelmed, and scared; knowing that she needed support, she went to Brownsville Multi-Service Family Health Center (BMS), a health care and social services organization near her home. Power of Two outreach workers were at BMS that day, talking with parents about ABC.

At that time, Vanessa was about to send her daughter to her high school prom. With her own children grown, she and her husband "were getting ready to live," as she put it. But that all changed when her 19-year-old son, who had a son of his own, was sentenced to 10 years in prison. Although Vanessa readily agreed to take in William, not yet 1 year old, she had mixed feelings about this role. She felt like it was her time to be a grandma—she had already raised her own children. The thought of doing it all over again felt overwhelming. "Here is this baby, my son's baby, and he's incarcerated. I'm dealing with the emotion of sadness—I'm not going to see my son for 10 years—and now I have this baby." Vanessa also had a tense relationship with William's mother, who was hostile and resistant to her but not able to care for William herself. On top of this, she was concerned about what her grandson had already been through. By her own observations, Vanessa had noted that William seemed "depressed" and didn't act like a typical 1-year-old. So Vanessa knew she needed help; she wasn't sure what that help might be, but she felt desperate. She wanted her grandson to know that he was loved and that he was safe, but she also knew that she needed support for herself too.

Vanessa went to BMS hoping to find something useful. That day, two parent coaches from Power of Two had set up a table in the waiting area, offering information to parents about ABC. Although many relative/kinship caregivers are referred to Power of Two directly from their foster care agency, Vanessa's grandson had not come to the attention of ACS and thus did not have an open case in the child welfare system. Upon hearing about ABC from the parent coaches, Vanessa felt a sense of hopefulness that the program could provide what she needed.

When her parent coach came for the first session, Vanessa expected that the session would primarily involve a discussion between the two of them. She immediately noticed her parent coach making comments such as, "Oh, you can go ahead and pick him up! Don't let me get in the way." She was thinking, "I don't want to pick him up—I want to talk to you!" and believed that William was just crying for attention, anyway. Vanessa's instinct was to tell William to be quiet—that he was fine. Vanessa's parent coach was persistent in supporting her in being nurturing, commenting at first on even small behaviors that communicated that she was available for William, such as looking at him when he was crying or reaching his arms out. Later in ABC sessions, Vanessa indicated that it was hard for her to be nurturing and that she had complicated feelings getting in the way. She felt upset at William's mother, disappointed that her son was incarcerated, and overwhelmed in her role as a parent. When her parent coach helped Vanessa identify these "voices from the past" (or present) that were getting in her way, Vanessa was able to override her responses that dismissed William's distress. After all, she wanted William to know that he was loved, whatever that took.

Whereas it was not her initial impulse to provide nurturance, following the lead was something that came naturally to Vanessa. The in-the-moment comments helped her do so more intentionally, especially after learning that following the lead communicated to her grandson that she was paying attention, that she valued what William did, and that he was important.

By the end of ABC, Vanessa showed notable shifts in being nurturing to William, and her family members noticed. Her husband and daughter told her that she was babying William. They would say, "Stop babying him," to which Vanessa confidently responded, "I don't care if you guys think I'm babying him. He's gonna get the comfort he needs right now. I need him to know Grandma is right here, and she isn't going anyplace."

After she graduated from ABC, Vanessa was hired as a foster care outreach liaison at Power of Two. As part of ACS's Strong Families New York City initiative, Power of Two's goal is to make ABC available to every infant and toddler involved in the foster care system in New York. Along with a team of about five foster care liaisons at Power of Two who work across New York City's five boroughs, Vanessa is tasked with engaging foster parents (and birth parents following reunification) in signing up for ABC. That is not an easy assignment. When talking with foster parents about the program, Vanessa often tells them about her own experiences. She has found that sometimes foster parents, especially kinship and older foster parents, aren't interested—they say they're too busy, or they don't need help. Sometimes they're frustrated with the foster care agency, or their case planner, or the judge, or the child's parent. Maybe they don't trust someone coming into their home. Whatever it is, she listens. "And I tell them about my story, about my son who is incarcerated, and my grandson, that I did ABC . . . and that it changed our lives."

Although Vanessa is employed at Power of Two, she still sees her first job as being a parent to William, a role that she now plans to continue as he gets older. She hopes she never has to give him back. She wants to send him to college someday, which she intends to pay for. But for now, William is young, and life is still unpredictable at times. William, now nearly 3 years old, has weekend visits with his mom. Recently, upon returning home from a weekend visit, Vanessa recalls, "He was crying—he wanted Mommy. I thought there was absolutely nothing I could do. . . . And then I remembered ABC, and I just held him and rubbed his back. And I told him, it will be OK. We're gonna do this together."

CHAPTER 13

Fostering Relationships

with Caroline K. P. Roben

LORETTA, APRIL, AND LEE

Loretta's 12-month-old son Lee was removed from her custody following a domestic violence incident. Lee was taken to a temporary foster home for the first weekend and then was placed with his current foster mother with whom he has lived since. April, Lee's foster mother, has raised two of her own biological children who are now grown. She has fostered only one other child, an 8-year-old, who continues to live with her. Lee has had two visitations with his mother during the past two weeks. The visitations have been hard on everyone.

Lee's Experience

Once a week Lee is picked up by a van from his foster mother's house and taken to the social services building in town. Each day when he arrives at visitation, it is clear he has been crying the entire way—the driver has tried various things to distract

---

Caroline K. P. Roben, PhD, is Director of Dissemination of the Attachment and Biobehavioral Catch-up Intervention at the University of Delaware.

him but to no avail. Lee has never met the driver outside of transportation to and from visitation, and it is not always the same driver. Once at the social services building, he waits (often with a different, unfamiliar staff member) for his mother to arrive. Unfortunately, his distress is not alleviated when he sees his mother. She comes on strong—trying to hug him at times and trying to get him to play at other times. He hasn't seen her for a week, and he is confused about how to respond to her and feels overwhelmed. He withdraws into himself, worried about where his foster mother is.

Loretta's Experience

Loretta has to ask for the afternoon off from work and take two buses to get from her home to the social services building. At each visitation, she hopes that Lee will remember her and come running to her, but each time she is disappointed. Even the very first week, Lee turned away when she arrived. She has done everything she can think of—she greets him as she always did when he lived with her, she tries to think of fun games to play with him, and she brings him toys and food—but nothing works.

She has wondered whether the foster parent is telling him things that make him doubt her love for him. She questions the relationship she had with Lee before he was removed from her care and feels hurt that he seems to have forgotten her.

As part of her reunification plans, she has been assigned parenting classes to attend and has been told it will be important for her to obtain stable housing, stay away from her boyfriend (who beat her up), and attend visitation sessions. She has been attending the group parenting classes even though they are often at inconvenient times. Although she hasn't yet found stable housing, she is hopeful that her attempts reflect her good intentions. Even though she is very concerned about doing everything she can to enhance her chances of reunification, visitation is so challenging for her that she is finding it difficult to go each week.

It's painful for her. She doesn't understand why Lee doesn't respond to her as he did before he was taken from her care.

April's Experience

April hates visitation days. She dreads the van's approach to her house, knowing that Lee will be crying hard by the time he is strapped into his car seat. She feels badly leaving him crying and doesn't like being separated from him. When he comes home, he is a wreck. She tries to comfort him, but he pushes her away. Last week he swatted at her face and scratched her cheek. She is concerned about what his birth mother may be doing to upset him so. She has noticed it takes several hours for him to return to normal, and then the next visitation comes much too soon.

From the perspective of the child, the birth mother, and the foster mother, not much about visitation is going well. From the child's perspective, visitation is a stressful experience without the buffering support of his attachment figure (his foster mother). The birth parent, Loretta, feels rejected by her child for reasons that she does not understand, and she does not feel supported by the foster parent. The foster mother, April, worries that Lee is being upset by the birth mother and that visitation is causing lasting problems.

FOSTERING RELATIONSHIPS

Fostering Relationships was adapted from ABC to address these issues. It represents a significant adaptation rather than a minor one, but it emerged out of ABC and shares some key principles. The intervention has several interrelated goals. For the child, the goal is to improve the experience so that he is supported by his foster parent throughout visitation and so that he has a positive interaction with his birth parent. For the birth parent, the goals are that she reinterpret her child's signals in such a way that she does not feel rejected, that she interact with her child in such a way that invites his involvement, and that she feel supported by the foster parent. For the foster parent, the goal is that she feel supportive of the birth parent and of the relationship between the child and parent.

Development of a Program to Improve Visitation

Fostering Relationships grew out of conversations with our colleague Carole Shauffer, who developed Quality Parenting Initiative. Quality Parenting Initiative, described in greater detail in Chapter 5, aims to strengthen and fundamentally change the nature of foster care. In many places, foster parents are not treated as partners by child welfare agencies; foster parents are not involved in decisions about children, are not kept informed about plans, and are not encouraged to provide long-term support to the children and their birth parents. This system may thus fail to attract the people who might be the strongest foster parents. Quality Parenting Initiative seeks to change this. One of the weaknesses in the child welfare system, as Quality Parenting Initiative saw it, was the strategy for visitation often employed. Carole recognized that an adaptation of ABC could serve as a model for visitation. Together with Carole, we developed a time- and cost-efficient intervention to address several notable challenges in visitation: child experiencing distress resulting from separation from the foster parent and interactions with an overwhelming birth parent; birth parent feeling rejected and inadequate in interactions with her child and judged by the foster parent; and foster parent feeling frustrated with the birth parent.

Child Distress during Visitation

When infants and young children arrive at visitation without their foster parents, they are usually highly distressed. Children are often transported by someone they do not know, to a place they do not know, to visit a parent they may not remember and have not seen in recent days.

Infants seem to form new attachments (i.e., stable attachment behaviors when distressed) relatively quickly (Stovall-McClough & McClough, 2004). From an evolutionary perspective, it makes sense that children would need to direct their attachment behaviors toward new caregivers quickly after losing parents. Although a week seems a short time from an adult's perspective, from an infant's perspective, it is an exceedingly long time. An infant would surely not have survived for a week if another adult did not step in as an alloparent. Thus, foster parents almost always become the primary attachment figures to infants quickly and usually before the first visitation with birth parents.

If young children are not accompanied by their foster parents, they will likely be distressed at visitation (Zeanah et al., 2011). In Fostering Relationships, we ask the foster parent to commit to accompanying the child to visitation and remaining present throughout the visit. Although some agencies encourage foster parents to accompany children to visitation, this encouragement is relatively rare. It can be challenging for foster parents to attend, as they often have other children in their care and other responsibilities—and in addition, they are often just not in the habit of attending.

Birth Parent Expectations and Behaviors

Having hoped for a warm reunion after a long separation, birth parents are often disappointed in their child's response to them. Although most infants certainly miss their parents, it is difficult for them to cope with separations of a week. Rather than going directly to their parents, they often show avoidant or resistant behavior. We found in our early work that when children behave in these avoidant or resistant ways, it has a powerful effect, with parents feeling rejected as a consequence (Stovall & Dozier, 2000). These feelings can lead birth parents to skip visitation sessions or to stop coming entirely (Haight, Kagle, & Black, 2003).

When birth parents anticipate that their child may not come running to them eagerly and have strategies for engaging them in play, the quality of the visit can be enhanced for both children and parents.

The Foster Parent–Birth Parent Relationship

Foster parents may be angry with birth parents because of the circumstances that led children to be placed in foster care, or they may attribute children's distress upon returning home from visitations to the behavior of birth parents (Erera, 1997; Sanchirico & Jablonka, 2000). Similarly, birth parents may resent foster parents for being with their children when they are not, or they may blame foster parents for their children's wary response to them during visitation. The foster–birth parent relationship can be challenging for many reasons. When foster parents take on the role of supporting birth parents, however, it can change this dynamic.

Fostering Relationships aims to create conditions such that visitation is not traumatic for children; help birth parents anticipate that they may feel rejected by their children and be prepared to follow their children's lead in play; and help foster parents learn to make in-the-moment comments to support birth parents in following their children's lead, thus enhancing the relationship between foster and birth parents.

Overview of Fostering Relationships

Fostering Relationships is intended specifically for visitation. The program is designed to be used during the first five visitation sessions following foster care placement, but the methods employed could certainly be used beyond the initial five visits. We would not expect Fostering Relationships to be effective if other reforms of the foster care system were not initiated. Perhaps most especially, foster parents need to be recruited who are willing to engage with and support birth parents and be part of a child welfare system that values foster parents as resource parents. Fostering Relationships seeks to enhance the experience of the child, the birth mother, and the foster mother during visitation in several ways.

Structural Change to Visit

Rather than send children off in a van to see birth parents, foster parents accompany children to visitation and stay with them throughout the visitation. Children thus supported are less likely to be distressed than they would be otherwise.

Birth Parent Mentor

Birth parents meet with a mentor before each of the five initial visits. The mentor helps birth parents with two issues. First, she helps birth parents anticipate that children may be distressed upon seeing them or may turn away from them. Anticipating this reaction, birth parents can be prepared and not feel as rejected as they would likely be otherwise. Second, the mentor helps birth parents learn to follow their children's lead, so that they will be more attractive play partners for their children than they would be otherwise.

Foster Parent as Support

Foster parents receive a half-day training from Fostering Relationships before they have a foster child placed with them. Training focuses on helping foster parents understand the importance of following a child's lead and helping them learn to make in-the-moment comments that will support birth parents. Comments are expected to be positive and analogous to in-the-moment comments made by parent coaches in ABC. However, we are aware that it is rarely possible to learn to do this quickly, and we do not expect foster parents to comment with the same frequency or quality as ABC parent coaches. Foster parents may make several comments about birth parents' following the lead during an hour session, whereas we would expect ABC coaches to make one comment per minute during a home visit. The point is to place foster parents in a supportive role to birth parents while also having them provide useful scaffolding to birth parents.

Fostering Relationships: April and Lee

April, Lee's foster mother, completed the training for Fostering Relationships. She had practiced making in-the-moment comments in the training session but was nervous as she took Lee to the visitation. She wasn't confident in her ability to make comments, she thought she might sound strange or insincere, and she worried that Lee's birth mother would be hostile in response. In addition, she had never met Loretta, Lee's birth mother, and expected that to be hard. It was a relief for her to take Lee to visitation, though, because she hated putting him in the van, knowing how upset it made him. She had to arrange for a babysitter for her older child, but it was worth it. Hearing in training that Loretta would also likely be nervous had helped take her mind off her own anxiety.

Loretta had dreaded the visitation when she heard that April would be there. She thought that April disliked her and looked down on her. In addition, she felt threatened by the idea of seeing her son with his foster parent. The mentoring session helped calm her down though. The mentor's explanation that, at this age, children may act as though they don't remember their parents from one week to the next had helped. Also, the tools the mentor gave her, showing videos of a parent following the lead and not following the lead, gave her a sense of having a strategy for playing with her child during the visit. She'd felt nervous that she'd have to play "just right," but she now saw that she didn't need to teach him or come up with a fun activity during the visit; she just needed to follow his lead.

Lee and April were already in the visitation room when Loretta came in from her meeting with the Fostering Relationships mentor. To Loretta's surprise, April greeted her warmly. Lee clung to April for a minute and April allowed it. Loretta wanted to rush toward Lee and pick him up, but she remembered the mentor's advice that it might overwhelm him. Instead, she overrode her desire to pick him up, knelt down near him, smiled, and waved. Then April said to Lee, "Why don't you check out the toys." Lee held on a minute longer and then ventured out. When Lee picked up a ball, Loretta said, "Hey, you got the ball!" April smiled and said, "Look what you just did. You're doing something that I just learned about in a foster parent training. You're following his lead." Loretta kept her head down and didn't reply. April was worried that she had annoyed her and let the next thing she noticed go by without a comment.

But then Lee pushed a plastic cow along the ground and Loretta said, "Mooo," and Lee looked up with a smile. April said, "Wow, he pushed his cow and you said moo! And what a smile on his face!" Loretta looked at Lee and then looked up at April with a shy smile herself. Some of April's comments weren't on the topic of following the lead. For example, she commented that Lee surely seemed to like yogurt and asked Loretta if he had a favorite flavor. But all of her comments were positive or were questions about Lee, and the tension in the room dissipated quickly. The play between Loretta and Lee seemed almost effortless. Once Loretta asked for a hug and Lee looked away, but otherwise, all went very smoothly.

Loretta came out of the session shocked at how well it had gone. Her first comment to her case worker was, "I think she likes me." April was also thrilled with how well the session had gone. Lee seemed himself afterward—there was not even a trace of the dysregulation he usually showed after coming home from visits in the van.

Subsequent sessions went well too. Loretta came every session and began to look to April for advice. She began to follow Lee's lead more frequently and found that Lee brought toys to her. At the start of the third session, Lee waved and smiled at her and even reached up for a hug. After the sixth session, Lee was moved from April's care to the care of a maternal grandmother. April stayed in touch with Loretta through texting and Facebook. She invited Lee, Loretta, and Loretta's mother over for a late celebration of Lee's birthday. Fostering Relationships had helped April and Loretta to forge a relationship that led to ongoing support and involvement.

Sometimes birth parents have taken longer to warm up to the foster parent than described for Loretta. For example, in the first session, a birth father reacted somewhat angrily to comments. The foster parent gently continued to comment, and by the third session, he became friendly and engaged with the foster parent. Also, foster parents are often not as adept at making comments as seen here with April. We continue to work on ways to facilitate comfort with and use of comments by foster parents, such as voice or text phone consultations between sessions.

INTERVENTION EFFECTS
OF FOSTERING RELATIONSHIPS

We have conducted a small pilot study on the effects of Fostering Relationships and have feasibility pilots ongoing across the country. In our pilot study, families were randomly assigned to receive Fostering Relationships or were placed on a waitlist. Although foster parents at this agency seldom accompany their children to visitation, we required them to do so in the waitlist control condition to allow us to examine the effects of the Fostering Relationship intervention very specifically. If we found differential effects of the intervention, we wanted to know that effects resulted from the Fostering Relationships intervention itself and not from the foster parent accompanying the child to visitation.

Following the Lead during Sessions

We conducted single-subject analyses to test whether parents followed their children's lead across the sessions. Participants included 11 foster children and their birth and foster parents. Figure 13.1 shows changes in following the lead (and not following the lead) behaviors across the five sessions for birth parents who received Fostering Relationships (including Loretta) and birth parents in the control group. At Session 1, parents in both groups followed their child's lead about as often as they failed to follow the lead. But for the Fostering Relationships group, there was a marked change after Session 1. In Sessions 2 through 5, Loretta and other parents receiving Fostering Relationships often followed their children's lead, rarely directing, teaching, or ignoring them. Overall, six out of seven Fostering Relationships families, and one out of four control families, demonstrated significantly

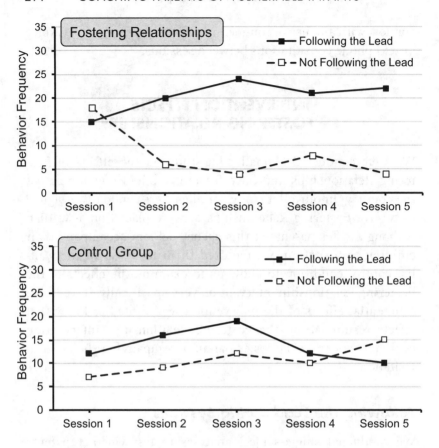

FIGURE 13.1. Changes in following the lead across sessions of Fostering Relationships. Data from Burtch, Roben, and Dozier (2018).

more following-the-lead behaviors than not following across the five sessions.

Sensitivity Assessment

After completion of Session 5, birth parents and foster parents each separately completed a semistructured sensitivity assessment with their children. Parents were provided with several toys and instructed to interact with their children as they normally would, with the interaction filmed for 7 minutes. We used the same coding system for this sensitivity assessment that we use when coding parent behavior in ABC cases (NICHD Early Child Care Research Network, 1999, 2003). Birth parents who completed Fostering Relationships were rated higher in sensitivity than the control group (3.71 vs. 2.0, on a scale from 1 to 5, which represents a large effect).

Birth Parent Attendance

All birth parents in the Fostering Relationships group attended all five sessions, whereas one of four parents in the control group discontinued visitation altogether after the second visit and a second attended only sporadically. We expect that better attendance by birth parents could be due to feeling more support from foster parents, having a better understanding of why their children may turn away initially, and feeling greater efficacy during play.

SUMMARY

Fostering Relationships shares several key aspects with ABC, although its mode of delivery is quite different. The first characteristic shared is the recognition that children who have experienced adversity may not always reach out to caregivers directly and be soothed, and this behavior can be offputting to caregivers. Second, it shares an emphasis on following the child's lead as a way to engage the child. And third, it shares an emphasis on commenting in-the-moment to build rapport and support parents' behaviors. We have been cautious about making adaptations to the ABC model, but the Fostering Relationships adaptation seemed important and apropos.

CHAPTER 14

Future Directions

In this chapter, we consider where the future may take us. ABC has emerged as a powerfully effective brief intervention that can be disseminated with fidelity. This evidence of effectiveness creates exciting opportunities for the future but also makes it important that we are cautious. Considering how to (and whether to) scale the intervention up is vital. ABC is being implemented in 18 states and eight countries, but is reaching only a small fraction of the parents who could benefit. Can it be scaled up while maintaining our approach to ensuring that it is implemented with fidelity? Or does scaling up entail the cost of letting go of the control we have maintained over fidelity monitoring? Second, does the intervention need to be adapted to individual needs? Although the intervention has been shown to enhance parent and child functioning when considering effects at the group level, there are likely moderators of treatment effectiveness—or factors that affect whether specific individuals benefit more or less. In this context, we consider whether important individual differences (e.g., substance use, being a teen parent) may moderate or affect whether the intervention has different effects for different individuals. And we discuss whether adaptations or augmentations to the intervention might be appropriate. We then consider extending or adapting the intervention to other populations. To this point, we have implemented the intervention in upper-middle- and upper-income countries, but we are only beginning

216

to implement it in lower- or lower-middle-income countries. The need is clearly great, making this an important issue. Populations such as Syrian refugee communities in Turkey and teen mothers in Guatemala are among those we are considering. We also discuss our choice not to extend the intervention to other contexts such as child care, congregate care (group residential care), and orphanage care.

SCALING INTERVENTION UP

We discussed some of the challenges involved in dissemination in Chapter 10. In thinking about what is involved in scaling up fully, some of the issues remain the same, but the scale is different.

Interventions that do not require supervision beyond the initial training, or interventions for which supervision is limited, can scale up more readily than an intervention such as ABC. Supervision needs in ABC are high: One PhD-level supervisor and one staff-level supervisor can together supervise about 25–30 parent coaches annually, with the PhD providing general clinical supervision in small groups and the staff member providing individual fidelity-focused supervision. It is easy to see how these supervisory demands would become unwieldy if we were training and supervising thousands of parent coaches rather than hundreds. The question, of course, is how to handle this challenge. Should we not try to scale up fully, or should we develop alternative strategies for supervision?

CPP is an intervention with a relatively heavy supervision load (although not as heavy as ABC) that has been disseminated more widely than ABC. Similarly, Parent–Child Interaction Therapy (not discussed in this book because it was developed for older children with behavior problems) has fidelity criteria similar to ABC's and relatively heavy supervision, yet it is implemented widely. Both of these models have developed systems of training master trainers such that the master trainers can train and supervise others. Without such a system, the ABC intervention will be necessarily limited in its reach.

We have experimented with training supervisors in other places, and just as with our experience with initial implementation challenges, we learned what not to do. Agencies often approach us with particular staff in mind for training as supervisors. These are typically individuals who fill supervisory roles at the organizations or who have higher educational levels or more experience than others. However, we have often found that it is critical that supervisors be selected from among those who emerge as the star parent coaches after training and supervision, and they may or may not be those who were originally in supervisory roles. When someone is chosen to be a supervisor without showing particular skill as a parent coach, the individual is sometimes poorly equipped to supervise on ABC. Therefore, a somewhat extended process is involved before we can indicate to agencies who we are recommending to fill supervisory roles. We are moving in the direction of training others to supervise, which is a critical next step for us.

OPTIMIZING INTERVENTION

Consider the examples of Crystal and Claudette described earlier. Crystal had many challenges, including intermittent homelessness, a partner who physically abused her, and struggles with substance use. She had not had a consistently available attachment figure as she was growing up. She needed help with all three intervention targets. She was not nurturing (e.g., she told her child not to be a baby if he cried), did not follow her child's lead, and was frightening to her child. In contrast, Claudette had difficult experiences as a child but also had a very loving, available grandmother. She had come away with a real valuing of a nurturing relationship with her own child. She was reassuring to her child when he was distressed and did not behave in frightening ways. Where she had trouble was following her child's lead. She was eager that her child become "smart," and she used every opportunity to teach, to ask questions, to push. In the process, she was not following her child's lead at all. Her child quickly lost focus in play interactions and sometimes showed frustration with his mother's questions.

We implemented the 10-session ABC intervention with both of these mothers, and single subject-level outcomes suggested that the intervention had been useful to both. But perhaps tailoring was warranted. Crystal could possibly use more support following the end of the 10 sessions. Although she had made substantial changes from the initial session to Session 10, her sensitivity and nurturance broke down at times. At the other extreme, Claudette did not really need the emphasis on nurturance or frightening behavior. Hearing about how well she was nurturing her child may have helped her to buy into following the lead, but there may have been a more efficient path for her.

At this point, we have empirical evidence supporting the efficacy of the full 10-session intervention. We do not have evidence, and have not yet piloted, a more tailored approach to individual needs. This approach of "personalized medicine" is gaining attention in the delivery of both health and mental health services. Testing an individualized (or modular) approach will be an important next step. Although intuitively it makes sense that a briefer version for one parent and a more intensive approach for another would be optimal, testing that approach is vital as opposed to individualizing without empirical evidence. Of course, Claudette might fail to show the benefits of ABC if the focus on following the lead is not embedded with other content. And Crystal might not show enhanced benefit from a longer sequence of sessions than the standard 10 sessions. For example, parent coaches may not work with the same urgency in an intervention that they know can be extended beyond 10 sessions as they do when they know their time is limited.

We can envision several ways to tailor the intervention to individual needs. A personalized approach could involve weekly assessments to determine whether parents show that they have met the criteria for engaging in sensitive and nurturing behavior and avoiding frightening behavior. There are many opportunities for following the lead in a relatively brief period of time (e.g., 5 minutes), but typically there are fewer opportunities for nurturance, and harsh or frightening behavior has a low base rate. Therefore, whereas assessing sensitivity is not difficult to accomplish on a weekly basis, assessing nurturance and frightening behavior is more difficult. Parent coaches could possibly become reliable assessors of nurturing and frightening behavior, such that these behaviors could be assessed on a weekly basis as well. Finding that parents had met criteria would not be enough. Rather, establishing an evidence base demonstrating that meeting criteria was associated with positive long-term outcomes would be critical.

A second approach would be to identify trajectories of change based on individual differences, such as risk, mental health problems, substance abuse problems, or parenting skills. For example, high-risk parents such as Crystal might show better outcomes when completing an enhanced version of ABC (e.g., the 10 sessions augmented by six additional sessions) than when completing an abbreviated version (e.g., three sessions) or the standard ABC (e.g., 10 sessions). Relatively low-risk parents such as Claudette might show similar outcomes whether they experience the abbreviated intervention or the standard ABC. Thus, based on initial characteristics, parents could be assigned to varying levels of ABC.

MODERATING VARIABLES

We have implemented ABC with parents who represent a wide range with regard to risk—parents who differ with respect to income, educational level, mental health problems, substance abuse problems, and parenting skills. ABC has been effective with parents who have low levels of resources and high risk, and with parents who have high levels of resources and low risk. At this point, we have not had success in identifying moderating variables—that is, individual differences that moderate the intervention's effectiveness. That is good news in suggesting that the intervention works well for everyone. But it is not an altogether satisfying conclusion. It seems likely that individual-difference variables are important to consider in augmenting or abbreviating the intervention, in prioritizing the intervention for some parents in the case of limited resources, or in combining with other services. Although we do not have data to support our speculation, we consider several of these possibilities.

Mental Health Issues

In our sample of CPS-involved parents, parents had elevated levels of depression, anxiety, and posttraumatic stress disorder. At Power of Two, approximately 40% of Brownsville parents enrolling in ABC reported elevated levels of depression at baseline.

Anecdotally, we have seen shifts in parents' moods *within* ABC sessions. Recall how Lenixia, a mother receiving ABC through Power of Two while living in a family shelter in Brownsville, could be pulled out of a depressed mood by seeing how Shafique lit up when she followed his lead for a few minutes. We have seen similar shifts with other parents.

Shanice

Shanice stands out as an example of a parent who often presented with blunted affect at the beginning of most sessions but showed a remarkable ability to light up in response to her son, Josiah. In Session 3, for example, the parent coach showed up and found Shanice sitting on her front porch. Shanice said she wasn't feeling well and she appeared depressed; she shared that she had had a fight with the child's father, was stressed about whether she could keep living with him, and had recently found out she was pregnant. Nevertheless, she agreed to do the session. The parent coach set up her camera on the porch and dumped out some toys. Josiah found a spoon and plate among the toys and handed them to his mom, saying, "Here you go!" Shanice took the toys, pretended to eat from the plate, said "All done!," and smiled at Josiah. "Nice responding to him and following his lead," said the parent coach, as Josiah smiled back at his mom as he dug in the pile of toys for something else to show her. "Did you see how he looked at you? He was so happy to see that delight from you!" A few min-utes later, Josiah tripped on the porch and lay flat on the floor, motionless. He didn't signal that he was upset, but Shanice got out of her chair, picked him up, and held him close. "That's per-fect, go right over to him—yes, pick him right up! All he needed was a hug and kiss, and knowing mom is there for him." Shanice looked like a different person than she had at the beginning of the session—she looked bright, open, and lively. Moments of nurtur-ance and following the lead (with delight) occurred frequently in each session, giving her many opportunities for getting back on her feet. What seemed important about Shanice and Lenixia, and other parents like them, is that interactions with their children and positive feedback from their coaches were powerful enough to pull them out of what appeared to be a depressed mood.

Sadie

Other parents, however, have shown signs of depression and appeared disengaged, flat, and unresponsive to their children and to parent-coach feedback during sessions. One example was Sadie, a second mother living in a motel room, this time with her husband and four children. She was able to engage with her baby but was listless and seemingly uninterested in the older children. We saw systematic change in Sadie's sensitivity over time, but her depression remained noticeable. When we returned for follow-up, we were concerned that her depression was likely interfering with her ability to stay engaged with her children.

Depression has been found to be a significant moderator of other home-visiting programs' effectiveness. For example, in a study of the Healthy Families America program, Anne Duggan and colleagues found that mothers' baseline depression and attach-ment anxiety interacted to predict the magnitude of changes in maternal sensitivity. Among nondepressed mothers, the interven-tion was effective, on average, with significant increases in mater-nal sensitivity, regardless of mothers' attachment anxiety. Among depressed mothers, however, the intervention was effective only if attachment anxiety was low (Duggan, Berlin, Cassidy, Burrell, &

Tandon, 2009). Thus, although we have no evidence that maternal depression influences the effectiveness of ABC, mental health may be an important factor to consider in future studies.

Substance Use

Substance use is one factor that could moderate the effectiveness of ABC. We have examined mothers' self-report of substance use and have not found evidence that mothers who report that they are using illicit substances benefit less from ABC than do other mothers. We are aware, however, that we are limited in our measurement of substance abuse problems. Parents reported their substance use on a self-report inventory. Oliveros and Kaufman (2011) reported that 60–70% of parents with substantiated maltreatment allegations have diagnosable substance abuse problems, which is a substantially higher rate than reported by our parents. Parents who are being monitored by the child welfare system may be motivated *not* to report substance use, so we cannot be confident in our null effects regarding substance use as a moderator.

Indeed, there are reasons to wonder whether substance-using parents may be less responsive to the intervention than other parents. Substance use and addiction can alter reward circuitry in the brain, affecting regions and processes known to be critical for parenting. For example, in an fMRI study of mothers receiving inpatient treatment for substance addiction, Kim and colleagues (2017) found reduced activation in reward regions of the brain when mothers viewed the emotional faces of their own babies relative to the faces of unfamiliar babies. Compared with non-substance-using mothers, substance-using mothers have also been found to show reduced activation to infant cries in brain regions implicated in reward and motivation, emotional processing, and auditory sensory processing (Landi et al., 2011). Such deficits in neural processing, resulting from substance abuse, may make substance-using parents less responsive during interactions with their infants than non-substance-using mothers.

Although we had limited data to examine substance abuse as a moderating factor of ABC's effectiveness, Lisa Berlin and colleagues conducted a pilot study examining the efficacy of ABC for 21 new mothers and their infants living together in a residential substance abuse treatment center. Mothers were receiving comprehensive services, including group therapy, individual counseling for substance abuse problems and other mental health issues, and case management. For their study, mothers were randomly assigned to receive ABC or a control intervention, the "Book-of-the-Week" program. For the control intervention, mothers received 10 brief weekly home visits, during which the clinician checked in to see how they were doing and gave the mothers a developmentally appropriate book. In this sample of substance-abusing mothers, ABC had a medium-to-large effect on maternal sensitivity (Berlin, Shanahan, & Carmody, 2014). Though limited by a small sample size, this study provides evidence that ABC is effective among mothers with histories of substance abuse.

Although we do not have empirical evidence that ABC is less effective with mothers abusing substances than with others, we have examples of times when the program was ineffective with some and not with others.

Gloria

Gloria was one of the first mothers with whom we implemented ABC. She lived with her two youngest children but had lost custody of her older children some years earlier. During our time working with her, her two remaining children were removed from her custody and returned twice.

Gloria was likely using heroin and perhaps other street drugs, although she did not admit use on self-report inventories. Her behavior was highly inconsistent from one week to another. In one session, she nodded off repeatedly, and in another she was barely dressed and highly dysregulated (e.g., yelling at the kids loudly), whereas in others, she was responsive to the parent coach and to her children. The progress made in one session seemed to have little bearing on where she would be in the following session. The parent coach tried a variety of approaches to engage Gloria in the sessions, but when she was high, things did not stick—and she was often high. In the sensitivity assessments conducted before and after the intervention, she was rated 1.5 on the 5-point scale (very insensitive). Her son was classified as having a disorganized attachment to her, showing odd movements followed by aimless wandering upon his reunion with her. He was behaviorally dysregulated in problem-solving tasks as a 3-year-old. Clearly, this case was a treatment failure. ABC did not change Gloria's behavior, and her child did not show gains. However, the treatment failure in this case illustrates the point that ABC is not effective for all parents, whether substance-using or not. And we reiterate that our evidence suggests that ABC is as effective among substance-using parents as among other parents.

Marissa

Marissa was addicted to methadone when her parent coach first met with her. She was jumpy and inattentive much of the time. She had three children, all of whom showed problems regulating their behavior. The middle child cried during at least half of the first five sessions, and the oldest child pushed the limits with one thing and then another. Marissa was problematic with regard to all intervention targets: She didn't follow her children's lead, didn't nurture consistently when her children were distressed, and was erratic in ways that frightened them. Her parent coach was pessimistic that she was influencing Marissa because Marissa's life remained highly chaotic and she remained agitated. Rather than focus attention on the one child in the ABC age range (the youngest of the three), she focused on helping Marissa in following the lead and nurturing all three children.

At least half of the sessions had to be rescheduled because Marissa and her children were not home at the agreed-upon time. Her parent coach tried to set up additional appointments the same week to avoid extended periods between sessions. By Session 7, as she prepared for the first "voices from the past" session, the parent coach found herself unsure as to which target she should focus on because Marissa needed to improve with regard to all three targets. Her parent coach managed to address all three, starting with frightening behavior. Whereas there is an "aha" moment for some parents, there was no such noticeable time for Marissa. But she changed nonetheless, at least in some ways. She noticed and commented on what the children were doing enough so that the oldest child settled down. Her son remained very rambunctious but became much less intense in seeking attention than he had been before. Marissa began to soothe her children at least some of the time when they were distressed. Because she was enrolled in a study in which we assessed sensitivity for each session, we could examine the course of her behavior over time. We saw that she behaved in largely insensitive ways through about Session 5 and then showed steady improvement throughout the remaining sessions. By the end of the 10 sessions, she was in the sensitive range. When assessed in the Strange Situation, her youngest was classified as having a secure attachment.

We felt that Marissa might benefit from an augmented ABC—that several more sessions could help further consolidate her gains. This is an empirical question, however, and one that we cannot answer at this point. Alternatively, an integrated ABC/substance abuse treatment could be powerful for her. Intervening with both parenting and substance abuse simultaneously could have synergistic effects, with motivation and ability to change parenting and gain control of substance use increasing through hormonal and self-regulatory mechanisms.

OPTIONS FOR ABC IN THE CONTEXT OF OTHER IDENTIFIED NEEDS

Implementing with Other Interventions

We recognize that parents often have a host of problems in addition to the need for help with sensitive parenting. They may have unstable financial and housing situations, mental health problems, substance abuse problems, and homes or environments that are unsafe for children. Our approach has been to focus on parenting with the belief that parental sensitivity can change children's lives, even if parents continue to have many other problems. But a coordinated effort may also make sense.

The availability of federal funding for home-visiting programs through MIECHV gives impetus to the need for a coordinated effort. One possibility suggested by the Home Visiting Applied Research Collaborative (HARC), funded to develop a research agenda to examine the impact of home-visiting programs, is to develop a precision medicine approach to home visiting. Parents could be assessed for need (i.e., need for help with sensitive parenting, safety, depression, substance use, housing) and be provided the service(s) for the identified need(s). For example, if a parent was identified as insensitive in interactions with children (through a 7-minute video-recorded observation), the parent would be referred to ABC; if also assessed as having an unsafe home, the parent would also be referred to SafeCare (a MIECHV-approved evidence-based program focused on safety) and also be referred for cognitive-behavioral therapy if identified as depressed.

Modified ABC

An alternative to implementing ABC as one of several modular interventions delivered to parents is to incorporate interventions that address other issues into the implementation of ABC. We are currently studying this idea with modified ABC (mABC), a version of ABC adapted for opioid-dependent mothers. The babies of opioid-dependent mothers are often born dependent on opioids themselves and are therefore dysregulated both biologically and behaviorally. Nurturing care and sensitive care are important for these newborns. In addition, several specific practices have been shown to enhance regulation and to reduce both length of time in the hospital and reliance on medication for babies. The practices, endorsed by a consensus panel (Reddy, Davis, Ren, & Green, 2017), include breastfeeding, kangaroo care (skin-to-skin contact), swaddling, and reduced stimulation.

ABC typically begins at about 6 months at the earliest because the intervention is so dependent on having an awake, behaving infant to allow practice of target behaviors. Given the challenges of dysregulation seen in the neonatal period, however, we identify opioid-dependent mothers prenatally. Indeed, helping prepare mothers to breastfeed and to engage in kangaroo care needs to begin prenatally. Therefore, mABC begins with two prenatal sessions that help mothers practice (with an infant simulator doll) nurturing care and swaddling, help them think through barriers to breastfeeding and kangaroo care, and help them anticipate the possibility that they may feel rejected by their infant if they cannot effectively soothe him or her. Postnatal sessions continue this hybrid of the opioid-specific and ABC foci, with ABC as the primary focus. We have extended the usual 10 sessions to 14 to allow extra time for the additional components. No results are available at this point, but we are hopeful that mABC will prove useful for this high-risk population of mothers and infants.

EXTENDING ABC TO OTHER CONTEXTS

As we have described in earlier chapters, we have extended the ABC intervention to some populations (toddlers, parents adopting internationally) and borrowed concepts for use in visitation. We have been invited to extend or adapt ABC to other contexts, such as intervening in groups rather than individually and intervening in the child-care setting and orphanage care. We approach extensions cautiously.

Group Context

Several interventions for high-risk parents are implemented in group contexts, including COS (Powell et al., 2016) and GABI (Steele et al., 2018). These interventions use the group to support parents' acknowledging and confronting challenging issues.

Intervening in the group context has important benefits. In the case of ABC, we can imagine that parents might find it useful to observe other parents behaving in ways that are sensitive or nurturing (or ways that are *not* sensitive or nurturing), to hear of other parents' struggles with the issues as they try to change their behaviors, and to receive support from other parents for their parenting and to provide support to others. Nonetheless, we feel we would lose too much if we implemented in a group context. Most importantly, we would lose the opportunity for parents to practice over and over again following their children's lead and nurturing their children while receiving feedback and scaffolding from the parent coach. Time for such targeted support would be much diluted in a group. The intervention could not occur in the mother's home, where she could learn the skills in the context where skills would most often be used (thus maximizing generalizability). And only those parents who could make it to a group meeting would receive the intervention. Many parents lead such disorganized lives that they would never or rarely make it to another facility.

Child Care

Colleagues have asked us about adapting ABC for use with child-care workers. We agree that the concepts of nurturing, following the lead, and not frightening the child are critical to the work of child-care workers. However, given that the ABC intervention is designed to work with individual families in their homes, we think it is not optimally suited to be adapted for work with child-care workers. The specific elements of ABC that make it work so effectively with individual families render it not as applicable to child-care workers. In-the-moment comments, which work so well in directing parents' attention to their own behaviors that are relevant to intervention targets, are not well suited to the child-care context. These are really dyadic comments (or family-level comments) that are part of a conversation.

Congregate Care and Orphanage Care

Based on the preponderance of evidence, we are convinced that children are best reared in homes by parents. When birth parents are not able to provide safe homes, foster care or adoptive care is the best option. With orphanage or institutional care, children are housed in a relatively large institutional setting. Staff members work shifts, so children do not consistently have the same caregivers. Thus, children may see many caregivers in a day, with no constant figure to whom the child can develop an attachment. Although virtually all infants raised by their parents show a clear attachment to their parents, Carlson and colleagues found that most children in orphanage care showed some variant of a limited attachment (Carlson, Hostinar, Mliner, & Gunnar, 2014; Zeanah et al., 2005).

In many cases, the child-to-caregiver ratio is quite high in orphanage care. This reality, combined with the philosophy of the setting, often leads to a host of practices that work well for minimizing the time required to care for children but are at odds with children's developmental needs. Among these practices are keeping children on a schedule for eating, sleeping, toileting, and playing, rather than following children's individual needs. Other practices include propping bottles up in the children's cribs so that the children do not need to be held while being fed. Children often spend extended periods of time alone in their cribs. In some facilities, the bars on cribs are covered to prevent children from seeing other children in nearby cribs.

Although large residential care is not used for young children in the United States (or used only rarely), congregate care sometimes is. Congregate care involves placement of children in relatively small group homes or shelters. In some instances, these resemble larger institutions in terms of staff members who work shifts, activities governed by set schedules rather than individual child needs, and children lacking attachment figures. In other instances, caregivers live with the children, and the environment looks somewhat more homelike. Nonetheless, even when caregivers live with children, we have found that the caregivers do not invest in them at the same level as foster parents (Lo et al., 2015). Although group care of infants and young children is often prohibited because of its deleterious consequences, congregate care continues to exist in the United States, and it is sometimes used for young children. In particular, young children who are part of sibling groups may be placed together in congregate care.

We have been invited to adapt the ABC intervention for use in congregate and institutional care many times, but we have steadfastly refused. We do not want to appear to condone the use of group care (congregate care or larger orphanages) through having ABC be part of what happens there. We consider group care of any size to be at odds with children's needs. (See Dozier et al., 2012, for a fuller discussion of these issues.)

IMPLEMENTING ABC IN OTHER CULTURES

Adapting to Cultural Context

When we implement the intervention in other cultures, people often ask whether the intervention may be at odds with the culture in which we are implementing. To some extent, challenging customary ways of parenting is the point. We want to help parents become more sensitive and nurturing even if sensitive, nurturing care is not in line with cultural expectations. We argue that the parental behaviors we are targeting are universal; these behaviors will enhance children's behavioral and self-regulatory capabilities in any culture.

We therefore do not adapt the major tenets of the intervention to different cultures. We do, however, present the message somewhat differently to make it attractive to people whose cultures may prioritize different values. For example, a parent living in Philadelphia worries that soothing her distressed child may not prepare her child for a "tough world." Her parent coach may tell her that her child will learn to be more independent and better equipped to face later challenges if she does in fact soothe him than if she does not. Another mother, a Guatemalan immigrant, raises the concern that parents should not follow their children's lead in her culture because people will think they are pushovers. As she is encouraged to follow her child's lead even though it doesn't fit with cultural norms, she is told that she is helping the child develop better behavioral control, which *is* a value in her culture. In Hawaii, parent coaches often use the example of a mythical figure that parents sometimes use to threaten their children when their children misbehave, helping parents recall their own fear of the figure when they were children. In Germany, the terminology for following the lead is altered because the connotation there is not what we intend when translated directly. In each case, the basic principles remain the same even though certain more superficial aspects are allowed to vary.

ETHAN

Ethan, an energetic 19-month-old, dumps out a bin of toy cars on the floor. He picks up his favorite red car and drives it along the edge of the couch, up his grandmother's leg, and then parks it on her lap. Grandma responds, "What a fast car you've got!" Ethan smiles and says, "Go go go!" He grabs two more cars, one in each hand, and zooms them along the imaginary road, parking them again in his grandma's lap as she makes noises to follow his game: "Vroom vroom! Beep beep! Make way for Ethan!"

Just as Ethan picks up the next car, the door opens and it's Ethan's dad, James. Ethan runs to him with his arms up. James scoops him up, gives him a hug, and says, "I see you're making Grandma into a parking lot again!" Back to his pile of cars, Ethan grabs a car for dad and hands it to him. James, now down on the floor, drives his car behind Ethan, expertly following his lead.

Suddenly a police car passes outside, its siren jarring. Ethan startles and looks immediately at James. "That scared you, didn't it?," James remarks as he reaches out and rubs Ethan's back, "Daddy's here, it's OK, buddy." Quickly reassured, Ethan resumes driving, with James close behind.

James doesn't remember that his mother received ABC when he was a baby. Sonya, now a grandmother, has some vivid memories of the 10 weeks with Gabriella nearly 25 years ago, but much of it is foggy. And yet, Sonya's and James's interactions with Ethan are rich with examples of following the lead, delight, and nurturance.

We haven't followed James and children who received ABC into adulthood—at least not yet. Maybe it is overly optimistic to think that the effects of ABC could extend to the next generation—but maybe not. Sonya provided James with a very different childhood than she had experienced herself, potentially disrupting the intergenerational cycle of toxic stress. James was exposed to significant stressors—poverty, instability, and seeing his mother go through periods of depression and violent relationships. But as a sensitive parent most of the time, Sonya buffered him from many of those threats. After ABC, we saw James develop a secure attachment, strong executive functioning, and good regulation of emotions—setting him up to face the challenges of the world. And maybe that foundation will also allow him be that same source of protection for Ethan as Sonya was for him.

SUMMARY

ABC has proven to be a remarkably powerful intervention. Developed initially for parents of foster infants, ABC was subsequently adapted for neglecting birth parents, then internationally adopting parents, and finally parents of toddlers. ABC's core mission is to help parents behave in sensitive and nurturing ways, with the different versions of the intervention retaining this focus. We were delighted to see the effects of the intervention emerge immediately following the intervention for such things as attachment quality and cortisol regulation. We have been both delighted and surprised to see the effects sustained through early and middle childhood. As preschoolers, children whose parents received the ABC intervention when they were infants show better behavioral regulation and continue to show better regulation of cortisol production than children whose parents received the control intervention. As middle school–aged children, children in the ABC group showed different and more optimal patterns of brain activation, as well as better regulation of cortisol production, and indicated that they could count on their parents for support more than children in the control group.

We look forward to figuring out ways to scale the intervention up so that it can be useful for more families and we look forward to adapting to the specific needs of different populations while retaining the focus on parental nurturance and sensitivity. The need for such an intervention is profound. Our data as well as our experiences with families like that of Sonya and James have convinced us that remarkable and lasting change is possible when parents become sensitive and responsive partners.

References

Adam, E. K., Quinn, M. E., Tavernier, R., McQuillan, M. T., Dahlke, K. A., & Gilbert, K. E. (2017). Diurnal cortisol slopes and mental and physical health outcomes: A systematic review and meta-analysis. *Psychoneuroendocrinology, 83,* 25–41.

Ainsworth, M. D. S., Blehar, M. C., Waters, E., & Wall, S. (1978) *Patterns of attachment: A psychological study of the Strange Situation.* Hillsdale, NJ: Erlbaum.

Allan, N. P., Hume, L. E., Allan, D. M., Farrington, A. L., & Lonigan, C. J. (2014). Relations between inhibitory control and the development of academic skills in preschool and kindergarten: A meta-analysis. *Developmental Psychology, 50,* 2368–2379.

American Psychiatric Association. (2000). *Diagnostic and statistical manual of mental disorders* (4th ed., text rev.). Washington, DC: Author.

American Psychiatric Association. (2013). *Diagnostic and statistical manual of mental disorders* (5th ed.). Arlington, VA: Author.

Ames, E. W. (1997). *The development of Romanian orphanage children adopted to Canada.* Ottawa, Ontario: Human Resources Development Canada.

Anda, R. F., Brown, D. W., Dube, S. R., Bremner, J. D., Felitti, V. J., & Giles, W. H. (2008). Adverse childhood experiences and chronic obstructive pulmonary disease in adults. *American Journal of Preventative Medicine, 34,* 396–403.

Anderson, S. E., Gooze, R. A., Lemeshow, S., & Whitaker, R. C. (2012). Quality of early maternal-child relationship and risk of adolescent obesity. *Pediatrics, 129,* 132–140.

Anderson, S., & Whitaker, R. (2011). Attachment security and obesity in US preschool-aged children. *Archives of Pediatrics and Adolescent Medicine, 165,* 235–242.

Bakermans-Kranenburg, M. J., van IJzendoorn, M. H., & Juffer, F. (2003). Less is more: Meta-analyses of sensitivity and attachment interventions in early childhood. *Psychological Bulletin, 129,* 195–215.

Bakermans-Kranenburg, M. J., van IJzendoorn, M. H., & Juffer, F. (2005). Disorganized infant attachment and preventive interventions: A review and meta-analysis. *Infant Mental Health Journal, 26,* 191–216.

Bandura, A. (1977). Self-efficacy: Toward a unifying theory of behavioral change. *Psychological Review, 84,* 191–215.

Bates, B., & Dozier, M. (1999). *Initial motivation for fostering unrelated to commitment.* Unpublished paper, University of Delaware.

Beauchaine, T. P. (2001). Vagal tone, development, and Gray's motivational theory: Toward an integrated model of autonomic nervous system functioning in psychopathology. *Development and Psychopathology, 13,* 183–214.

Beck, D. M., Schaefer, C., Pang, K., & Carlson, S. M. (2011). Executive function in preschool children: Test-retest reliability. *Journal of Cognition and Development, 12,* 169–193.

Beebe, B., Jaffe, J., Markese, S., Buck, K., Chen, H., Cohen, P., et al. (2010). The origins of 12-month attachment: A microanalysis of 4-month mother–infant interaction. *Attachment and Human Development, 12,* 3–141.

Bell, M. A. (1998). The ontogeny of the EEG during infancy and childhood: Implications for cognitive development. In B. Barreau (Ed.), *Neuroimaging in child neuropsychiatric disorders* (pp. 97–111). Berlin: Springer.

Berlin, L. J., Martoccio, T. L., & Jones Harden, B. (2018). Improving Early Head Start's impacts on parenting through atachment-based intervention: A randomized controlled trial. *Developmental Psychology.* [Epub ahead of print]

Berlin, L. J., Shanahan, M., & Carmody, K. A. (2014). Promoting supporting parenting in new mothers with substance-use problems: A pilot randomized trial of residential treatment plus and attachment-based parenting program. *Infant Mental Health Journal, 35,* 81–85.

Bernard, K., Butzin-Dozier, Z., Rittenhouse, J., & Dozier, M. (2010). Cortisol production patterns in young children living with birth parents vs children placed in foster care following involvement of Child Protective Services. *Archives of Pediatrics and Adolescent Medicine, 164,* 438–443.

Bernard, K., Caron, E. B., Imrisek, S., Dash, A., Rodriguez, M., & Dozier, M. (2017). *Longitudinal examination of parent coach fidelity in community-based implementation efforts of Attachment and Biobehavioral Catch-Up.* Paper presented at the International Attachment Conference, London.

Bernard, K., & Dozier, M. (2010). Examining infants' cortisol responses to laboratory tasks among children varying in attachment disorganization: Stress reactivity or return to baseline? *Developmental Psychology, 46,* 1771–1778.

Bernard, K., & Dozier, M. (2011). This is my baby: Foster parent's feelings of commitment and displays of delight. *Infant Mental Health Journal, 32,* 251–262.

Bernard, K., Dozier, M., Bick, J., & Gordon, M. K. (2015). Intervening to enhance cortisol regulation among children at risk for neglect: Results of a randomized clinical trial. *Development and Psychopathology, 27,* 829–841.

Bernard, K., Dozier, M., Bick, J., Lewis-Morrarty, E., Lindheim, O., & Carlson, E. (2012). Enhancing attachment organization among maltreated children: Results of a randomized clinical trial. *Child Development, 83,* 623–636.

Bernard, K., Hostinar, C. E., & Dozier, M. (2015). Intervention effects on diurnal cortisol rhythms of child protective services-referred infants in early childhood: Preschool follow-up results of a randomized clinical trial. *JAMA Pediatrics, 169,* 112–119.

Bernard, K., Lee, A. H., & Dozier, M. (2017). Effects of the ABC Intervention on foster children's receptive vocabulary: Results from a randomized clinical trial. *Child Maltreatment, 22,* 174–179.

Bernard, K., Nissim, G., Vaccaro, S., Harris, J., & Lindhiem, O. (2018). Association between maternal depression and maternal sensitivity from birth to 12 months: A meta-analysis. *Attachment and Human Development.* [Epub ahead of print]

Bernard, K., Simons, R., & Dozier, M. (2015). Effects of an attachment-based intervention on child protective services–referred mothers' event-related potentials to children's emotions. *Child Development, 86,* 1673–1684.

Bernstein, V. J., Jeremy, R. K., & Marcus, J. (1986). Mother–infant interaction in multiproblem families: Finding those at risk. *Journal of the American Academy of Child Psychiatry, 25,* 631–640.

Bick, J., & Dozier, M. (2013). The effectiveness of an attachment-based intervention in promoting foster mothers' sensitivity toward foster infants. *Infant Mental Health Journal, 34,* 95–103.

Bick, J., Palmwood, E., Zajac, L., Simons, R., & Dozier, M. (2018). Early parenting intervention and adverse family environments affect neural function in middle childhood. *Biological Psychiatry.* [Epub ahead of print]

Blair, C., Ursache, A., Greenberg, M., Vernon-Feagans, L., & Family Life Project Investigators. (2015). Multiple aspects of self-regulation uniquely predict mathematics but not letter–word knowledge in the early elementary grades. *Developmental Psychology, 51,* 459–472.

Bowlby, J. (1982). *Attachment and loss: Vol. 1. Attachment.* New York: Basic Books. (Original work published 1969)

Bowlby, J. (1990). *Charles Darwin: A new life.* New York: Norton.

Boyle, M. H., & Pickles, A. (1997). Maternal depressive symptoms and ratings of emotional disorder symptoms in children and adolescents. *Child Psychology and Psychiatry and Allied Disciplines, 38,* 981–992.

Bretherton, I. (1985). Attachment theory: Retrospect and prospect. *Monographs of the Society for Research in Child Development, 50,* 3–35.

Bronfenbrenner, U. (1979). Contexts of child rearing: Problems and prospects. *American Psychologist, 34,* 844–850.

Bruce, J., Fisher, P. A., Pears, K. C., & Levine, S. (2009). Morning cortisol levels in preschool-aged foster children: Differential effects of maltreatment type. *Developmental Psychobiology, 51,* 14–23.

Burtch, E. N., Roben, C. K. P., & Dozier, M. (2018). *Preliminary results assessing the efficacy of Fostering Relationships, an intervention designed to enhance visitation.* Manuscript in preparation.

Carlson, E. A. (1998). A prospective longitudinal study of attachment disorganization/disorientation. *Child Development, 69,* 1107–1128.

Carlson, E. A., Hostinar, C., Mliner, S. B., & Gunnar, M. R. (2014). The emergence of attachment following early social deprivation. *Development and Psychopathology, 26,* 479–489.

Carlson, M., & Earls, F. (1997). Psychological and neuroendocrinological sequelae of early social deprivation in institutionalized children in Romania. In C. S. Carter, I. I. Lederhandler, & B. Kirkpatrick (Eds.), *The integrative neurobiology of affiliation* (pp. 419–428). New York: New York Academy of Sciences.

Caron, E. B., Bernard, K., & Dozier, M. (2016). In vivo feedback predicts behavioral change in the Attachment and Biobehavioral Catch-Up Intervention. *Journal of Clinical Child and Adolescent Psychology.* [Epub ahead of print]

Caron, E. B., Roben, C. K. P., Yarger, H., & Dozier, M. (2018). Novel methods for screening: Contributions from Attachment and Biobehavioral Catch-Up. *Prevention Science, 19,* 894–903.

Cassidy, J. (1994). Emotion regulation: Influences of attachment relationships. *Monographs of the Society for Research in Child Development, 59,* 228–283.

Centers for Disease Control and Prevention. (2014, March 27). CDC estimates 1 in 68 children has been identified with autism spectrum disorder. Retrieved from *www.cdc.gov/media/releases/2014/p0327-autism-spectrum-disorder.html.*

Chilcoat, H. D., & Breslau, N. (1997). Does psychiatric history bias mothers' reports?: An application of a new analytic approach. *Journal of the American Academy of Child and Adolescent Psychiatry, 36,* 971–979.

Chisholm, K. (1998). A three year follow-up of attachment and indiscriminate friendliness in children adopted from Romanian orphanages. *Child Development, 69,* 1092–1106.

Chisholm, K., Carter, M. C., Ames, E., & Morison, S. J. (1995). Attachment security and indiscriminately friendly behavior in children adopted from Romanian orphanages. *Development and Psychopathology, 7,* 283–294.

Cicchetti, D., Rogosch, F. A., & Toth, S. L. (2000). The efficacy of toddler–parent psychotherapy for fostering cognitive development in offspring. *Journal of Abnormal Child Psychology, 28,* 135–148.

Cicchetti, D., Rogosch, F. A., Toth, S. L., & Sturge-Apple, M. L. (2011). Normalizing the development of cortisol regulation in maltreated infants through preventive interventions. *Development and Psychopathology, 23,* 789–800.

Cicchetti, D., Toth, S. L., & Rogosch, F. A. (1999). The efficacy of toddler–parent psychotherapy to increase attachment security in offspring of depressed mothers. *Attachment and Human Development, 1,* 34–66.

Citizens' Committee for Children of New York. (2017). *From strengths to solutions: An asset-based approach to meeting community needs in Brownsville.* New York: Author.

Cohen, J. (1992). A power primer. *Psychological Bulletin, 112,* 155–159.

Cole, P. M., Tan, P. Z., Hall, S. E., Zhang, Y., Crnic, K. A., Blair, C. B., et al. (2011). Developmental changes in anger expression and attention focus: Learning to wait. *Developmental Psychology, 47,* 1078–1089.

Connell, C. M., Bergerson, N., Katz, K. H., Saunders, L., & Tebes, J. K. (2007). Re-referral to child protective services: The influence of child, family, and case characteristics on risk status. *Child Abuse and Neglect, 31,* 573–588.

Dash, A., Rodriguez, M., Imrisek, S., & Bernard, K. (2018). *ABC intervention for high-risk infants: Examining effects on maternal depression in the context of community-based implementation.* Poster presented at the International Congress of Infant Studies, Baltimore, MD.

Dickerson, S. S., & Kemeny, M. E. (2004). Acute stressors and cortisol responses: A theoretical integration and synthesis of laboratory research. *Psychological Bulletin, 130,* 355–391.

Donelan-McCall, N., & Olds, D. (2018). The Nurse–Family Partnership. In H. Steele & M. Steele (Eds.), *Handbook of attachment-based interventions* (pp. 79–103). New York: Guilford Press.

Dozier, M. (1990). Attachment organization and treatment use for adults with serious psychopathological disorders. *Development and Psychopathology, 2,* 47–60.

Dozier, M., & Attachment and Biobehavioral Catch-up Lab. (2015). *Attachment and Biobehavioral Catch-up.* Unpublished document, University of Delaware.

Dozier, M., & Bick, J. (2007). Changing caregivers: Coping with early adversity. *Psychiatric Annals, 37,* 411–415.

Dozier, M., Kaufman, J., Kobak, R., O'Connor, T. G., Sagi-Schwartz, A., Scott, S., et al. (2014). Consensus statement on group care for children and adolescents: A statement of policy of the American Orthopsychiatric Assocation. *American Journal of Orthopsychiatry, 84,* 219–225.

Dozier, M., & Lindhiem, O. (2006). This is my child: Differences among foster parents in commitment to their young children. *Child Maltreatment, 11,* 338–345.

Dozier, M., Lindhiem, O., Lewis, E., Bick, J., Bernard, K., & Peloso, E. (2009). Effects of a foster parent training program on young children's attachment behaviors: Preliminary evidence from a randomized clinical trial. *Child and Adolescent Social Work Journal, 26,* 321–332.

Dozier, M., Lomax, L., Tyrell, C. L., & Lee, S. (2001). The challenge of treatment for clients with dismissing states of mind. *Attachment and Human Development, 3,* 62–76.

Dozier, M., Manni, M., Gordon, M. K., Peloso, E., Gunnar, M. R., Stovall-McClough, K. C., et al. (2006). Foster children's diurnal production of cortisol: An exploratory study. *Child Maltreatment, 11,* 189–197.

Dozier, M., Peloso, E., Lewis, E., Laurenceau, J., & Levine, S. (2008). Effects of an attachment-based intervention on the cortisol production of infants and toddlers in foster care. *Development and Psychopathology, 20,* 845–859.

Dozier, M., Stovall, K. C., Albus, K. E., & Bates, B. (2001). Attachment for infants in foster care: The role of caregiver state of mind. *Child Development, 72,* 1467–1477.

Dozier, M., Zeanah, C. H., Wallin, A. R., & Shauffer, C. (2012). Institutional care for young children: Review of literature and policy implications. *Social Issues and Policy Review, 6,* 1–25.

Dube, S. R., Anda, R. F., Felitti, V. J., Croft, J. B., Edwards, V. J., & Giles, W. H. (2001). Growing up with parental alcohol abuse: Exposure to childhood abuse, neglect, and household dysfunction. *Child Abuse and Neglect, 25,* 1627–1640.

Dubowitz, H., Kim, J., Black, M., Weisbart, C., Semiatin, J., & Magder, L. (2011). Identifying children at high risk for a child maltreatment report. *Child Abuse and Neglect, 35,* 96–104.

Duggan, A. K., Berlin, L. J., Cassidy, J., Burrell, L., & Tandon, S. D. (2009). Examining maternal depression and attachment insecurity as moderators of the impacts of home visiting for at-risk mothers and infants. *Journal of Consulting and Clinical Psychology, 77,* 788–799.

Dunn, M. G., Tarter, R. E., Mezzich, A. C., Vanyukov, M., Krisci, L., & Kirillova, G. (2002). Origins and consequences of child neglect in substance abuse families. *Clinical Psychology Review, 22,* 1063–1090.

Durlak, J. A., & DuPre, E. P. (2008). Implementation matters: A review of research on the influence of implementation on program outcomes and the factors affecting implementation. *American Journal of Community Psychology, 41,* 327–350.

Egeland, B., Jacobvitz, D., & Sroufe, L. A. (1988). Breaking the cycle of abuse: Relationship predictions. *Child Development, 59,* 1080–1088.

Erera, P. I. (1997). Foster parents' attitudes toward birth parents and caseworkers: Implications for visitations. *Families in Society, 78,* 511–519.

Fabes, R. A., Leonard, S. A., Kupanoff, K., & Martin, C. L. (2001). Parental coping with children's negative emotions: Relations with children's emotional and social responding. *Child Development, 72,* 907–920.

Facompre, C., Bernard, K., & Waters, T. (2018). Effectiveness of interventions in preventing disorganized attachment: A meta-analysis. *Development and Psychopathology, 30,* 1–11.

Fearon, R. P., Bakermans-Kranenburg, M. J., van IJzendoorn, M. H., Lapsley, A. M., & Roisman, G. I. (2010). The significance of insecure attachment and disorganization in the development of children's externalizing behavior: A meta-analytic study. *Child Development, 81,* 435–456.

Felitti, V. J., Anda, R. F., Nordenberg, D., Williamson, D. F., Spitz, A. M., Edwards, V., et al. (1998). Relationship of childhood abuse and household dysfunction to many of the leading causes of death in adults: The Adverse Childhood Experiences (ACE) Study. *American Journal of Preventative Medicine, 14,* 245–258.

Field, T. (1984). Early interactions between infants and their postpartum depressed mothers. *Infant Behavior and Development, 7,* 517–522.

Fisher, L., Ames, E. W., Chisholm, K., & Savole, L. (1997). Problems reported by parents of Romanian orphans adopted to British Columbia. *International Journal of Behavioral Development, 20,* 67–82.

Fisher, P. A., Stoolmiller, M., Gunnar, M. R., & Burraston, B. O. (2007). Effects of a therapeutic intervention for foster preschoolers on diurnal cortisol activity. *Psychoneuroendocrinology, 32,* 892–905.

Francis, D. D., Diorio, J., Plotsky, P. M., & Meaney, M. J. (2002). Environmental enrichment reverses the effects of maternal separation on stress reactivity. *Journal of Neuroscience, 15,* 7840–7843.

Fuhs, M. W., Nesbitt, K. T., Farran, D. C., & Dong, N. (2014). Longitudinal associations between executive functioning and academic skills across content areas. *Developmental Psychology, 50,* 1698–1709.

Garnett, M., Bernard, K., Zajac, L., & Dozier, M. (2018). *Parental sensitivity mediates the effects of an attachment-based intervention on children's diurnal cortisol pattern in middle childhood.* Manuscript in preparation.

George, C., Kaplan, N., & Main, M. (1985). *Adult Attachment Interview protocol* (2nd ed.). Unpublished manuscript, University of California, Berkeley, CA.

Golinkoff, R. M., Can, D. D., Soderstrom, M., & Hirsh-Pasek, K. (2015). (Baby)talk to me: The social context of infant-directed speech and its effects on early language acquisition. *Current Directions in Psychological Science, 24,* 339–344.

Goodman, S. (2007). Depression in mothers. *Annual Review of Clinical Psychology, 3,* 107–135.

Green, J. G., McLaughlin, K. A., Berglund, P. A., Gruber, M. J., Sampson, N. A., Zaslavsky, A. M., et al. (2010). Childhood adversities and adult psychiatric disorders in the national comorbidity survey replication I: Associations with first onset of DSM-IV disorders. *Archives of General Psychiatry, 67,* 113–123.

Greenough, W. T., Black, J. E., & Wallace, C. S. (1987). Experience and brain development. *Child Development, 58,* 539–559.

Groark, C. J., Muhamedrahimov, R. J., Palmov, O. I., Nikiforova, N. V., & McCall, R. B. (2005). Improvements in early care in Russian orphanages and their relationship to observed behaviors. *Infant Mental Health Journal, 26,* 96–109.

Groh, A. M., Fearon, R. P., Bakermans-Kranenburg, M. J., van IJzendoorn, M. H., Steele, R. D., & Roisman, G. I. (2014). The significance of attachment security for children's social competence with peers: A meta-analytic study. *Attachment and Human Development, 16,* 103–136.

Groh, A. M., Roisman, G. I., van IJzendoorn, M. H., Bakermans-Kranenburg, M. J., & Fearon, R. P. (2012). The significance of insecure and disorganized attachment for children's internalizing symptoms: A meta-analytic study. *Child Development, 83,* 591–610.

Grossman, P., & Taylor, E. W. (2007). Toward understanding respiratory sinus arrhythmia: Relations to cardiac vagal tone, evolution and biobehavioral functions. *Biological Psychology, 74,* 263–285.

Gunnar, M. R., Bruce, J., & Grotevant, H. D. (2000). International adoption of institutionally reared children: Research and policy. *Development and Psychopathology, 12,* 677–693.

Gunnar, M. R., Morison, S. J., Chisholm, K., & Schuder, M. (2001). Salivary cortisol levels in children adopted from Romanian orphanages. *Development and Psychopathology, 13,* 611–628.

Gunnar, M. R., van Dulmen, M. H. M., & the International Adoption Project Team. (2007). Behavior problems in postinstitutionalized internationally adopted children. *Development and Psychopathology, 19,* 129–148.

Gustafsson, H. C., Coffman, J. L., & Cox, M. J. (2015). Intimate partner violence, maternal sensitive parenting behaviors, and children's executive functioning. *Psychology of Violence, 5,* 266–274.

Haga, S. M., Ulleberg, P., Slinning, K., Kraft, P., Steen, T. B., & Staff, A. (2012). A longitudinal study of postpartum depressive symptoms: Multilevel growth curve analyses of emotion regulation strategies, breastfeeding self-efficacy, and social support. *Archives of Women's Mental Health, 15,* 175–184.

Haight, W. L., Kagle, J. D., & Black, J. E. (2003). Understanding and supporting parent–child relationships during foster care visits: Attachment theory and research. *Social Work, 48,* 195–207.

Hajcak, G., Jackson, F., Ferri, J., & Weinberg, A. (2016). Emotion and attention. In L. F. Barrett, M. Lewis, & J. M. Haviland-Jones (Eds.), *Handbook of emotions* (4th ed., pp. 595–605). New York: Guilford Press.

Hart, B., & Risley, T. R. (1995). *Meaningful differences in the everyday experience of young American children.* Baltimore: Brookes.

Hazan, C., & Shaver, P. R. (1987). Romantic love conceptualized as an attachment process. *Journal of Personality and Social Psychology, 52,* 511–524.

Hazen, A. L., Connelly, C. D., Kelleher, K., Landsverk, J., & Barth, R. (2004). Intimate partner violence among female caregivers of children reported for child maltreatment. *Child Abuse and Neglect, 28,* 301–319.

Heckman, J. J. (2012). The developmental origins of health. *Health Economics, 21,* 24–29.

Hertsgaard, L., Gunnar, M., Erickson, M. F., & Nachmias, M. (1995). Adrenocortical responses to the Strange Situation in infants with disorganized/disoriented attachment relationships. *Child Development, 66,* 1100–1106.

Hesse, E., & Main, M. (2006). Frightened, threatening, and dissociative parental behavior in low-risk samples: Description, discussion, and interpretations. *Development and Psychopathology, 18,* 309–343.

Hirsh-Pasek, K., Adamson, L. N., Bakeman, R., Owen, M. T., Golinkoff, R. M., Pace, A., et al. (2015). The contribution of early communication quality to low-income children's language success. *Psychological Science, 26,* 1071–1083.

Hofer, M. A. (1994). Hidden regulators in attachment, separation, and loss. *Monographs of the Society for Research in Child Development, 59,* 192–207, 250–283.

Infurna, M. R., Reichl, C., Parzer, P., Schimmenti, A., Bifulco, A., & Kaess, M. (2016). Associations between depression and specific childhood experiences of abuse and neglect: A meta-analysis. *Journal of Affective Disorders, 190,* 47–55.

Jacobvitz, D., Leon, K., & Hazan, N. (2006). Does expectant mothers' unresolved trauma predict frightened/frightening maternal behavior?: Risk and protective factors. *Development and Psychopathology, 18,* 363–379.

Johnson, D. E. (2000). Medical and developmental sequelae of early childhood institutionalization in European adoptees. In C. A. Nelson (Ed.), *Minnesota Symposia on Child Psychology: Vol. 31. The effects of early adversity on neurobehavioral development* (pp. 113–162). Mahwah, NJ: Erlbaum.

Jones, J. D., Cassidy, J., & Shaver, P. R. (2015). Parents' self-reported attachment styles: A review of links with parenting behaviors, emotions, and cognitions. *Personality and Social Psychology Review, 19,* 14–76.

Juffer, F., Bakermans-Kranenburg, M. J., & van IJzendoorn, M. H. (2005). The importance of parenting in the development of disorganized attachment: Evidence from a preventive intervention study in adoptive families. *Journal of Child Psychology and Psychiatry, 46,* 263–274.

Juffer, F., Bakermans-Kranenburg, M. J., & van IJzendoorn, M. H. (2008). *Promoting positive parenting: An attachment-based intervention.* New York: Taylor & Francis Group/Erlbaum.

Juffer, F., Bakermans-Kranenburg, M. J., & van IJzendoorn, M. H. (2018). Video-feedback intervention to promote positive parenting and sensitive discipline: Development and meta-analytic evidence for its effectiveness. In H. Steele & M. Steele (Eds.), *Handbook of attachment-based interventions* (pp. 1–26). New York: Guilford Press.

Keck, G., & Kupecky, R. (1995). *Adopting the hurt child.* Colorado Springs, CO: Pinon Press.

Kerns, K. A., Aspelmeier, J. E., Gentzler, A. L., & Grabill, C. M. (2001). Parent–child attachment and monitoring in middle childhood. *Journal of Family Psychology, 15,* 69–81.

Kim, S., Iyengar, U., Mayes, L. C., Potenza, M. N., Rutherford, H. J. V., & Strathearn, L. (2017). Mothers with substance addictions show reduced reward responses when viewing their own infant's face. *Human Brain Mapping, 38,* 5421–5439.

Kim, S., Nordling, J. K., Yoon, J. E., Boldt, L. J., & Kochanska, G. (2013). Effortful control in "hot" and "cool" tasks differentially predicts children's behavior problems and academic performance. *Journal of Abnormal Child Psychology, 41,* 43–56.

Kitzman, H., Olds, D., Cole, R. E., Hanks, C. A., Anson, E. A., Arcoleo, K. K., et al. (2010). Enduring effects of prenatal and infancy home visiting by nurses on children: Follow-up of a randomized trial among children at age 12 years. *Archives of Pediatrics and Adolescent Medicine, 164,* 412–418.

Kitzman, H., Olds D. L., Henderson, C. R., Jr., Hanks, C., Cole, R., Tatelbaum, R., et al. (1997). Effect of prenatal and infancy home visitation by nurses on pregnancy outcomes, childhood injuries, and repeated childbearing: A randomized controlled trial. *Journal of the American Medical Association, 27,* 644–652.

Klebanov, P. K., Brooks-Gunn, J., McCarton, C. M., & McCormick, M. C. (1998). The contribution of neighborhood and family income upon developmental test scores over the first three years of life. *Child Development, 69,* 1420–1436.

Kopp, C. B. (1982). Antecedents of self-regulation: A developmental perspective. *Developmental Psychology, 18,* 199–214.

Kreppner, J. M., O'Connor, T. G., Rutter, M., Beckett, C., Castle, J., Croft,

C., et al. (2001). Can inattention/overactivity be an institutional deprivation syndrome? *Journal of Abnormal Child Psychology, 29,* 513–528.

Kreppner, J. M., Rutter, M., Beckett, C., Castle, J., Colvert, E., Groothues, C., et al. (2007). Normality and impairment following profound early institutional deprivation: A longitudinal follow-up into early adolescence. *Developmental Psychology, 43,* 931–946.

Landi, N., Montoya, J., Kober, H., Rutherford, H. J. V., Mencl, W. E., Worhunsky, P. D., et al. (2011). Maternal neural responses to infant cries and faces: Relationships with substance use. *Frontiers in Psychiatry, 2,* 32.

Laurent, H. K., & Ablow, J. C. (2013). A face a mother could love: Depression-related maternal neural responses to infant emotion faces. *Social Neuroscience, 8,* 228–239.

Leerkes, E. M., Supple, A. J., O'Brien, M., Calkins, S. D., Haltigan, J. D., Wong, M. S., et al. (2015). Antecedents of maternal sensitivity during distressing tasks: Integrating attachment, social information processing, and psychobiological perspectives. *Child Development, 86,* 94–111.

Levy, T. M. (2000). *Handbook of attachment interventions.* San Diego, CA: Academic Press.

Lewis, E., Dozier, M., Ackerman, J., & Sepulveda-Kozakowski, S. (2007). The effect of caregiving instability on adopted children's inhibitory control abilities and oppositional behavior. *Developmental Psychology, 43,* 1415–1427.

Lewis-Morrarty, E., Dozier, M., Bernard, K., Moore, S., & Terraciano, S. (2012). Cognitive flexibility and theory of mind outcomes among foster children: Preschool follow-up results of a randomized clinical trial. *Journal of Adolescent Health, 51,* 17–22.

Lieberman, A. F., Ghosh Ippen, C., & Van Horn, P. (2006). Child–parent psychotherapy: 6-month follow-up of a randomized controlled trial. *Journal of the American Academy of Child and Adolescent Psychiatry, 45,* 913–918.

Lilienfeld, S. O. (2007). Psychological treatments that cause harm. *Perspectives on Psychological Science, 2,* 53–70.

Lind, T., Bernard, K., Ross, E., & Dozier, M. (2014). Intervention effects on negative affect of CPS-referred children: Results of a randomized clinical trial. *Child Abuse and Neglect, 38,* 1459–1467.

Lind, T., Bernard, K., Yarger, H., & Dozier, M. (in press). Promoting compliance in children referred to Child Protective Services (CPS): A randomized clinical trial. *Child Development.*

Lind, T. A., Goldstein, A., Bernard, K., & Dozier, M. (2018). *CPS-involved children remaining with birth parents show more behavioral dysregulation than children in foster care.* Unpublished manuscript, University of Delaware.

Lind, T. A., Raby, K. L., Caron, E. B., Roben, C. K. P., & Dozier, M. (2017). Enhancing executive functioning among toddlers in foster care with an attachment-based intervention. *Development and Psychopathology, 29*, 575–586.

Lindhiem, O., & Dozier, M. (2007). Caregiver commitment to foster children: The role of child behavior. *Child Abuse and Neglect, 31*, 361–374.

Lindsey, D. (1991). Factors affecting the foster care placement decision: An analysis of national survey data. *American Journal of Orthopsychiatry, 61*, 272–281.

Lo, A., Roben, C. K. P., Maier, C., Fabian, K., Shauffer, C., & Dozier, M. (2015). "I want to be there when he graduates": Foster parents show higher levels of commitment than group care providers. *Children and Youth Services Review, 51*, 95–100.

MacLean, K. (2003). The impact of institutionalization on child development. *Development and Psychopathology, 15*, 853–884.

Main, M. (1990). Cross-cultural studies of attachment organization: Recent studies, changing methodologies, and the concept of conditional strategies. *Human Development, 33*, 48–61.

Main, M., & Hesse, E. (1990). Parents' unresolved traumatic experiences are related to infant disorganized attachment status: Is frightening and/or frightened parental behavior the linking mechanism? In M. T. Greenberg, D. Cicchetti, & E. M. Cummings (Eds.), *Attachment in the preschool years: Theory, research, and intervention* (pp. 161–182). Chicago: University of Chicago Press.

Main, M., & Solomon, J. (1986). Discovery of a new, insecure-disorganized/disoriented attachment pattern. In T. B. Brazelton & M. W. Yogman (Eds.), *Affective development in infancy* (pp. 95–124). Norwood, NJ: Ablex.

Main, M., & Solomon, J. (1990). Procedures for identifying infants as disorganized/disoriented during the Ainsworth Strange Situation. In M. T. Greenberg, D. Cicchetti, & E. M. Cummings (Eds.), *Attachment in the preschool years: Theory, research, and intervention* (pp. 121–160). Chicago: University of Chicago Press.

Matas, L., Arend, R. A., & Sroufe, L. A. (1978). Continuity of adaptation in the second year: The relationship between quality of attachment and later competence. *Child Development, 49*, 547–556.

Mayes, L. C., & Turman, S. D. (2002). Substance abuse and parenting. In M. H. Bornstein (Eds.), *Handbook of parenting: Vol. 4. Social conditions and applied parenting* (2nd ed., pp. 329–359). Mahwah, NJ: Erlbaum.

McCall, R. B., Muhamedrahimov, R. J., Groark, C. J., Palmov, O. I., Nikiforova, N. V., Salaway, J. L., et al. (2016). The development of children placed into different types of Russian families following an institutional intervention. *International Perspectives in Psychology: Research, Practice, Consultation, 5,* 255–270.

McGregor, I. S., & Bowen, M. T. (2012). Breaking the loop: Oxytocin as a potential treatment for drug addiction. *Hormones and Behavior, 61,* 331–339.

McLaughlin, A. A., Minnes, S., Singer, L. T., Min, M., Short, E. J., Scott, T. L., et al. (2011). Caregiver and self-report of mental health symptoms in 9-year-old children with prenatal cocaine exposure. *Neurotoxicology and Teratology, 33,* 582–591.

McLaughlin, K. A., Zeanah, C. H., Fox, N. A., & Nelson, C. A. (2012). Attachment security as a mechanism linking foster care placement to improved mental health outcomes in previously institutionalized children. *Journal of Child Psychology and Psychiatry, 53,* 46–55.

Meade, E. B., Dozier, M., & Bernard, K. (2014). Using video feedback as a tool in training parent coaches: Promising results from a single-case design. *Attachment and Human Development, 16,* 356–370.

Mikulincer, M., & Shaver, P. R. (2016). *Attachment in adulthood: Structure, dynamics, and change* (2nd ed.). New York: Guilford Press.

Mischel, W. (2014). *The marshmallow test.* New York: Little, Brown.

Moffitt, T. E., Arseneault, L., Belsky, D., Dickson, N., Hancox, R. J., Harrington, H., et al. (2011). A gradient of childhood self-control predicts health, wealth, and public safety. *Proceedings of the National Academy of Sciences of the USA, 108,* 2693–2698.

Najman, J. M., Williams, G. M., Nikles, J., Spence, S., Bor, W., O'Callaghan, M., et al. (2000). Mothers' mental illness and child behavior problems: Cause–effect association or observation bias? *Journal of the American Academy of Child and Adolescent Psychiatry, 39,* 592–602.

Nelson, C. A., Zeanah, C. H., Fox, N. A., Marshall, P. J., Smyke, A. T., & Guthrie, D. (2007). Cognitive recovery in socially deprived young children: The Bucharest Early Intervention Project. *Science, 318,* 1937–1940.

NICHD Early Child Care Research Network. (1999). Child care and mother–child interaction in the first three years of life. *Developmental Psychology, 35,* 1399–1413.

NICHD Early Child Care Research Network. (2003). Early child care and mother–child interaction from 36 months through first grade. *Infant Behavior and Development, 26,* 345–370.

O'Connor, T. G., Rutter, M., Beckett, C., Keaveney, L., & Kreppner, J. M. (2000). The effects of global severe privation on cognitive competence: Extension and longitudinal follow-up. *Child Development, 71,* 376–390.

Olds, D. L. (2002). Prenatal and infancy home visiting by nurses: From randomized trials to community replication. *Prevention Science, 3,* 153–172.

Olds, D. L., Eckenrode, J., Henderson, C. L., Jr., Kitzman, H., Powers, J., Cole, R., et al. (1997). Long-term effects of home visitation on maternal life course and child abuse and neglect. Fifteen-year follow-up of a randomized trial. *Journal of the American Medical Association, 278,* 637–643.

Olds, D. L., Henderson, C. L., Jr., Chamberlain, R., & Tatelbaum, R. (1986). Preventing child abuse and neglect: A randomized trial of nurse home visitation. *Pediatrics, 78,* 65–78.

Olds, D. L., Henderson, C. L., Jr., Tatelbaum, R., & Chamberlain, R. (1988). Improving the life-course development of socially disadvantaged mothers: A randomized trial of nurse home visitation. *American Journal of Public Health, 78,* 1436–1445.

Olds, D. L., Kitzman, H., Cole, R., Robinson, J., Sidora, K., Luckey, D. W., et al. (2004). Effects of nurse home-visiting on maternal life course and child development: Age 6 follow-up results of a randomized trial. *Pediatrics, 114,* 1550–1559.

Olds, D. L., Kitzman, H., Hanks, C., Cole, R., Anson, E., Sidora-Arcoleo, K., et al. (2007). Effects of nurse home visiting on maternal and child functioning: Age 9 follow-up of a randomized trial. *Pediatrics, 120,* e832–e845.

Oliveros, A., & Kaufman, J. (2011). Addressing substance abuse treatment needs of parents involved with the child welfare system. *Child Welfare, 90,* 25–41.

Oosterman, M., De Schipper, J. C., Fisher, P., & Dozier, M. (2010). Autonomic reactivity in relation to attachment and early adversity among foster children. *Development and Psychopathology, 22,* 109–118.

Panlilio, C. C., Jones Harden, B., & Harring, J. (2018). School readiness of maltreated preschoolers and later school achievement: The role of emotion regulation, language, and context. *Child Abuse and Neglect, 75,* 82–91.

Patterson, G. R. (1982). Coercion theory: The study of change. In T. J.

Dishion & J. J. Snyder (Eds.), *The Oxford handbook of coercive relationship dynamics* (pp. 7–22). New York: Oxford University Press.

Pears, K. C., Kim, H. K., Buchanan, R., & Fisher, P. A. (2015). Adverse consequences of school mobility for children in foster care: A prospective longitudinal study. *Child Development, 86,* 1210–1226.

Penela, E. C., Walker, O. L., Degnan, K., Fox, N. A., & Henderson, H. A. (2015). Early behavioral inhibition and emotion regulation: Pathways toward social competence in middle childhood. *Child Development, 86,* 1227–1240.

Pignotti, M., & Mercer, J. (2007). Holding therapy and dyadic developmental psychotherapy are not supported and acceptable social work interventions: A systematic research synthesis revisited. *Research on Social Work Practice, 17,* 513–519.

Powell, B., Cooper, G., Hoffman, K., & Marvin, B. (2016). *The Circle of Security intervention: Enhancing attachment in early parent–child relationships.* New York: Guilford Press.

Raby, K. L., Carlson, E., & Dozier, M. (2018). *ABC effects on adopted children's disorganized attachment.* Manuscript under review.

Raby, K. L., Freedman, E., Yarger, H. A., Lind, T., & Dozier, M. (in press). Enhancing the language development of toddlers in foster care by promoting foster parents' sensitivity: Results from a randomized control trial. *Developmental Science.*

Raby, K. L., Roisman, G. I., Fraley, F. R., & Simpson, J. A. (2015). The enduring predictive significance of early maternal sensitivity: Social and academic competence through age 32 years. *Child Development, 86,* 695–708.

Raby, K. L., Yarger, H. A., Lind, T., Fraley, R. C., Leerkes, E., & Dozier, M. (2017). Attachment states of mind among internationally adoptive and foster parents. *Developmental Psychopathology, 29,* 365–378.

Raby, K. L., Zajac, L., & Dozier, M. (2018). *ABC enhances secure base script knowledge among mothers with child welfare system involvement.* Manuscript in preparation.

Raver, C. C. (1996). Relations between social contingency in mother–child interaction and 2-year-olds' social competence. *Developmental Psychology, 32,* 850–859.

Reddy, U. M., Davis, J. M., Ren, Z., & Greene, M. F. (2017). Opioid epidemic: executive summary: Opioid use in pregnancy, neonatal abstinence syndrome, and childhood outcomes. *Obstetrics and Gynecology, 130,* 10–28.

Rivaux, S. L., James, J., Wittenstrom, K., Baumann, D., Sheets, J., Henry, J., et al. (2008). The intersection of race, poverty, and risk:

Understanding the decision to provide services to clients and to remove children. *Child Welfare, 87,* 151–168.

Rodrigo, M. J., Leon, I., Quinones, I., Lage, A., Byrne, S., & Bobes, M. A. (2011). Brain and personality bases of insensitivity to infant cues in neglectful mothers: An event-related potential study. *Development and Psychopathology, 23,* 163–176.

Roisman, G. I., Holland, A., Fortuna, K., Fraley, C. R., Clausell, E., & Clarke, A. (2007). The Adult Attachment Interview and self-reports of attachment style: An empirical rapprochement. *Journal of Personality and Social Psychology, 92,* 678–697.

Rutherford, H. J. V., & Mayes, L. C. (2017). Parenting and addiction: Neurobiological insights. *Current Opinion in Psychology, 15,* 55–60.

Rutter, M. (1998). Developmental catch-up, and deficit, following adoption after severe global early privation. *Journal of Child Psychology and Psychiatry, 39,* 465–476.

Rutter, M., Andersen-Wood, L., Beckett, C., Bredrenkamp, D., Castle, J., Groothues, C., et al. (1999). Quasi-autistic patterns following severe early global privation. *Journal of Child Psychology and Psychiatry, 40,* 537–549.

Rutter, M., Colvert, E., Kreppner, J., Beckett, C., Castle, J., Groothues, C., et al. (2007). Early adolescent outcomes for institutionally-deprived and non-deprived adoptees: I. Disinhibited attachment. *Journal of Child Psychology and Psychiatry, 48,* 17–30.

Sadler, L. S., Slade, A., Close, N., Webb, D. L., Simpson, T., Fennie, K., et al. (2013). Minding the baby: Enhancing reflectiveness to improve early health and relationship outcomes in an interdisciplinary home-visiting program. *Infant Mental Health Journal, 34,* 391–405.

Sadler, L. S., Slade, A., & Mayes, L. C. (2006). Minding the baby: A mentalization-based parenting program. In J. G. Allen & P. Fonagy (Eds.), *The handbook of mentalization-based treatment* (pp. 271–288). Hoboken, NJ: Wiley.

Sanchirico, A., & Jablonka, K. (2000). Keeping foster children connected to their biological parents: The impact of foster parent training and support. *Child and Adolescent Social Work Journal, 17,* 185–203.

Santa Ana, E. J., Martino, S., Ball, S. A., Nich, C., Frankforter, T. L., & Carroll, K. M. (2008). What is usual about "treatment-as-usual"?: Data from two multisite effectiveness trials. *Journal of Substance Abuse Treatment, 35,* 369–379.

Sapolsky, R. M. (2017). *Behave: The biology of humans at our best and worst.* New York: Penguin.

Scheeringa, M. S., Peebles, C. D., Cook, C. A., & Zeanah, C. H. (2001).

Toward establishing procedural, criterion, and discriminant validity for PTSD in early childhood. *Journal of the American Academy of Child and Adolescent Psychiatry, 40,* 52–60.

Schlam, T. R., Wilson, N. L., Shoda, Y., Mischel, W., & Ayduk, O. (2013). Preschoolers' delay of gratification predicts their body mass 30 years later. *Journal of Pediatrics, 162,* 90–93.

Schuengel, C., Bakermans-Kranenburg, M. J., & van IJzendoorn, M. H. (1999). Frightening maternal behavior linking unresolved loss and disorganized infant attachment. *Journal of Consulting and Clinical Psychology, 67,* 54–64.

Seifer, R., & Dickstein, S. (1993). Parental mental illness and infant development. In C. H. Zeanah (Ed.), *Handbook of infant mental health* (pp. 120–142). New York: Guilford Press.

Shaw, D. S., Bell, R. Q., & Gilliom, M. (2000). A truly early starter model of antisocial behavior revisited. *Clinical Child and Family Psychology Review, 3,* 155–172.

Smyke, A. T., Koga, S. F., Johnson, D. E., Fox, N. A., Marshall, P. K., Nelson, C. A., et al. (2007). The caregiving context in institution-reared and family-reared infants and toddlers in Romania. *Journal of Child Psychology and Psychiatry, 48,* 210–218.

Spangler, G., & Grossman, K. E. (1993). Biobehavioral organization in securely and insecurely attached infants. *Child Development, 64,* 1439–1450.

Sroufe, L. A. (2016). The place of attachment in development. In J. Cassidy & P. R. Shaver (Eds.), *Handbook of attachment: Theory, research, and clinical applications* (3rd ed., pp. 997–1011). New York: Guilford Press.

Sroufe, L. A., Egeland, B., Carlson, E., & Collins, W. A. (2005). *The development of the person: The Minnesota Study of Risk and Adaptation from Birth to Adulthood.* New York: Guilford Press.

Sroufe, L. A., & Waters, E. (1977). Attachment as an organizational construct. *Child Development, 48,* 1184–1199.

Steele, H., & Steele, M. (Eds.). (2018). *Handbook of attachment-based interventions.* New York: Guilford Press.

Steele, H., Steele, M., Bonuck, K., Meissner, P., & Murphy, A. (2018). Group attachment-based intervention: A multifamily trauma-informed intervention. In H. Steele & M. Steele (Eds.), *Handbook of attachment-based interventions* (pp. 198–219). New York: Guilford Press.

Stokes, J., Pogge, D., Wecksell, B., & Zaccario, M. (2011). Parent–child discrepancies in report of psychopathology: The contributions of response bias and parenting stress. *Journal of Personality Assessment, 93,* 527–536.

Stovall, K. C., & Dozier, M. (2000). The development of attachment in new relationships: Single subject analyses for 10 foster infants. *Development and Psychopathology, 12,* 133–156.

Stovall-McClough, K. C., & Dozier, M. (2004). Forming attachments in foster care: Infant attachment behaviors during the first 2 months of placement. *Development and Psychopathology, 16,* 253–271.

Stronach, E. P., Toth, S. L., Rogosch, F., & Cicchetti, D. (2013). Preventive interventions and sustained attachment security in maltreated children. *Development and Psychopathology, 25,* 919–930.

Suchman, N. E., Ordway, M. R., de las Heras, L., & McMahon, T. J. (2016). Mothering from the Inside Out: Results of a pilot study testing a mentalization-based therapy for mothers enrolled in mental health services. *Attachment and Human Development, 18,* 596–617.

Tabachnick, L., Raby, K. L., Goldstein, A., Zajac, L., & Dozier, M. (2018). *Effects of an attachment-based intervention in infancy on children's autonomic regulation during middle childhood.* Manuscript under review.

Tamis-LeMonda, C. S., Kuchirko, Y., & Song, L. (2014). Why is infant language learning facilitated by parental responsiveness? *Current Directions in Psychological Science, 23,* 121–126.

Thomas, K. A., & Spieker, S. (2016). Sleep, depression, and fatigue in late postpartum. *American Journal of Maternal/Child Nursing, 41,* 104–109.

Toth, S. L., Michl-Petzing, L. C., Guild, D., & Lieberman, A. F. (2018). Child–parent psychotherapy: Theoretical bases, clinical applications, and empirical support. In H. Steele & M. Steele (Eds.), *Handbook of attachment-based interventions* (pp. 296–317). New York: Guilford Press.

Toth, S. L., Rogosch, F. A., Manly, J. T., & Cicchetti, D. (2006). The efficacy of toddler–parent psychotherapy to reorganize attachment in the young offspring of mothers with major depressive disorder: A randomized preventive trial. *Journal of Consulting and Clinical Psychology, 74,* 1006–1016.

Tottenham, N., Hare, T. A., Quinn, B. T., McCarry, T. W., Nurse, M., Gilhooly, T., et al. (2010). Prolonged institutional rearing is associated with atypically large amygdala volume and difficulties in emotion regulation. *Developmental Science, 13,* 46–61.

Tronick, E. Z., & Cohn, J. F. (1989). Infant–mother face-to-face interaction: Age and gender differences in coordination and the occurrence of miscoordination. *Child Development, 60,* 85–92.

Tyrell, C. L., Dozier, M., Teague, G. B., & Fallor, R. D. (1999). Effective treatment relationships for persons with serious psychiatric disorders: The importance of attachment states of mind. *Journal of Consulting and Clinical Psychology, 67,* 725–733.

U.S. Department of Health and Human Services, Administration for Children and Families, Administration on Children, Youth and Families, Children's Bureau. (2013). Child maltreatment 2012. Available at *www.acf.hhs.gov/programs/cb/research-data-technology/statistics-research/child-maltreatment.*

Valadez, E., Tottenham, N., & Dozier, M. (2018). *Early intervention effects on neural hemodynamic reactivity to fear and mother faces.* Manuscript in preparation.

van den Dries, L., Juffer, F., van IJzendoorn, M. H., & Bakermans-Kranenburg, M. J. (2009). Fostering security?: A meta-analysis of attachment in adopted children. *Children and Youth Services Review, 31,* 410–421.

van IJzendoorn, M. H., Bakermans-Kranenburg, M. J., & Juffer, F. (2007). Plasticity of growth in height, weight, and head circumference: Meta-analytic evidence of massive catch-up after international adoption. *Journal of Developmental and Behavioral Pediatrics, 28,* 334–343.

van IJzendoorn, M. H., & Juffer, F. (2006). The Emanuel Miller Memorial Lecture 2006: Adoption as intervention: Meta-analytic evidence for massive catch-up and plasticity in physical, socio-emotional, and cognitive development. *Journal of Child Psychology and Psychiatry, 47,* 1228–1245.

van IJzendoorn, M. H., Schuengel, C., & Bakermans-Kranenburg, M. J. (1999). Disorganized attachment in early childhood: Meta-analysis of precursors, concomitants, and sequelae. *Development and Psychopathology, 11,* 225–249.

Vandell, D. L. (1979). Effects of a playgroup experience on mother–son and father–son interaction. *Developmental Psychology, 15,* 379–385.

Vanderwert, R. E., Marshall, P. J., Nelson, C. A., Zeanah, C. H., & Fox, N. A. (2010). Timing of intervention affects brain electrical activity in children exposed to severe psychosocial neglect. *PLOS ONE, 5,* e11415.

Velderman, M. K., Bakermans-Kranenburg, M. J., Juffer, F., van IJzendoorn, M. H., Mangeldorf, S. C., & Zevalkink, J. (2006). Preventing preschool externalizing behavior problems through video-feedback intervention in infancy. *Infant Mental Health Journal, 27,* 466–493.

Verhage, M. L., Schuengel, C., Madigan, S., Fearon, R. M. P., Oosterman, M., Cassibba, R., et al. (2016). Narrowing the transmission gap: A synthesis of three decades of research on intergenerational transmission of attachment. *Psychological Bulletin, 142,* 337–366.

Vernon-Feagons, L., & Cox, M. (2013). The Family Life Project: An epidemiological and developmental study of young children living in poor rural communities: I. Poverty, rurality, parenting, and risk: An introduction. *Monographs of the Society for Research in Child Development, 78,* 1–23.

Vu, N. L., Jouriles, E. N., McDonald, R., & Rosenfield, D. (2016). Children's exposure to intimate partner violence: A meta-analysis of longitudinal association with child adjustment problems. *Clinical Psychology Review, 46,* 25–33.

Wakschlag, L. S., Hill, C., Carter, A. S., Danis, B., Egger, H. L., Keenan, K., et al. (2008). Observational assessment of preschool disruptive behavior: Part I. Reliability of the Disruptive Behavior Diagnostic Observation Schedule (DB-DOS). *Journal of the American Academy of Child and Adolescent Psychiatry, 47,* 622–631.

Wald, M. S. (2015). Beyond CPS: Developing an effective system for helping children in "neglectful" families: Policymakers have failed to address the neglect of neglect. *Child Abuse and Neglect, 41,* 49–66.

Waters, H. S., & Rodrigues-Doolabh, L. (2001, April). *Are attachment scripts the builing blocks of attachment representations?* Paper presented at the annual meeting for the Society for Research in Child Development.

Waters, H. S., & Waters, E. (2006). The attachment working models concept: Among other things, we build script-like representations of secure base experiences. *Attachment and Human Development, 8,* 185–197.

Weinberg, K. M., & Tronick, E. Z. (1996). Infant affective reactions to the resumption of maternal interaction after the StillFace. *Child Development, 67,* 905–914.

Weisz, J. R., Jensen-Doss, A., & Hawley, K. M. (2006). Evidence-based youth psychotherapies versus usual clinical care: A meta-analysis of direct comparisons. *American Psychologist, 61,* 671–689.

Yang, M. (2015). The effect of material hardship on child protective services involvement. *Child Abuse and Neglect, 41,* 113–125.

Yarger, H. A., Bernard, K., Caron, E. B., Wallin, A., & Dozier, M. (in press). Attachment and Biobehavioral Catch-Up for parents adopting internationally: Enhancing parenting quality. *Journal of Clinical Child and Adolescent Psychology.*

Zeanah, C. H., Humphreys, K. L., Fox, N. A., & Nelson, C. A. (2017). Alternatives for abandoned children: Insights from the Bucharest Early Intervention Project. *Current Opinion in Psychology, 15,* 182–188.

Zeanah, C. H., Shauffer, C., & Dozier, M. (2011). Foster care for young children: Why it must be developmentally informed. *Journal of the American Academy of Child and Adolescent Psychiatry, 50,* 1199–1201.

Zeanah, C. H., & Smyke, A. T. (2005). Building attachment relationships following maltreatment and severe deprivation. In. L. J. Berlin, Y. Ziv, L. Amaya-Jackson, & M. T. Greenberg (Eds.), *Enhancing early attachments: Theory, research, intervention, and policy* (pp. 195–216). New York: Guilford Press.

Zeanah, C. H., Smyke, A. T., & Dumitrescu, A. (2002). Attachment disturbances in young children: II. Indiscriminate behavior and institutional care. *Journal of the American Academy of Child and Adolescent Psychiatry, 41,* 983–989.

Zeanah, C. H., Smyke, A. T., Koga, S. F., Carlson, E., & the Bucharest Early Intervention Project Core Group. (2005). Attachment in institutionalized and community children in Romania. *Child Development, 76,* 1015–1028.

Zelazo, P. D., Frye, D., & Rapus, T. (1996). An age-related dissociation between knowing rules and using them. *Cognitive Development, 11,* 37–63.

Zeman, J., Shipman, K., & Suveg, C. (2002). Anger and sadness regulation: Predictions to internalizing and externalizing symptoms in children. *Journal of Clinical Child and Adolescent Psychology, 31,* 393–398.

ZERO TO THREE. (2016, March 18). Stop the cuts!: Babies can't wait. Available at *www.zerotothree.org/resources/541-stop-the-cuts-babies-can-t-wait.*

Index

Note. *f* or *t* following a page number indicates a figure or a table.

257